Capital in Disequilibrium

Capital in Disequilibrium

The Role of Capital in a Changing World

Second Edition

PETER LEWIN

Copyright © 2011 by the Ludwig von Mises Institute

Published under the Creative Commons Attribution License 3.0.
http://creativecommons.org/licenses/by/3.0/

Ludwig von Mises Institute
518 West Magnolia Avenue
Auburn, Alabama 36832
Ph: (334) 844-2500
Fax: (334) 844-2583
mises.org

Large Print Edition published 2012 by Skyler J. Collins.
Visit: www.skylerjcollins.com

Cover image by StockFreeImages.com

ISBN-13: 978-1479323869
ISBN-10: 1479323861

Contents

Acknowledgments vii

Preface to the Second Edition xi

  1. Introduction and Outline. 1

Part I. Background: Equilibrium and Change

  2. What Does Equilibrium Mean? A Discussion in the Context of Modern Austrian Ideas 15

  3. Equilibrium and Expectations Re-Examined: A Different Perspective 31

Part II. Capital, Interest, and Profits

  4. Capital in Historical Perspective 51

  5. Modern Capital Theory 79

  6. The Hicksian Marriage of Capital and Time 93

  7. The Nature of Interest and Profits 109

Part III. Capital in a Dynamic World

  8. Modern Mengerian Capital Theory 125

  9. Capital and Business Organizations 147

10. Organizations, Money, and Calculation 177

11. Human Capital 193

12. Human Capital, the Nature of Knowledge, and the Value of Knowledge 225

Conclusion 237

Bibliography 243

Index 259

Acknowledgments

I owe a large intellectual debt to two remarkable and very different teachers.

The spark of interest, of which this book is the culmination, was ignited when, as an undergraduate (in 1968), I took a course in capital theory from my teacher Ludwig Lachmann, at the University of the Witwatersrand in Johannesburg, South Africa. Lachmann's ideas have influenced the writing of almost every page of this work. From him I learned at a young and impressionable age to think critically about the implications of time for human action. From him I inherited an enduring fascination with the questions posed by capital theory, a fascination enhanced by the very complexity of the subject. I suspect that it would not have troubled him in the least that his student presumed to differ from him in some ways and to extend his approach into novel areas; on the contrary, I imagine he would have been quite pleased. In particular, Lachmann's influence as an economist was limited by the absence of concrete or practical implications of his work. Yet, as I have tried to show, his general insights have specific applications in the areas of the theory of the firm, in human capital, and many other areas.

Professor Lachmann, in addition to providing a crucial component of my education, helped me in other ways at the beginning of my professional career. He was always considerate and respectful of his students and his memory inspires and sustains me.

I am indebted in a less personal, but nevertheless important, way to Gary Becker. Professor Becker was my PhD thesis committee chairman and my teacher for a number of graduate courses. The opportunity to study with him was of inestimable value to me in my training as an economist and, more particularly, in gaining an appreciation of the importance of human capital (and related subject areas, like the economics of the family). His influence will be particularly apparent in the chapters that deal with human capital.

This work, then, has been in the pipeline for many years, during which time I have benefited from talking to many individuals. I cannot hope to recall them all, at least not without engaging in an inappropriate exercise of intellectual autobiography. However, they include Karl Mittermaier, Landis Gabel, Sam Weston, Bob Formaini, Roger Garrison, Richard Ebeling, Don Lavoie, and Karen Vaughn. I have benefited from comments on presentations at the Colloquium on Austrian economics at New York University, most notably from comments by Mario Rizzo, Israel Kirzner, Peter Boettke, Joe Salerno, Bill Butos, Roger Koppl, David Harper, Don Boudreaux, Frederic Sautet, and Sanford Ikeda. I also benefited from comments received at presentations at the Southern Economic Association and the History of Economics Association meetings. Larry White provided very useful comments.

I am very grateful to Steven Horwitz who read the entire manuscript of an early version and provided numerous stylistic and substantive corrections.

This book would not have been written without the efforts and encouragement of Mario Rizzo. It was he who first suggested it and provided important directional indicators. In addition, his work in Austrian economics has been an important source of inspiration for me and has helped me to gain greater insight into and appreciation of many of the themes that appear in the pages that follow.

In the years since the first edition of this book I have benefited from too many individuals to name. My coauthor Howard Baetjer cannot go unmentioned however. His work on capital and knowledge is crucial to my current understanding of the subject. For editorial assistance at the Mises Institute I thank Jeffrey Tucker and Paul Foley.

I need hardly add that none of the individuals mentioned above is to be implicated in any of the errors that may be found in this work, especially where they are the result of my stubborn refusal to follow their advice.

In addition to colleagues and teachers, I have been fortunate to have had the support of friends and family, without which I could not have found the time and resolve to complete this work. My parents, Merle and Herman Lewin, have been a constant source of support and have stood by me in my obstinate determination to follow the calling of academe. To my father-in-law Felix Shapiro, also my constant friend and admirer, I owe more than I can say. And finally and mostly, my family, my children Dan, Andy, Shiralee and Gabbi, each in their own way has helped me in this "strange" project (as they must see it); and my wife Beverley, my partner in life, who has struggled valiantly to identify with her husband's determination to complete this weird time- and energy-consuming project.

Preface to the Second Edition

It has been twelve years since the original publication of this book in 1999. Much has happened in the intervening years to affect its relevance.

In the world of economic policy, the relevance of (Austrian type) capital theory has increased dramatically. The appeal of what Ludwig Lachmann referred to as "neoclassical formalism" has not diminished. Policy-makers, following the counsel of their economic advisors, who are ruled by a belief in the significance of economic aggregates, have persistently ignored, indeed precipitated, capital structure distortions; the results of which have been two major domestic economic crises (the dot-com bust and the housing-bubble meltdown), a global credit crisis, a chronic fiscal deficit and an exploding debt burden that threatens to destroy the very fabric of the economy's value-creating potential. This book is designed for those who wish to understand, in a thorough and fundamental way, the nature and significance of capital. What makes an economy "capitalist"? How does value get created over time? If we get this wrong we may end up paying a high price indeed.

The erroneous ideas upon which disastrous economic policy has been based have come down from the intellectual forebears of the current generation of economic advisors. A full appreciation of this entails understanding the nature of battles fought long ago over the nature and significance of capital and capital theory. Accordingly, the focus of this book on this particular aspect of the history of economic thought remains very relevant.

In the world of economic theory, though the majority of the economics profession remains oblivious of, and contemptuous of, anything outside of its narrow quantitative orientation, and, indeed, has become even more finely specialized and technically esoteric, so that its members know more and more about less and less over time, on the growing fringes of the profession a number of "heterodox" approaches have prospered and are growing. One of these heterodox approaches is that of Austrian economics, which has continued to gain adherents, including from young, energetic graduates who are beginning to make their marks. I hope that the re-publication of this book in a more accessible form will serve to encourage this development and provide a firm foundation for the diverse applications of capital theory that are now becoming evident.

One area in which such applications have been growing apace is that of management and business studies, particularly in the areas of strategic-management, organization studies and entrepreneurship. The Austrian ideas most relevant to this line of research concern the nature of resources and how they can be organized in productive combinations to produce value. The "capital-nature" of productive resources has pointed in the direction of the Austrians. Though long interested in Schumpeter, scholars in this area have recently enthusiastically embraced the ideas of Hayek, Kirzner, and, most recently, Lachmann. In particular, understanding resources as capital has led to an appreciation of the importance of time and knowledge in productive processes, and of social institutions—connected themes examined below, especially in Chapter 9. This literature stream has grown rapidly since 1999. An indication of some of this work and its connection to the work below can be found in Lewin and Baetjer (2011).

This book is about capital in a disequilibrium world, a dynamic world. In the years since its first publication the world in which we live has become even more dynamic. The pace of change has accelerated. The "digital-age" works its magic every day in the form of new products, new organizations, new production techniques, new modes of communication, and who knows what else. This increased dynamism has enhanced the relevance of the capital-based framework developed in this book. One shortcoming that is glaringly obvious to me now in retrospect is the insufficient attention paid to an understanding of capital as a form of "embodied knowledge," as first developed by Howard Baetjer, to whose work I enthusiastically refer the interested reader (Baetjer 1998, 2000; Lewin and Baetjer 2011).

I have made very few changes to the original text. I have added some references to work published since the first edition, I have added some explanatory footnotes and deleted some others (deemed obsolete or unnecessary) and I have taken the opportunity to make a few stylistic improvements. One major advantage of the new edition is that the footnotes are now found below the text rather than at the back of the book.

Peter Lewin,
Dallas, June 2011

CHAPTER 1

Introduction and Outline

"Case Study"

This book is the result of a capital project, a production plan. More accurately it is the final product of a series of related intertemporal plans, and is the intermediate product of some higher level plans. This structure of plans encompasses both my own particular plans and the plans of others, like the publisher and the editors. As I write this, it is still too early to say whether the project is to be judged a success, by me or the other planners. But, whatever the final judgment, the planning process is illustrative of the ingredients of capital planning in general.

I am writing this introduction having already completed (at least a first draft of) the rest of the book, save for the conclusion. This means that you, the reader, are going to read the introduction and the rest of the book to which it refers in reverse order from the way in which they were written. The reason for this is obvious. I could not have written the introduction first, or at least not most of it with all the details and the outline to follow, because I did not know what I was going to write in the book. To be sure, I did have a general idea of the chapter layout and the points that I wanted to establish in each chapter, but I was unable to imagine in any kind of detail the words and sentences that would eventually fill the pages. This is in part due to the fact that the writing was a kind of learning experience, a kind of spontaneous unfolding of ideas that depend sequentially on one another, a kind of "learning by doing." And in part this was also because of the occurrence of events that could not be anticipated in any detail. I shall argue that all planning is like this to some degree. Because of the way that we experience time, plans are necessarily incompletely specified. (We may say that planning for production is an "emergent" process.)

Nevertheless, my inability to completely visualize the unfolding of my production plan, which depended in part on the fulfillment of the plans of others, and influenced the plans of still others, will not, in itself, prevent its fulfillment. It is not necessary that every aspect of the plan turn out as expected, especially as there are many aspects that could not be expected. But some things *must* turn out as expected. Among these are the crucial actions of mine and others which conform to certain preconceived or tacitly held notions of how people do and will behave in certain types of circumstances. This plan, like any other that is to have a chance of success, proceeded within an institutional framework of shared "ways of doing things."

This book, the product of a capital project, is the result of "team production." I did the writing, my editor did the guiding and the nudging, and the publisher did a number of things including overseeing the whole project, providing the necessary financial capital and equipment and the support staff. This "team" transcends the boundaries of the "firm." In a sense there are a number of "firms" involved; myself, the editor, the publisher, the publisher's suppliers and customers, and so on. We are all part of a grand matrix of organizations, some of whose employees are part of the "team." So the book is in reality a team product. Each member's contribution helped to facilitate its production. The value of the final product is thus causally attributable to these efforts and, therefore, the value of these joint efforts can be imputed from a knowledge of the value of the product.

Team production has to be coordinated, and in order to facilitate this coordination efficiently it may be argued that the members of the team should receive the full value of their marginal contribution to the product. This turns out to be quite problematic, especially when the extent or the value of the contribution of any team member is wholly or partially indeterminate (difficult or impossible to measure). But, as a practical matter, the existence of certain types of organizations and institutions—like a firm that specializes in publishing, and a market economy, where contracts and promises are made and honored and are expected to be honored, and in which money is used and understood, so that decision-makers can attribute a value to the efforts of the team members even though there may be a large element of indeterminacy surrounding each one's contribution—helps to facilitate the necessary coordination.

So capitalistic production is about more than the existence of capital goods. It involves in addition the social and institutional framework that I have mentioned and the human capital of the individual team members.

These are also indispensable parts of the capital structure, and thus of the value of any project. It is true, for example, that my prior conscious investments in human capital (generally in learning to read and write and more specifically in the studying of economics) helped to equip me for the task of writing this book. "Knowledge capital" is a crucial part of capital in general. (For a discussion of the relationship between knowledge and capital see Lewin and Baetjer 2011.)

In this "case study" I anticipate some of the themes that I shall examine in this book:

- The complexity of plans and the inevitable existence of disequilibrium does not imply the failure of all plans, or of all aspects of plans. Production occurs in a changing world, but this can only happen if some aspects of that world are relatively stable and ordered.
- Capital is more than an array of capital equipment and involves an understanding of how value gets created by a combination of human and physical resources over time in an organizational structure that facilitates that creation.
- Organizational form, routines, habits, rules, norms, and mores are thus part of the social capital of any society. And the knowledge of its members is part of its human capital. And both are part of its capital structure.
- Any social policy that involves regulating or substituting for these largely spontaneous value-creating structures should, at the very least, be aware of the complexity of this all-encompassing capital structure.

Some more detail is provided in the rest of this chapter.

A Disequilibrium Approach to Capital

Most students of economics encounter the theory of capital as part of a theory of finance and/or project evaluation. When considering the question of how to measure (known or estimated) values that occur at different points in time, they get introduced to the arithmetic of present values. And while the notion of present value can be elaborated and dissected in many subtle ways, its basics derive from some very straightforward, intuitive ideas. It is surprising, then, to find that capital theory is regarded as a particularly esoteric and largely irrelevant part of economics.

Obviously, although present-value arithmetic is an important part of an understanding of capital, it is only a part of that understanding. It is the other parts that have been regarded as obscure and irrelevant. Although capital theory may be difficult, it is hard to see that it could justifiably be judged as irrelevant. After all, the market economies of the world are often referred to as "capitalist" economies. Surely a good understanding of the meaning and significance of the "capital" in "capitalist" is of some importance, for history and for policy. If capital is that phenomenon that makes market economies different, ought we not to accord it a prominent place in the education of an economist?

As will become clear from the discussion below (Chapter 4), much of the reluctance of economists to deal with the theory of capital is a result of the historical context in which it was developed. The history of thought in capital theory contains volumes of discussion on intricate technical and sometimes philosophical issues that modern economists have come to think they can do quite well without. This impression was strongly reinforced by the Keynesian revolution and Keynes's summary dismissal of capital theory as irrelevant. Even with the emergence of a more critical approach to Keynesian macroeconomics, this habit of ignoring the deeper issues that a consideration of the nature of capital invites was not broken. Capital theory is widely (if tacitly) regarded as a topic in the history of economic thought.

This book is an attempt to reawaken to some extent an interest in the kind of issues that emerged in the historical capital theory discussions. While it cannot be denied that much of those discussions meandered into areas of dubious relevance to the functioning of modern capitalist economies, it also remains true that many of the issues emerged and continue to emerge from *any* careful consideration of the nature and significance of capital. A good understanding of these issues would hopefully enhance our ability to talk intelligently about our economies and to make wise policy.

The history of capital theory contains relevant lessons and I examine this history in an attempt to understand it and to free capital theory from it, in the sense that its significance will be seen to extend far beyond the concerns to be found in those historical discussions. Those concerns, it seems to me, are largely the result of a particular approach to capital theory, a particular mindset, which we may call an equilibrium approach. Dating at least from Ricardo, economists have become accustomed to thinking about economic concepts in the context of a world in which individual plans largely dovetailed. This enabled them to build grand systems in which economic aggregates, including capital (the value of capital for the economy as a whole), made perfect sense. Even with the advent of the marginalist revolution, and the related discovery of subjective utility, the assumption of equilibrium enabled the construction of logically consistent and contextually meaningful aggregates like national income, wealth and capital.

The debates in capital theory thus took it for granted that it was relevant to discuss such things as the correct way to measure the capital stock theoretically. So while some (like Böhm-Bawerk) tried to argue for a simple logical formula involving production time (although, as we shall see, this was only a small part of his theory), others (like Clark and Knight) tried to finesse or banish the problem (of how capital should be valued) by assuming that the market "takes care of it," by assuring that the multitude of heterogeneous capital items in existence are all somehow consistently and spontaneously integrated into the large, permanent organic network of production which had no beginning or end. These latter theorists thus wondered about the meaning and relevance of "production time" and quite predictably the discussion progressed into the realm of metaphysics.

In a world in which individual plans may embody disparate views of that world, which the unfolding of time would put to the test, as is the case in the real world, the value of capital has no objective meaning. Yet capital evaluation is performed all the time and is a crucial and indispensable part of the market process. One might do well, therefore, to abandon any search for the appropriate method to measure economic aggregates like the capital stock and focus instead on understanding how the process of capital valuation actually functions as part of the market process as a whole. This is the approach taken in this book.

Capital as Value

Physical analogies featured heavily in the capital theory debates. This probably reflects not only the difficulty of the subject in which analogies based on familiar physical processes helped to simplify, but also the natural tendency to think about production as a physical process. Production, after all, (often) involves the physical transformation of matter from one form into a more useful one. And since these physical processes were seen to be involved, it was but a small step to seeing them as the essence of the process. Yet, I shall argue, these engineering aspects of production are among the least important for an understanding of the social significance of capital. Production technologies exist within a social framework. It is the value that is placed on these technologies, under different circumstances, that needs to be explained. Indeed, the evaluation of technologies is also a large part of the story of their discovery and adoption.

We see capital as an aspect of wealth, the result of the creation of value. Value is created in the context of trade (except in the unlikely instance of completely autarkic production, "trading with nature"). And trade occurs in an institutional context. Instead of focusing on the meaning and measurement of capital as an aggregate category, we shall focus on the individual capital evaluation decision. From the perspective of the individual, capital value is the perceived value of a particular production plan or set of plans. We examine therefore the logic of this individual evaluation, where we find the arithmetic of present value to be indispensable, and we examine the institutional context in which these evaluations, and the decisions to which they lead, occur.

Out of these individual decisions emerge the results of the market process. And these results are most often at some variance with the imagined and expected results of the planners whose combined and interacting actions gave rise to them. These planners thus experience capital gains and losses, that is, revisions to the capital evaluations embodied in original plans. These capital gains and losses are a crucial part of the market process. They are indispensable guides to ongoing decision-making in a changing world. It is thus startling to recall that capital gains and losses were taken out of capital theory in the traditional approaches to capital. This is related to the banishment of profit in the same context. It is a context of the banishment of change. The absence of change means no more (and no less) than the coinciding of the expected with the actual, and this must mean that everyone plans on the basis of accurate and consistent expectations. So if we are to understand why profits are earned, we must understand why people make capital gains—why some people are able to evaluate combinations of productive resources—capital combinations—more accurately than others, according to their judgment of the market. That is, we must recognize the existence and importance of *different* individual evaluations, even of the same things. Capitalist economies are changing economies. How do they cope with change?

Outline

The main body of this book is divided into three parts. Part I, consisting of two chapters, examines the concept of equilibrium and its relationship to change. Chapter 2 investigates the concept of equilibrium in the context of the enduring debate in modern Austrian economics about the presence or absence of equilibrating tendencies. This exercise in the "history of thought" has relevance beyond Austrian circles, however, as the issues involved are intrinsic to the subject. For example, it is at the heart of much of the debate in macroeconomics between the English Keynesians (see, for example, Kaldor 1985:60ff.) and the American neoclassicals. What is at stake are the implications of the fact that different individuals have different and often inconsistent expectations. Is there a tendency for these expectations to become more consistent over time as a result of the market process? If yes, what does this mean? If no, does this matter? How do individuals make decisions on the basis of inconsistent plans? The inescapable and troubling "loose ends" of mainstream economics are nicely brought out in this debate, particularly in the insightful analysis of Israel Kirzner. If we want to assume that markets are either in, or are in the process of approaching, equilibrium, ought we not to be able to explain how they get into equilibrium or are able to approach it?

In Chapter 3 I suggest that it is the adoption of an insufficiently examined concept of equilibrium that is behind the apparent impasse that this and related debates have reached. Specifically, if equilibrium is defined, along with Hayek, as a situation in which individual plans are mutually consistent (and realistic), then a closer examination of the way in which individuals plan will reveal that economies are at any time both in and out of equilibrium and are tending toward and away from equilibrium at the same time. This paradoxical conclusion is the result of a semantical sleight of hand. The Hayekian definition of equilibrium does not examine the limits and dimensions of the individual plans that feature in it. Once we realize that individual plans are, of necessity, based on different types of knowledge, are incomplete in crucial respects, and are multidimensional in nature, we realize that some aspects or plans are, and must be, highly, or even completely, consistent; while, at the same time, other aspects of plans are (and must be, if we are to have the kind of change necessary for dynamic market processes) inconsistent. And we shall see that equilibrium in relation to some aspects, or levels, of plans is a necessary condition for the toleration of disequilibrium in others, the levels at which innovation occurs. The insights derived in this chapter provide a necessary general backdrop for the consideration of capital evaluation and the decisions to which they give rise in a changing economy, which occupy the rest of the book.

Part II, Chapters 4 through 7, consists of investigations into the nature of capital and the related concepts of interest and profits. These concepts cannot be adequately considered apart from their development in the history of economic thought. Chapter 4 is an impressionistic historical outline of the development of the concept of capital. It is suggestive rather than accurate or complete. I examine the "model" offered by Adam Smith in the *Wealth of Nations* as a prototype "corn economy," an agrarian economy devoid of disruptive innovation in productive methods. In this corn economy, capital is a homogeneous circulating fund. (Adam Smith's contributions to the notion of the division of labor will occupy us later in a different context.) When we move from Smith's world to the world of Ricardo's *Principles* we find that things are not so simple. Ricardo strove valiantly to apply Smith's insights and method to a world in which much of the productive equipment was in the form of heterogeneous "machinery." He salvaged homogeneity by banishing considerations of change, by focusing on the conditions of the "long-run" stationary state. Those who followed Ricardo thus came to see this long-run equilibrium not only as the condition toward which the economy was always moving, but also as a sort of essential reality that characterized the market system below the surface reality of which our senses may at any time be aware.

In this sense, all modern-day theorists who work in terms of stationary or steady-state economics are "Ricardians." Their approach is to be contrasted with that of Carl Menger who, while also following Adam Smith in some respects, offered a different vision of the economy and of the process of production. For Menger production was characterized by a time structure of production that was the result of individual intertemporal planning. There is no suggestion that the economy is in a stationary-state equilibrium.

These two approaches exist in uneasy combination in the work of perhaps the most famous capital theorist in economics, Eugen von Böhm-Bawerk. Though a disciple of Menger's, Böhm-Bawerk's work has been adopted by neoclassicals, neo-Ricardians, and Austrians alike as embodying their particular approaches. We thus examine how it is that these apparently conflicting visions could coexist in the work of the same theorist. From Böhm-Bawerk's work we will learn a great deal about the ways in which time is seen to be involved in the process of production. In particular, his assertion that the essence of capitalist production is the adoption of increasingly "roundabout" methods will be seen to be of enduring relevance.

One way of reading Böhm-Bawerk can be seen to be consistent with the modern "production function" approach to capital. This is examined in Chapter 5. The production function story rests on some particular assumptions: production is an unvarying input-output scheme in which both inputs and outputs are unambiguous aggregate values. The logic of the production function approach is informative and yields some important insights into the meaning of constant returns to scale, diminishing returns, and technological change. It has also recently focused attention on the important phenomenon of endogenous change. But these insights come only by straining to the limit the bounds within which the production function makes any sense.

The debate between the Cambridges in the 1950s, 1960s, and 1970s featured the English neo-Ricardians against the American neoclassicals. Taking the production function approach to be definitive of production economics, the neo-Ricardians relentlessly picked at its logical limits in an effort to discredit it and seem to have been largely successful in this. But what they gained in logical consistency, they arguably lost in relevance. Both the Cambridges implicitly assumed a Ricardian equilibrium world in which the "rate of profit" was uniformly equal to the rate of interest. From the perspective of a technologically dynamic market economy, both approaches would appear to be largely irrelevant.

John Hicks was a penetrating thinker, an economist who helped to guide his colleagues through the difficult issues of the day. He did considerable work on the theory of capital over his long and productive career and, although his work as a whole defies easy categorization, he had an abiding sympathy for the Austrian approach, as exemplified particularly by Carl Menger. In Chapter 6 I examine his last full length work on capital theory (Hicks 1973b), which he called a neo-Austrian approach. In it we shall find a convenient expression of the type of evaluation arithmetic facilitated by a money-using market economy. Although we cannot follow Hicks into his world of social accounting, we shall find much that is useful in his insights.

In the development of capital theory various approaches to the characterization of profits and interest have emerged. In Chapter 7 I briefly review this and give prominence to one particular approach, the "pure time preference theory" (PTPT) of interest. The most notable aspect of this view is the careful separation of the concepts of profit and interest. The former is seen to be the result of changes in the value of capital combinations in a world of change and uncertainty, while the latter is an expression of time preference. While time preference is indeed (and contrary to some approaches) to be seen as an expression of individuals' feelings of uncertainty, it is to be very carefully distinguished from the concept of profit. Although they may be difficult to disentangle in practice, profit, rent, and interest are separate and distinct concepts.

In Part III, Chapters 8 through 12, I turn to an examination of capital in a dynamic world. In Chapter 8 we look at a Mengerian approach to capital theory. We take Hayek to be the modern pioneer, in his writings in the 1930s culminating in his *Pure Theory of Capital* (1941). The *Pure Theory* in itself is not a work about capital in a changing world but it points in that direction. In particular, in his extended analysis of the so-called problem of "imputation," Hayek raises questions of relevance to such a changing world. Ludwig Lachmann's work on capital theory may be seen as picking up Hayek's cue. Lachmann consciously adopts a disequilibrium framework to re-examine what he takes to be the valid insights of Böhm-Bawerk. He ends up with a fascinating synthesis of Adam Smith and Böhm-Bawerk, one that sees in the growing complexity of modern productive structures a representation of Böhm-Bawerk's increasingly roundabout methods of production and Adam Smith's division of labor.

As mentioned above, capital evaluation decisions occur within an institutional-organizational framework. In Chapter 9 I explore the link between capital structures (narrowly understood) and organizational structures. The original pioneering work of G. B. Richardson and Edith Penrose is seen to have much in common with Lachmann's Mengerian approach, and from this a link is forged to some later work in the areas of production and organizations. In Chapter 10 this is seen to be relevant to the work of Mises and others on the question of capital calculation in market economies.

In Chapter 11 I turn to an examination of human capital. The human capital "revolution" in economic theory sometimes seems to have had more of an impact in adjacent fields like sociology and anthropology than in economics itself. It is true that the concept of human capital has now permeated the mainstream in many areas; for example in growth theory, in the theory of the firm, and, of course, in labor economics. Its application to a consideration of the dynamics of market economies has, however, been surprisingly limited. In this chapter I attempt to draw out some implications along these lines while summarizing some of the keynotes of the literature, deriving primarily from the work of Gary Becker, T. W. Schultz, and Jacob Mincer. In Chapter 12 I confront some subtle issues arising out of the special nature of knowledge as a phenomenon that would seem to be relevant to human capital as a product. In observing that knowledge is at once fallible, unfathomable, and tacit, we are drawn full circle back to a discussion of equilibrium in a changing world.

The book closes with a concluding chapter that summarizes the work and explores some implications for economic policy.

PART I

BACKGROUND: EQUILIBRIUM AND CHANGE

This first part of this work consists of two chapters (2 and 3).[1] In Chapter 2 I summarize briefly some issues connected with the meaning and existence of equilibrium. This controversial area has been made difficult by the fact that the term "equilibrium" is often used in an inconsistent manner, either by a single theorist in different places and times or as between different theorists. So I try first to clarify what is meant (or what should be meant) by equilibrium. I adopt the Hayekian definition—the mutual consistency of individual plans. From this point of view I examine a current debate, one that is specific to modern Austrian (market process) economics, but is relevant to and, in many ways, reflective of, economics in general. This is the debate about the presence or absence (and, indeed, meaning) of equilibrating tendencies in the economy. The chief (friendly) protagonists in this discussion are Ludwig Lachmann and Israel Kirzner. The legacy of this debate is still with us.

In Chapter 3 I turn to the question of what really is at stake here. I offer a different perspective, a different approach to the question of equilibrium. If we say that the economy is always in disequilibrium, because plans must be inconsistent to some degree, then are we not undermining our ability to do economics, to understand human action in the economy? Or is action possible and understandable in disequilibrium? I shall contend that if we wish to adopt Hayek's approach to equilibrium, we must mean that we can act in a world where the plans that motivate and define those actions are not mutually compatible. This is hardly controversial. After all, the market process features

---

[1] A shorter version of some of the material in this part appears in Lewin (1997c).

rivalrous actions, that is, actions that are part of mutually inconsistent plans. Successful plans tend to displace unsuccessful ones. But can we therefore say that, overall, plans tend to become more consistent so that there is a 'tendency' toward equilibrium? Is this important? I shall answer both in the negative. Furthermore, I shall maintain that capital accumulation and economic progress depend in a crucial way on the absence of equilibrium and in no way on our ability to discern equilibrium tendencies. More specifically, I shall argue that the Hayekian definition requires too much. Plans are complex, multilayered constructs. Overall "plan consistency" is, therefore, either impossible or hopelessly imprecise. I shall argue that at some levels plans are and must be highly compatible, while at other levels (as part of the market process, for example) they are and, if we are to have economic progress, they must be, incompatible.

The issues discussed in this part and the resolutions offered provide an important backdrop for the consideration of capital in a dynamic world.

CHAPTER 2

What Does Equilibrium Mean? A Discussion in the Context of Modern Austrian Ideas

Equilibrium Examined and Defined

> A term which has so many meanings that we never know what its users are talking about should be either dropped from the vocabulary of the scholar or "purified" of confusing connotations.
> (Machlup 1958:43)

The continuing use of the word "equilibrium" by different people to mean different things justifies yet another brief examination. No pretense, however, is made at completeness.

I can think of at least seven different approaches to equilibrium. These are not mutually exclusive and are, indeed, related in important ways:

1. equilibrium as a balance of forces
2. equilibrium as a state of rest (a stationary state)
3. equilibrium as a state of uniform movement (a steady state—of which 2 is a special case)
4. equilibrium as a constrained maximum
5. equilibrium as an optimum
6. equilibrium as rational action
7. equilibrium as a situation of consistent plans.

In each case at least two dimensions can be identified. Equilibrium can relate to the entire economy (general equilibrium) or to a subset of the economy (partial equilibrium) or to the individual. Equilibrium can be considered for a single all-encompassing period (static equilibrium), or for a succession of self-contained periods (temporary equilibrium) or for a succession of related sub-periods (intertemporal equilibrium).

Examining this further, we note that equilibrium as a balance of forces (as the word implies)[1] *in some sense* is at the base of all other equilibrium concepts. And if "change" (and its absence) is defined appropriately, definitions 1 and 2 are seen to be equivalent. So, for example, the traditional supply and demand equilibrium is a balance of forces that acts to keep prices stable (at rest). In the case of the price of an asset, we may say that if the price is stable, the bulls balance the bears.[2] In the case of a perishable good, those forces (whatever they are: technology, price expectations, etc.) which tend to influence the amounts offered for sale and purchase at various prices in a way that tends to push the price up are balanced by those that tend to push it down. This is one way to think of stable prices. If neither supply nor demand change, price (once in equilibrium) will not change. It is also an optimum (definition 5) of sorts in the well-understood sense that, given the fundamental conditions of supply and demand, buyers and sellers are doing the best they can. From another perspective, it is a

---

[1] Interestingly *The New Shorter Oxford English Dictionary* offers a number of definitions:

> 1. A well balanced state of mind or feeling.... 2. A condition of balance between opposing physical forces.... 3. A state in which the influences or processes to which a thing is subject cancel one another and produce no overall change or variation.... *Econ.* A situation in which supply and demand are matched and prices stable.

Although 2 and 3 are probably the most intuitive colloquially, 1 comes closest to our usage, as we shall see.

[2]
> [The market] cannot make bulls and bears change their expectations but it nevertheless can coordinate these. To coordinate bullish and bearish expectations is, ... the economic function of the Stock Exchange and of asset markets in general. This is achieved because in such markets the price will move until the whole market is divided into equal halves of bulls and bears. In this way divergent expectations are cast into a coherent pattern and a measure of coordination is accomplished ... asset markets are inherently 'restless,' and equilibrium prices established in them reflect nothing but the daily *balance* of expectations. (Lachmann 1976b:237–238, italics added)

Clearly Lachmann is here using the term "coordination" in a rather limited sense and in no way to suggest a rendering of expectations compatible.

constrained maximum (definition 4) in that buyers and sellers maximize the perceived opportunities to buy and sell, and thereby achieve a maximum of "satisfaction" as determined by their preferences in relation to the (perceived) opportunities. It may not be an optimum, however, if there are opportunities of which the economic agents are unaware (see Kirzner 1990), or if their actions affect opportunities in other markets adversely. Also, it is possible to see how momentary equilibrium can be generalized to a situation of uniform change (definition 3) — for example, where demand and supply increase proportionately.

So while, in an appropriate sense, equilibrium as a balance of forces is also a state of rest (or a situation of uniform change) and a constrained maximum, it may not be an optimum. Also, in each case it is possible to conceive of situations that are not in equilibrium. Some theorists have found it helpful, however, to define the constraints so broadly as to conceive of individuals as being *always* in equilibrium (see Shmanske 1994). So, again using the example of simple supply and demand, a situation of non-price rationing, not allowing the price to rise and clear the market, can be seen as an equilibrium situation if we include in all individual decisions the costs imposed by rationing—like waiting in line. Indeed, using this approach, one may predict that the lines at the checkout counter of a supermarket would tend to an "equilibrium" size that equalizes waiting time. Thus the supply curve becomes vertical at the fixed price below the market-clearing price. In effect, the money price has been reduced, but the real price (including waiting cost) has gone up because of a "shift" in the supply curve to the left (from an upward slope to a vertical one). So demand *always* equals supply if we are careful to include all relevant factors.[3] While it is clear that this approach may prove enlightening in some cases, when extended to the level of all agents for the entire economy it can involve disturbing and paradoxical implications. Thus, considering all possible costs and benefits, the world is at all times in a Pareto optimal equilibrium, a Panglosian "best of all possible worlds" given the relevant constraints. Things are what they are because we understand how individuals had to act the way they acted in order to max-

---

[3]Becker (and others using the 'Chicago approach') have used this type of reasoning to explain regulation-busting behavior (bribes, black markets, etc.) where individuals are seen as weighing all of the costs and benefits involved in violating regulations, etc. (Becker 1971:106ff.)

imize, given the constraints that existed and were perceived by them (again see Shmanske 1994 for a complete discussion). This approach uses equilibrium to characterize rational action (definition 6) where "rational" is understood to refer to the system as a whole and not just to individuals. For normative (policy) purposes this is obviously not very helpful. The policy-maker is, after all, subject to the same, universally perceived, constraints. We shall see that the difficulty arises because of the lack of a distinction between individual and system equilibrium.

In a lecture delivered in 1936, Hayek defined equilibrium as a situation in which "the different plans which the individuals composing [a society] have made for action in time are mutually compatible" (Hayek 1937b:41). This is my definition 7. As this is the definition that we shall adopt in the rest of this work, it is worth examining in some detail. An important aspect is the move away from the purely physical dimensions of equilibrium as a state of rest or balance of forces, to one firmly based in the human mind. Equilibrium is here conceived as a situation in which individual knowledge and expectations, and the actions based on these, are compatible with the "data," where the "data" for one individual include the actions of other individuals. Scratching the surface of any of the definitions offered above indeed reveals that it is impossible to think of equilibrium in economics without bringing in the perceptions of individuals. After all, we are dealing with human actions and these are determined by the perceptions of the actors. So, in the case of the supply and demand of a single well-defined market, for example, the price will not be observed to change when all individuals are fulfilling their mutually related plans to buy and sell; and where such plans are not fulfilled we may expect these plans to be revised.[4]

The volitional, intentional aspect of equilibrium is likewise obvious in all of the other approaches. This is widely recognized, although in

---

[4]It is possible to conceive of a situation of "statistical" equilibrium where mutually offsetting individual errors are such as to leave the price unchanged. In such a situation, although individual plans are not mutually compatible, we have equilibrium as a kind of balance of forces. Individuals are right "on average." Hayek discusses this case in passing (Hayek 1937b:43n.) In a way this anticipates aspects of the rational expectations literature developed since the 1970s. As we shall be concerned with equilibrium in terms of its implications for individual perceptions, we shall not consider this case in any more detail. A sufficient, though not necessary, condition for price stability in the partial equilibrium static (non-growth) case, is the compatibility of plans to buy and sell.

the formal technical treatments of modern economics one is often apt to lose sight of it, as for example in the case of neo-Ricardian capital theory and general equilibrium theory. There is no doubt, however, that Hayek's insights have been accepted in principle and have been variously endorsed by a number of eminent neoclassical economists. For example:

> [Equilibrium refers to] those states in which the intended actions of rational economic agents are mutually consistent and can, therefore, be implemented. (Hahn 1984:44)

> [Equilibrium is a] state where no economic agents have an incentive to change their behavior ... the equality of demand and supply should not be taken as a definition of equilibrium, but rather as a consequence following from more primitive behavioral postulates. (Stiglitz 1987:28)

Thus we shall say that an equilibrium situation is one in which individual plans are fully coordinated. Each plan can be successfully executed. Means are exactly matched to ends.

Implications of Equilibrium

It will be immediately apparent that equilibrium *thus defined* is an extremely unlikely event. It is patently unrealistic. One might wonder at its widespread acceptance as a standard of reference. This raises the important question of the function of equilibrium constructs in economic theory. Obviously, theoretical constructs are, to a greater or lesser extent, unrealistic. They all abstract from reality in order to illuminate it. For example, one common use to which equilibrium constructs are put is the tracing of the (ultimate) consequences of any change while imagining all other possible relevant changes to be absent. In this way a general idea of cause and effect can be built up by isolating the effects of different causes.[5] The crucial question is: what are

---

[5] Machlup identifies four basic steps in equilibrium analysis:

1. Initial position—everything could go on as it is.
2. A disequilibrating change.
3. Adjusting changes.
4. Final position—new equilibrium.

Comparing 4 with 1 establishes cause–effect (see the discussion in Machlup 1958:47ff.).

permissible abstractions, and what abstractions render a theoretical construct useless? When is the usefulness of the model compromised so that its results (the cause–effect connections that it suggests) are no longer reliable guides to reality? This is an involved question that we shall not be able to answer here in any detail. I shall contend, however, and hopefully motivate in the course of our discussion, that theoretical constructs that abstract completely from the implications for human action of the passage of time and its implications for changes in knowledge are not likely to be very helpful in understanding economic processes. While it is true that equilibrium "is in the model and not in the world,"[6] I want to build a bridge between the "model" and the "world" and maintain that timeless models cannot do this.[7] This is most clearly seen in discussing the stability of equilibrium.

Before turning to this, however, we should pause to note some other aspects of equilibrium, understood as the mutual compatibility of individual plans, including the relationship between micro and macro equilibrium, or between individual and system equilibrium.[8] Hayek makes an important distinction between these:

> I have long felt that the concept of equilibrium itself and the methods which we employ in pure analysis have a clear meaning only when confined to the analysis of the action of a single person and that we are really passing into a different sphere and silently introducing a new element of altogether different character when we apply it to the explanation of the interactions of a number of different individuals. (Hayek 1937b:35)

It is from a careful consideration of the meaning of individual equilibrium that a number of implications for our understanding of system equilibrium emerge. First, Hayek argues that the "tautological propositions of pure equilibrium analysis" are not directly applicable to the explanation of social relations. Examining individual equilibrium shows

---

[6] This phrase is from O'Driscoll and Rizzo (1996:24). See generally Machlup (1958).

[7] See also the discussions in Rizzo (1990, 1992).

[8] I will use this designation to distinguish in general a higher level than individual equilibrium, whether it be the entire economic system or a subsystem of it (for example, an isolated market). As will become clear from the text, the crucial distinction is between equilibrium as it applies to an individual mind and as it applies to the interaction between two or more minds.

it to be equivalent to rational action. "What is relevant [however] is not whether a person as such is or is not in equilibrium but which of his actions stand in equilibrium in so far as they can be understood as part of one plan" (ibid.:36). Second, the role of the individuals' knowledge and, therefore, the knowledge of all individuals, is of crucial importance. "It is important to remember that the so-called 'data,' from which we set out in this sort of analysis, are (apart from his tastes) all facts given to the person in question, the things as they are known to (or believed by) him to exist, are not, strictly speaking, objective facts" (ibid.:36). So it is quite conceivable, and likely, that in some respects different individuals' "knowledge" of the same circumstance will be not only different but inconsistent. And some types of knowledge are likely to be more reliable guides to action than others.

Third:

> since equilibrium relations exist between the successive actions of a person only in so far as they are part of the execution of the same plan, any change in the relevant knowledge of the person, that is, any change which leads him to alter his plan, disrupts the equilibrium relations between his actions taken before and those taken after the change in his knowledge. In other words, the equilibrium relationship comprises only his actions during the period in which his anticipations prove correct. [And] since equilibrium is a relationship between actions, and since the actions of one person must necessarily take place successively in time, it is obvious that *the passage of time is essential to give the concept of equilibrium any meaning.*
>
> (ibid.:36–37, italics added)

So equilibrium is not only a relationship between individuals at a point of time, it is necessarily also a relationship between actions over time. For equilibrium to exist during a period of time it must exist at every point of time within that period. If equilibrium exists at a point of time, then individuals' plans are consistent with each other and with the technical facts of the world such that each plan can be successfully implemented. This means that in the absence of any change (meaning the arrival of new knowledge) equilibrium will exist at *every* point of time. This definition of equilibrium thus implies intertemporal equilibrium.[9]

---

[9] See also (Hicks 1965:24).

A Tendency Towards Equilibrium?

Hayek on Equilibrium Tendencies

In the history of the development of the equilibrium concept economists have been concerned with certain basic properties that equilibria may or may not exhibit. The most basic is the question of *existence*—whether or not an equilibrium can be shown logically to exist. According to our definition this involves showing that a situation exists (logically) such that all plans can be implemented. In the voluminous mathematical literature on general equilibrium such a proof was ultimately discovered, but at the expense of the imposition of a set of heroic restrictions on knowledge, preferences and technology. It was also possible to show that under certain even more restrictive conditions such an equilibrium was *unique* (Ingrao and Israel 1990). It is clear, however, that the importance that these properties assumed is directly related to the formal, technical, mechanistic nature of the conception of equilibrium that tended to dominate this literature (and still does). For Hayek, equilibrium was never understood as a state that could ever actually be said to exist, although its logical existence is clearly implied. He was more concerned with the question of whether or not it could be shown or argued that a *tendency* toward equilibrium ("a greater degree of plan coordination") characterized the actual market process. This is related to the questions of *stability* and/or *convergence* that the mathematical economists have been unable to answer satisfactorily.[10] But for Hayek (and those who followed his lead) it was not a theoretical matter. As this will be quite important, I will quote at some length from Hayek:

> We shall not get much further here unless we ask for the reasons for our concern with the admittedly fictitious state of equilibrium. Whatever may occasionally have been said by overpure economists, there seems to be no possible doubt that the only justification for this is the supposed existence of a tendency toward equilibrium. It is only by this assertion that such a tendency exists that economics ceases to be an exercise in pure logic and becomes an empirical science....

---

[10] Once in equilibrium, will the system remain there (stability); and starting from any arbitrary point, will it converge to equilibrium?

> In the light of our analysis of the meaning of a state of equilibrium it should be easy to say what is the real content of the assertion that a tendency toward equilibrium exists. It can hardly mean anything but that, under certain conditions, the knowledge and intentions of the different members of society are supposed to come more and more into agreement or, ... that the expectations of the people and particularly of the entrepreneurs will become more and more correct. In this form the assertion of the existence of a tendency toward equilibrium is clearly an empirical proposition, that is, an assertion about what happens in the real world.... And it gives our somewhat abstract statement a rather plausible common-sense meaning. The only trouble is that we are still pretty much in the dark about (a) the *conditions* under which this tendency is supposed to exist and (b) the nature of the *process* by which individual knowledge is changed. (Hayek 1937b:44–45)

This was a preoccupation of Hayek's throughout his career even as he moved beyond economics narrowly understood. Whether or not he was able to provide a satisfactory answer to items (a) and (b) in the quotation above is a matter of some debate (see, for example, Rizzo 1990, 1992; Lewin 1994).

Lachmann versus Kirzner

The revival of the Austrian research program, in its market process variety, since the 1970s, has seen a return to this issue of equilibrating tendencies in a more energetic fashion. In particular, it has emerged as a defining issue *within* the Austrian School of economics in a way that was clearly foreshadowed during some historical moments in June 1974 in South Royalton, Vermont, at a conference marking the start of this revival (Dolan 1976). At that conference two papers in particular outlined the two key perspectives that have appeared to be in conflict ever since—by Ludwig Lachmann and Israel Kirzner (Lachmann 1976a; Kirzner 1976). In these two papers (and some others by the same authors in the conference volume) we find a clear, concise articulation of the issues.[11] Both Kirzner and Lachmann regard the market as a

---

[11] In particular, Lachmann's analysis of equilibrium appears in its most uncompromising version. It is probably from here, more than from any other time and place, that Lachmann's reputation as a "radical subjectivist" gained momentum and has since tended to dominate in evaluations of his work.

process in time, out of equilibrium. Both regard the question of equilibrating tendencies to be problematic. But for Kirzner the problem is resolved by the actions of the entrepreneur in noticing disequilibrium situations and profiting by their removal, thus providing a reason to believe in, and an explanation of, a tendency in markets towards equilibrium.

The problem is most simply seen once again in the supply and demand analysis of an isolated market. As Kirzner remarks, often our explanations proceed no further than an identification of the market-clearing price at the intersection point — "almost implying that the only possible price is the market clearing price." Our common-sense explanations proceed in terms of familiar Walrasian equilibrating processes. At prices below market clearing, there is an excess supply in the aggregate (unsold stocks) and this will tend to force prices down; while the opposite is true for a situation of excess demand (unsatisfied buyers). "Thus, we explain there will be a tendency for price to gravitate toward the equilibrium level." We should note that it is implicitly assumed that there is always only one price in the market. "One uncomfortable question, then, is whether we may assume that a single price emerges before equilibrium is attained. Surely a single price can be postulated only as a result of the process of equilibration itself." Various explanations have been offered and devices suggested for dealing with this problem, including Marshallian adjustment processes and perfect competition, none successfully. The problem remains because "disequilibrium occurs precisely because market participants do not know what the market-clearing price is" (Kirzner 1976:116–117).

This approach can be generalized to equilibrium in contexts other than the isolated market. The problem of explaining convergence to equilibrium is a problem of explaining how individuals out of equilibrium obtain the information necessary for them to have knowledge of, and incentives to make, the appropriate adjustments. In the process of developing the solution Kirzner reaffirms the Hayekian definition of (dis)equilibrium. "Disequilibrium is a situation in which not all plans can be carried out together; it reflects mistakes in the price information on which individual plans were made" (ibid.:118). It is the Kirznerian entrepreneur who notices these mistakes and is able to take advantage of them. Kirzner's well-known, and justly admired, theory of entrepreneurial action in the removal of all manner of price discrepancies will not be summarized here.[12] Suffice it to say that the entrepreneur is "an all-purpose arbitrageur" (my term) who is alert to profit opportunities that exist as a result of price differences at a point of time, price differences between two points in time (after accounting for interest and holding costs), or price and cost differences (that is the price of a finished product and the cost of all the resources, including interest, necessary to produce it). By exploiting these generalized price discrepancies the entrepreneur tends to remove them, thus providing the answer to the original uncomfortable question. The tendency to equilibrium is supplied by entrepreneurial action. Kirzner then states clearly the issue that we are investigating:

> Disequilibrium represents a situation of widespread market ignorance. This ignorance is responsible for the emergence of profitable opportunities. Entrepreneurial alertness exploits these opportunities when others pass them by. G. L. S. Shackle and Lachmann emphasized the unpredictability of human knowledge, and indeed we do not clearly understand how entrepreneurs get their flashes of superior foresight. We cannot explain how some men discover what is around the corner before others do so.... As an empirical matter, however, opportunities do tend to be perceived and exploited. And it is on this observed tendency that our belief in a determinate market process is founded. (ibid.:121)

Lachmann makes it clear that he does not believe in a "determinate market process." While he is readily prepared to endorse the notion of individual equilibrium, he has no use for general equilibrium (and, as is clear from the context, any equilibrium other than that of the individual) or tendencies toward it. "The notion of general equilibrium is to be abandoned, but that of *individual equilibrium* is to be retained at all costs. It is simply tantamount to *rational action*. Without it we should lose our 'sense of direction'" (Lachmann 1976a:131). The reason for his rejection of market equilibrium is his understanding

---

[12]For a recent statement see Kirzner (1992). Since the first edition of this book was published in 1999, Kirzner has continued to explain and refine his ideas as they have gained in exposure and popularity especially in the field of management studies. See Kirzner (2009).

of the implications for action of the passage of time. Once again, as with Kirzner, I shall not stop to summarize in any detail Lachmann's well-known views in this regard. I merely note some implications. He considers it axiomatic that the passage of time cannot occur without the arrival of new knowledge. Each moment in time is unique and time is irreversible. "As soon as we permit time to elapse, we must permit knowledge to change" (ibid.:127–128, italics removed). I have referred to this as Lachmann's axiom.[13]

> Although old knowledge is continually being superseded by new knowledge, though nobody knows which piece will be obsolete tomorrow, men have to act with regard to the future and make plans based on expectations. Experience teaches us that in an uncertain world different men hold different expectations about the same future event ... divergent expectations entail incoherent plans ... what keeps this process in continuous motion is the occurrence of unexpected change as well as the inconsistency of human plans.... Are we entitled, then, to be confident that the market process will in the end eliminate incoherence of plans...? To say that the market gradually produces a consistency among plans is to say that the divergence of expectations, on which the initial incoherence of plans rests, will gradually be turned into convergence. But to reach this conclusion we must deny the autonomous character of expectations.... Expectations are autonomous. We cannot predict their mode of change as prompted by failure or success. (ibid.:128–129)

There is thus no way to know which of the "opportunities" perceived by the Kirznerian entrepreneurs are "real" and which are (perhaps inconsistent) figments of their disparate expectations. In this way Lachmann departed company from Kirzner and Hayek and was not prepared to assert the existence of any tendency toward equilibrium. "What emerges from our reflections is an image of the market as a particular kind of process, a continuous process without beginning or end, propelled by the interaction between the forces of equilibrium and the forces of change" (Lachmann 1976b:61).[14]

---

[13] Lewin (1994:236). "According to a well-known Austrian axiom, 'Time cannot elapse without the state of knowledge changing'" (Lachmann 1986:95).

[14] For an in-depth examination of this debate, see Karen Vaughn (1992; 1994:ch. 7). The debate continues, though in muted terms since Lachmann's death in 1990. Kirzner has attempted to restate and refine his position (1992) and Mario Rizzo has provided a

The issue of convergence, of a tendency toward equilibrium,[15] thus remains a contentious issue in which a lot is perceived to be at stake. From Lachmann's lead, further investigations of the meaning and implications of Lachmann's axiom have followed, the most elaborate of which is the in-depth examination by O'Driscoll and Rizzo (1996). The varying reactions to this book bear testimony to the depth of the rift within the subjectivist Austrian family. This is well captured in the two reviews by Kirzner (1994a) and Lachmann (1994).[16] Although intrafamily disputes are often the most vociferous, where there is so much agreement on everything else of significance it is perhaps surprising. Yet it appears to be fundamental.

Hayekian equilibrium is a state of complete coordination of plans (and the expectations on which they depend). An equilibrating tendency is thus a tendency of markets to coordinate human affairs. By denying the existence of equilibrating tendencies, Kirzner worries, one may be led to deny the "plausibility of possible systematic processes of market coordination" and in the extreme "render economic science non-existent" (Kirzner 1994a:40–41). On the other hand, Lachmann worries that by affirming the existence of persistent equilibrating tendencies "we are playing right into the hands of our opponents who merely have to point to obvious instances of malcoordination to win debating points" (Lachmann and White 1979:7). Further, "the root of our difficulty lies in this: in a market ... all coordinating activity must engender some discoordination of existing relations" (Lachmann 1986:11) hence endogenous change. Those who take Lachmann's axiom seriously see no way to avoid the conclusion that change is endogenous and continuous, thus making any statement about equilibrating tendencies inherently suspect. At the heart of the problem is the "autonomy of individual expectations" and the choices to which they lead. Lachmann's axiom follows from the inability to deny its implication that individual behavior cannot be predicted because future

---

further critique (Rizzo 1996). For a summary of Kirzner's position, see Kirzner (1997). For a more recent summary, see Kirzner (2009).

[15]See the appendix to this chapter.

[16]Originally published soon after O'Driscoll and Rizzo (1996, first edition 1985) in the *Market Process Newsletter*. For references to some of the contributions to this debate see Boettke, Prychitko, and Horwitz (1994).

knowledge cannot be predicted (O'Driscoll and Rizzo 1996). Expectations relating to the choices of other individuals must be diverse and, therefore, are bound to be falsified. But if expectations are bound to be falsified, implying that prediction is impossible, how do we do economics? Indeed how do we act at all? Is life possible without equilibrium?

Appendix: Equilibrium, Time and Expectations

The problem of convergence to equilibrium revolves essentially around the prior problem of *how economic agents in a disequilibrium situation acquire information that would motivate them to take actions that would result in the economy moving toward equilibrium*. They cannot be presumed to know what the equilibrium price is, since this would assume away the entire problem. Kirzner's answer, as we have seen, is that the entrepreneur, the important economic agent in this context, acts on the basis of price discrepancies—"buying low and selling high"—thus moving prices toward the establishment of one price. But how do we know that this will be the equilibrium price? The problem may be seen most simply if we once again use the simple supply and demand case of an isolated market.

The simplest case is the one where we assume that the positions of the supply and demand curves are unaffected by the actions of individuals in the market. That is to say, the effects of trading at "false prices" must be assumed to be negligible—small enough to be ignored. We thus ignore any possible income effects that might give rise to path dependence. We rule out changes in the "data" as a result of the actions of the market participants themselves—we rule out *endogenous* change; and we rule out changes that emanate from outside of this market, like changes in technology—we rule out *exogenous* change. In this case the equilibrium price is a fixed target, an unmoving attractor. Should the market arrive at it, it will stay there in the absence of any exogenous change. The question is: if the price is not at the equilibrium price, will it move towards it?

Traditionally, and predictably, this problem has been answered by attempting to investigate how individuals might react to the information they receive in disequilibrium. So for example, when the price is above the equilibrium price, there will be more available for sale than is demanded. The existence of excess supply will tend plausibly to suggest to economic agents (or an entrepreneur will suggest to them) that they reduce the price that they offer or ask, and in this way the price will tend to fall. But to what level will the price fall; how do agents form their expectation of what the price should be? These "reaction functions" can be of greater or lesser complexity, and depending on their properties the problem will exhibit a "smooth" transition toward the equilibrium price in each successive "period," an oscillating approach, a perpetual circling around it, or an explosive divergence away from it.

This is the familiar corn–hog cycle. It suffers from pretending to know how individuals will react in any given disequilibrium situation. It is not plausible to suggest that individual reaction functions that depend on each other's reaction to ever increasing higher levels can be mathematically modeled in a satisfactory way. However, it may be argued that another route is available. Whatever the precise way in which individuals react, as long as there is *enough variation in reactions*, and as long as we allow *enough time to elapse* in the absence of fundamental change, we may argue that as a result of sheer "trial and error," propelled by varying reactions to disequilibrium prices, the market will eventually, if not sooner then later, "hit" on the equilibrium price. It is hard to believe that an unmoving equilibrium price will not eventually be discovered and established. It is, after all, a "preferred" price in the sense that it results in the mutual fulfillment of all buy and sell plans and we reasonably expect it to emerge out of individual free trades.

Now of course the problem is that it is not at all plausible to assume that the supply and demand curves are fixed for the duration. The above exercise may establish a convergence in principle (not a "rigorous" proof, but a suggestive argument), and this may suggest further that, as an empirical matter, reactions are such in the real world that a "tendency" toward the equilibrium price will prevail even though it is continually being thwarted by shifts in supply and demand. The argument is that the tendency in the market is toward equilibrium. To the extent that this is disturbed it is as a result of exogenous changes in supply and demand forces, like a new technology, new products, etc. Thus, it is the presence or absence of endogenous change that has emerged as a critical issue.

The simple supply–demand case is suggestive in two ways. First, where the world is such that the "underlying realities" (in this case the positions of the supply and demand curves or, more accurately, the contingent trades that they represent) are constant, it seems natural to argue that convergence will occur. So even if, for centuries, most people believe erroneously that the world is flat, and for some time there is a variation of beliefs, since the world remains round no matter what we believe or how we act messages from our experience will eventually convince us (all of us?!) that it is round. There is a notable convergence of expectations as a result of experience. No one now expects to fall off the edge. Generally a stable (constant) decision environment is conducive to convergence, exhibiting the required feedback. Second, the simple supply–demand case can be generalized to situations of multiple markets as long as we continue to ignore income or wealth effects and rule out exogenous changes. Then the entrepreneur becomes key. Price discrepancies in geographically separated markets or for inputs versus outputs will then tend to be eradicated even as each market is "groping" its way to isolated equilibrium. And in this case it is easy to see how prices are powerful transmitters of information. Once again, the result is ideal, depending as it does on the assumption of unvarying underlying realities and sufficient variation in individual reaction.

CHAPTER 3

Equilibrium and Expectations Re-Examined: A Different Perspective

> [F]rom time to time it is probably necessary to detach oneself from the technicalities of the argument and to ask quite naively what it is all about. (Hayek 1937b:54)

The debate referred to in the previous chapter is in many ways related to the general problem in economics of dealing adequately with the phenomenon of time. It seems that every economist of note has, in one way or another, perceived some difficulty associated with accounting for the passage of time while maintaining equilibrium and has wrestled with it (Currie and Steedman 1990). On the one hand there is the undeniable fact of human action in an ordered society. On the other hand there are the undeniable facts of novelty and disequilibrium and the inability to foresee all consequences. All action is future oriented—it rests on connecting present causes to future effects, which seems to imply successful prediction. How is one to reconcile these apparently irreconcilable perspectives?

Describing and Understanding Action

One possible resolution may lie in re-examining the concept of "expectations" and concepts related to it. I offer a scheme that will include an articulation of the following concepts: *events/occurrences, laws of nature, social "laws," acts/actions, plans, knowledge and expectations*. We take note of the passage of time by recording *occurrences* or *events* that we categorize according to our understanding of them. Events that occur in nature, that do not involve humans, are understood according to what we think of as the *forces (or laws) of nature*. Events that occur in society, that relate to humans, are understood according to the intentions and meanings of the individuals involved. At one level it is possible to describe human events as part of events in nature; physiologically for example. So it is possible to examine human acts in terms of the biological processes, in the brain and in the rest of the body, that brought them about. But the nature of the understanding we achieve by this is of the same type as of events in nature. To acquire an understanding of events as *human or social events* requires examining (inter)subjective intentions and meanings.[1] We may say that events in society are the results of *actions*. They involve human acts.[2] To describe an act satisfactorily, recourse must be had to motives, means and outcomes—even if the latter are unintended. Outcomes are connected to (understood in terms of) a multitude of actions, related and unrelated. This seems to me what we mean when we talk about equilibrium in terms of the consistency, compatibility and coordination of *plans*. Plans embody a number of related acts. They are related by *purpose*. Thus different acts may be *complementary*, when they work towards the same purpose, or *competitive*, when they work for conflicting purposes, or they may be unrelated.[3] The notion of "plan," so widely used by economists, is in need of further examination.

---

[1] While differing from his approach in some respects, this echoes Mises' insistence on "methodological dualism" (see for example Mises 1957:ch. 1). Mises' approach to this can be described as somewhat "pragmatic."

> What the sciences of human action must reject is not determinism but the positivistic and panphysicalistic distortion of determinism. They stress the fact that ideas determine human action and that at least in the present state of human science it is impossible to reduce the emergence and transformation of ideas to physical, chemical or biological factors. It is this impossibility that constitutes the autonomy of the sciences of human action. (ibid.:93)

The ultimate givens in social science are the ideas of individuals, including their judgments of value. There is no accounting for these in terms of more ultimate (physical) causes. "Saying that judgments of value are ultimately given facts means that the human mind is unable to trace them back to those facts and happenings with which the natural sciences deal" (ibid.:69).

[2] "Act *noun* 1 A thing done; a deed ▸b An operation of the mind" (*The New Shorter Oxford English Dictionary*).

[3] This chapter uses material from Lewin (1997c). An anonymous referee has pointed out that an important distinction must be made between the plans of a given individual and the plans made by different individuals. A question arises whether an

What Do We Mean by Consistency of Plans?

There are three important things to note about plans:

1. *Plans depend on different kinds of knowledge.* As already indicated, a plan is defined by its purpose or set of purposes. Its formulation depends on its purpose and on the desires (*preferences*) and *knowledge* of the planner. This knowledge is an infinitely complex phenomenon, and operates at many levels, as we shall later remark in some detail in our discussion of human capital. For the moment we note simply three types or "levels:"

   (a) The individual will have knowledge of those laws of nature to which we referred earlier — *knowledge type 1*. This knowledge will have been gained in a variety of ways according to the individual's perceptions and experience (and may be to some extent a priori).

   (b) Second, the individual will have knowledge of the social world, "social laws" — *knowledge type 2*. This knowledge will depend on the existence of, and the individual's perception and experience of, social *institutions*. By "institutions" we mean here those typical and stable features of the social world on which individuals come to rely. So they include rules of behavior, standard categories, habits, customs, and the like. We will discuss this in greater detail in a moment.

   (c) Third, the individual will have knowledge of specific and unique events that have occurred (history) and in order to carry out the actions constituting the plan, the individual must form some mental picture of the specific possible consequences of those actions and decide on which are more or less likely. To be sure, some actions will involve greater and lesser degrees of conscious anticipation, and some may

---

individual is always aware of the complementary or contradictory nature of his or her plans. Does the harboring of plans contradictory in their likely outcomes imply irrationality or just ignorance? Presumably a "rational" individual would not knowingly adopt contradictory plans. For groups of individuals, contradictions are inevitable in market economies. These contradictions, and also some complementarities, are mostly unknowable to individuals *ex ante* and are only revealed (if at all) *ex post* with the unfolding of the market process.

be so habitual as to seem almost reflexive. Nevertheless, even these *implicitly* involve imagined consequences, as would presumably be brought to the fore upon interrogation. We may hesitate to group these anticipations or *expectations* in the category of knowledge, but we do so, as a third level of knowledge (*knowledge type 3*), in the conviction that expectations may be held with greater or lesser confidence. (In the case of habitual actions referred to just now, we may imagine the relevant expectations to be held so confidently as to be indistinguishable from (tacit) knowledge as usually understood as some sort of absolute confidence.) Expectations are thus here considered to be a special aspect of knowledge. Type 1 and 2 knowledge is knowledge of an abstract kind, knowledge of general principles (related to the natural world—apples fall from trees to the ground, exposure to bacteria can cause infection; or related to the social world—people stop at red lights, dollar notes are a generally accepted means of payment), whereas knowledge type 3—historical knowledge and expectations/anticipations—is knowledge of specific unique events.[4]

2. *Plans cannot be completely specified, they cannot include a specification of everything that can happen (imagined or unimagined).*

---

[4]This discussion is, in many ways, similar to (perhaps the same as) O'Driscoll and Rizzo's distinction between typical and unique elements in any situation and between pattern and detail prediction (1996:76–91). And, once again, there are close similarities to and differences from Mises. Mises was concerned with the sources of knowledge. I am less so. So his distinction is twofold, first on the basis of whether or not knowledge can be considered a priori, and second, whether or not it yields certain (unambiguous, eternal) knowledge. My scheme is elaborated very specifically in the service of trying to describe how action is possible in disequilibrium (with reference to a Hayekian equilibrium of consistency of plans). So I distinguish between different types of knowledge, not according to their sources, but according to their degree of certitude, and second, according to their subject matter (human or natural). In this latter regard my methodological dualism is not that different from Mises'. So I lump together knowledge that is (or might be) a priori with that gained by experience, but distinguish it according to whether it is about the social or natural world. Mises would put mathematics in praxeology together with economics, whereas I put mathematics in natural (nonhuman) science.

The notion of "plan" in the literature is very vague. Lindahl (1929 and especially 1939b)[5] and Lachmann spent some time talking about aspects of individual plans. Of these, Lindahl's formulation is the most developed.[6] He distinguishes, for example, between three types of actions that affect the plan's *"degree of definiteness"* (Lindahl 1939a:45) thus conceiving of some flexibility in the execution of the plan. This means that even if some anticipations are not fulfilled, if the plan contains sufficient flexibility, that is, sufficient room for contingencies, it may not be disappointed and thus need not be revised or abandoned. It may be accommodated within equilibrium. Likewise Lachmann, in different (but similar) ways, attempted to account for plans that contained contingencies.[7] But neither of these authors, nor anyone else to my knowledge, has remedied the vagueness that continues to surround the concept. There is an aspect of paradox in this. It is because theorists have failed to make clear that *real-world plans* are necessarily vague and often only dimly perceived by the planners, that the plans in the theorist's discussion have assumed a specious, but unarticulated, precision. They have fostered the (unconscious) impression that they are meant to depict detailed project analysis–type means–ends schemes, even though such details are never provided, even by way of example. The necessary vagueness of real-world plans is implied by the nature of time and the way in which we experience it; in short, by Lachmann's axiom. As future knowledge cannot be gained before its time, and as plans must inevitably depend to some degree on future knowledge, many of the aspects of a plan must simply be unspecified. We do not plan in terms of "micro"

---

[5] See also Currie and Steedman (1990:chs 4 and 5).

[6] "It can hardly be pretended that every individual has a clear conception of the economic actions that he is going to perform in a future period. Nevertheless, in the greater number of cases it will certainly be found that underlying such actions there are habits and persistent tendencies which have a definite and calculable character comparable to … explicit plans … we may accordingly without danger proceed to generalize our notion of 'plans', so that they will include such actions. Plans are thus the explicit expression of the economic motive of man, as they become evident in his economic actions" (Lindahl 1939b:93).

[7] See Lachmann (1978:4, 53; 1971:40) and Lewin (1994:247–250).

details, but rather in terms of "macro" categories. We cannot experience future events before their time and the experience is never an exact correspondence of the anticipation, both because the difference is a matter of degree and because some of the aspects of the event *could not have been imagined.*[8]

3. Plans are *multilayered*; that is to say, an individual at any one time will have a very large number of plans by which he conducts his life. Each will relate to a different purpose and usually will have very different frames of reference including a different time frame. So for example, I may at a moment of time be acting *within* plans to teach my class (as planned) today, finish a first draft of this chapter this week, fulfill the expectations of my children to help them with their homework this entire year and save enough money to see them through college over the next ten years. Plans may be nested (within one another) or parallel. And while it might be possible ideally to conceive of all of an individuals plans as existing within one giant "life plan," this, as we shall see, can hardly advance our understanding. Rather we should realize that although the plans may exist in a structure of sorts, one being related to the other in terms of purposes and means, this relationship, this structure, is likely to be only dimly and partially perceived and is, moreover, likely to be ever changing as individual plans are adopted, revised and abandoned. So when we speak of plan coordination across individuals, and whether or not there is a necessary tendency for them to become more coordinated, our disagreement may be related to the fact that the concept of plan coordination has not been clearly understood. It may be that some *types* of plans do exhibit such a tendency while others do not; and that the functioning of the market system depends crucially on this difference. In particular, it may be, as

---

[8]"No matter how I try to imagine in detail what is going to happen to me, still how inadequate, how abstract and stilted is the thing I have imagined in comparison to what actually happens! ... For example, I am to be present at a gathering; I know what people I shall find there, around what table, in what order, to discuss what problem. But let them come, be seated and chat as I expected, let them say what I was sure they would say: the whole gives me an impression at once novel and unique.... Gone is the image I had conceived of it, a mere pre-arrangeable juxtaposition of things already known!" (Bergson 1965:91, quoted in Rizzo 1994:117n.).

we shall argue, that plans based heavily on knowledge types 1 and 2 are very likely to cohere and that the opposite is true for plans that depend heavily on knowledge type 3.

Before continuing it may be useful to approach this from a slightly different angle. Plans are based, to a greater or lesser extent, on expectations (knowledge type 3). Expectations are, of course, widely believed to influence actions, and the essential difference between theories is often to be found in the different way in which expectations are treated. While the rational expectations (RE) approach implicitly assumes that everyone has the same expectations, at the other extreme Lachmann emphasizes the dire consequences of expectations that necessarily diverge. But we may now pause to ask: expectations of what? RE approaches relate primarily to prices (or price indexes)—they refer to individuals' expectations of prices. Lachmann is less specific except to say that they are bound to be disappointed, from which we should infer that he is referring to expectations of the things about which individuals differ. Realizing that expectations, like the plans in which they are embodied, are *multidimensional* makes us realize that *the expectations concerning the vast majority of things (events) about which we have expectations will be fulfilled.* We may thus question whether Lachmann's statement that "experience teaches us that in an uncertain world different men hold different expectations about the same future event" is universally true and realize that it depends crucially on the type of event in question. For a large number of events there is widespread agreement of expectations.

How are Activities Synchronized and Coordinated?

We may be more specific. Expectations and plans are, for the most part, fulfilled because of the existence in the social world of shared categories and standards that facilitate the synchronization and coordination of activities. These operate to give individuals hard knowledge (type 2) of the actions of others on which these plans and expectations (type 3 knowledge) depend. This is most obvious and most crucial with regard to the way in which we cope with time. Currie and Steedman have drawn attention to a remarkable work by P. A. Sorokin originally published in 1943 (Currie and Steedman 1990:201–203; Sorokin 1964).

In this work Sorokin points out that the devices we use to organize and cope with time are cultural (rather than natural). We invent (or, more accurately, we "evolve") *cultural time units.* Thus Sorokin contrasts "sociocultural time" with "continuous, infinitely divisible, uniformly flowing, purely quantitative time of classical mechanics" (Currie and Steedman 1990:201). Consider the week.

> Factually, our living time does not flow evenly, is discontinuous, and is cut into various qualitative links of different value. The first form of this qualitative division is given by our week. Mathematical or cosmic time flows evenly, and no weeks are given in it. Our time is broken into weeks and week links. We live week by week; we are paid and hired by the week; we compute time by weeks; … we walk and exercise or rest so many times a week. In brief, our life has a weekly rhythm. More than that: within a week, the days have a different physiognomy, structure, and tempo of activities. Sunday especially stands alone, being quite different from the weekdays as regards activities, occupations, sleep, recreation, meals, social enjoyments, dress, reading, even radio programs and newspapers…. A week of any kind is a purely sociocultural creation, reflecting the rhythm of sociocultural life but not the revolution of the moon, sun, or other natural phenomena. Most human societies have some kind of week, and their very difference between weeks is evidence of their independence from astronomical phenomena. The constant feature of virtually all … is that they were always found to have been originally associated with the market … our week is not a natural time period but a reflection of the social rhythm of our life. It functions in hundreds of forms as an indivisible unit of time…. Imagine for a moment that the week suddenly disappeared. *What havoc would be created in our time organization, in our behavior, in the coordination and synchronization of collective activities and social life, and especially in our time apprehension?*
> (Sorokin 1964:190–193, italics added in the last sentence)

What is true of the week is equally true of other shared time unit categories, like days, months, seasons and years, even though these may have an original basis in astronomical regularities. In their evolved, developed state they provide us with predictable social rhythms. And this is even more true of the division of days into hours, minutes and seconds. In our interactions we all mark time in the same way and with reference to the same clock so that we are able to synchronize (consciously and subconsciously, overtly and tacitly) most of our actions or, more accurately, our *activities* (referring to action types or repeated actions).

> The knowledge of the main kinds of sociocultural rhythms—no matter whether periodical or not—is by itself very important knowledge.... Stripped of their specific qualities, all rhythms and punctuations would disappear, and the whole sociocultural life would turn into a kind of gray flowing fog in which nothing would appear distinct. (ibid.: 201)

The synchronization of activities is most obvious in contracts, which often refer to units of time. For example, we rent space by the day, week, month or year. But it occurs in all spheres of life where contracts are implicit or nonexistent. We expect people to work between the hours of 8 a.m. and 6 p.m. and not usually outside of that. We expect people to be asleep between midnight and daylight. The few exceptions give rise to disappointed expectations and discoordination. But the overwhelming conformity ensures routine expectation fulfillment. Knowledge of these time categories is a prerequisite for, and gives rise to, knowledge of people's typical activities.

This insight may be extended to other types of shared categories. For example, we share categories for measuring space—distance (miles and kilometers), area (acres of land), and volume (gallons of gasoline)—and weight (pounds of sugar), figuring accounts, classifying occupations,[9] driving on the roads, walking along pathways, and innumerable other conventions, customs, habits, and the like, which make our actions predictable to others. These institutionalized categories and modes of behavior (which we may designate as institutions broadly understood) are the cumulative unintended results of individual actions and they represent a real convergence of expectations. Starting out from a position of many different standards or modes of behavior that converge to one or a few implies that individuals come to expect certain kinds of behavior, with a degree of confidence related to degree of conformity of the particular standard. These institutions

---

[9] See Ebeling (1986:48).

enable each of us to rely on the actions of thousands of anonymous others about whose individual purposes and plans we can know nothing. They are the nodal points of society, *coordinating the actions of millions whom they relieve of the need to acquire and digest detailed knowledge about others and form detailed expectations about their further action.*

(Lachmann 1971:50, italics added)

Processes of Convergence

We have a fairly good idea of how social processes that converge work. A prototype case has been provided in the emergence of a single medium of exchange (Menger 1976:248ff.; Selgin 1988:ch. 2; Horwitz 1992:ch. 2). Money is the unintended result of individuals adopting one out of many goods as the preferred medium of exchange. Its spontaneous emergence is facilitated by the property that the more people use it, the greater its advantage for further use. It is a graphic case, but only one case, of similar processes where the advantages of the adoption of a particular standard—for example of a particular product or set of products to accomplish given tasks, like playing video cassettes, word processing, software development—as well as geographical location, language, and many other things, depend positively on the extent to which it has already been adopted (Arthur 1994; Krugman 1991; Kirzner 1990; Liebowitz and Margolis 1994;[10] see also Horwitz 1992). In such processes, once a critical level of adoption has been achieved adoption tends to be cumulative. Individuals are led by the clearly perceived advantages of adoption to follow suit, and the process feeds on itself until it has become an institution. Not all institutions emerge in this way, but many do.

It should be clear that these convergent processes do not exist in isolation but are crucially related to each other. So, for example, the emergence of money depends on the prior existence of established practices of trade, in particular the tacit or conscious enforcement of contracts. The institution of repeat purchase tends to enforce certain

---

[10]There is a growing literature on the many aspects and implications of these cumulative processes. We shall have occasion later to take note of some of them. For now we shall be content to note their existence and culmination in social institutions.

practices of honest dealing. And the existence of money, of course, supports a number of dependent institutions, like financial accounting practices (see Chapter 10 below). There is, in short, an intricate *institutional structure*. There is an essential complementarity between enduring institutions (Horwitz 1994).[11] The market system is itself dependent on the existence of important aspects of the legal structure. This brings up the question of institutional change.

The designation "institution" connotes an image of permanence, of reliability. The institutions that we have been talking about exist as fixed points in the landscape of time within which individuals can make their choices in the knowledge (knowledge type 2) that they, the institutions, at least, will remain unchanged. We will look at this a little more closely in a moment. It is evident, however, that this permanence must be relative, for we have the fact of institutional change. Standards come and go. Categories change. Rules appropriate to one society often disappear as the society changes. Even language evolves. How does this affect the functioning of institutions as facilitators of coordination? The answer must be in the rapidity of change. A society in which everything changed rapidly would be one devoid of any perceptible order. History is possible only because the historian is able to know something about the enduring orientations inside people's minds. The historical context is defined by the *meaning* of the institutions of the society under examination. But as the context changes, institutions may be seen at one point in time as fixed points, while at another they may be seen as aspects of change. It depends on the purpose of the analysis and the time span involved. What is fixed and what evolves is itself a matter of context. There seems to be a continuing interaction between the foreground and the background, and which is moving depends very much on which you have in focus, much like a three-dimensional holographic picture. Commercial law is necessary for the conduct of economic life and indeed facilitates the emergence of unpredictable novelty in economic life. But economic (and technological) changes of certain types put a strain on aspects of the law that prompt it to change. For example, the emergence of

---

[11]"Company Law, as it has emerged in the Western world in the course of time, is a delicate web within which many interests, some conflicting, some complementary, have been woven into a pattern of harmony...." (Lachmann 1979:254)

electronic communications has suggested the acceptance of facsimile signatures and has raised difficult legal questions relating to copyright and privacy on the Internet.

So convergence and permanence are relative phenomena. Nevertheless such permanence is necessary for the existence of and for our understanding of dynamic economic processes. The hectic procession of new products and productive processes—that is, the result of the activities of a multitude of individuals organized as companies, operating within the constraints of contract law, and so on, some of whom succeed in their endeavors, many of whom do not (as defined by the ability to earn positive accounting profits)—is dependent on these underlying institutions. While we cannot predict who will succeed and who will not, while we cannot predict which products will emerge and be popular, while we cannot foresee the nature of future technologies, we strongly believe that the process will be peaceful and will be orderly; we confidently expect those who are unsuccessful to accept their losses peacefully and perhaps try something else, those who lose their jobs to move on in the hope of greener pastures, and those who do succeed to continue to try to do so. The fruits of this dynamic process depend crucially on our willingness to accept the consequences of its unpredictability. That willingness is the vital predictable part. We have the emergence of "chaos out of order."[12]

The analogy with organized sports has been suggested by a number of theorists (for example Hayek 1973:115; Loasby 1994:32). The game is played according to certain fixed rules (although from time to time the rules "evolve" to reflect new realities). The rules (both written and unwritten) are highly predictable. Given a hypothetical contingency, we can predict its resolution. The actual outcomes are uncertain and infinitely variable. That is the point of playing the game. By "outcome" we mean not only the score, but also the pattern of the game in its infinite detail, which is part of the attraction. If we cared only about the score it would be a simple betting game; we are also interested in seeing how it is played and what unexpected variations are around the corner to delight, intrigue, shock, or disgust us. The game of life, and

---

[12]With apologies to Progogine and Stengers (1984). The market process is not chaotic in the colloquial sense, but it is complex and unpredictable.

the game of economic life in particular, is like this in many respects. Most notably it depends on written and unwritten rules and on the resources (the abilities, the equipment, and the experience) of the players. We hope that our team will win, but we usually do not go to war if they do not. If we did, the game would not exist and we would not be able to enjoy it.

We cope with the complexity in the world by converging on institutions. Thus once the arrival of a new range of products, made possible by the development of a new technology, has been digested, new categories of classification tend to be developed, into which these products are grouped. The categories emerge spontaneously out of individual attempts to communicate the attributes of the new products. A good example is the products of the computer industry. A whole range of products exist, whose workings remain a mystery to the vast majority of people, but whose purposes needed to be explained. Laptops evolved into notebooks, microcomputers into desktops. At another level a series of technical standards and categories has been developed in order to cope with the complexity. The attributes of computer monitors include its refresh rate, its dot pitch as well as simply its screen size. All these shorthands provide the increasingly informed public with a way to tailor their expectations when choosing between products. They enhance predictability by enhancing the interpretability of information. But these relatively predictable elements change with time and it is no accident that conscious innovation involving product differentiation is often referred to using the phrase "category killer."

Novelty and Equilibrium

About some events there is no predicting. These are the specifics of any given (future) historical situation. Lachmann's axiom implies the uniqueness of every experience. Perhaps it is better to say that each experience contains unique elements, although we are able in retrospect to describe it in terms of recognizable categories. Describing a situation is never the same as being there. Each moment is unique and therefore cannot be *precisely* predicted. Thus plans are never coordinated in every detail. Such a situation is inconceivable, it is a world without time. In that sense we are never in equilibrium. Nevertheless, in peaceful, lawful societies behavior is *ordered*. Hayek, in his later work, spoke less of equilibrium and more of order. He quotes from "a distinguished social anthropologist":

> that there is some order, consistency and constancy in social life is obvious. If there were not, none of us would be able to go about our affairs or satisfy our most elementary needs.
> (Evans-Prichard 1951:49, quoted by Hayek 1973:36)

> It is evident that there must be uniformities and regularities in social life, that society must have some sort of order, or its members could not live together. It is only because people know the kind of behavior expected of them, and what kind of behavior to expect from others, in the various situations of life, and coordinate their activities in submission to rules and under the guidance of values that each and all are able to go about their affairs. They can make predictions, anticipate events, and lead their lives in harmony with their fellows because every society has a form or pattern which allows us to speak of it as a system, or structure, within which, and in accordance with which, its members live their lives.
> (Evans-Prichard 1951:19, quoted by Hayek 1973:155n.)

Thus:

> By "order" we shall ... describe a state of affairs in which a multiplicity of elements of various kinds are so related to each other that we may learn from our acquaintance with some spatial or temporal part of the whole to form correct expectations concerning the rest, or at least expectations which have a good chance of proving correct. (Hayek 1973:36, italics removed)

The (extended) order which is the society is clearly a result of the component orders which we have called institutions. And the latter indeed are the results of a process by which society has (without planning to do so) converged towards their adoption. They are "spontaneous orders" and they represent equilibria of a sort, in that they are states of convergence (rest) around which expectations are formed and conform. In this sense, we may say that the social process is composed of equilibrating, disequilibrating and non-equilibrating sub-processes. Economic growth, the arrival of new and better products and better methods of production is the result of unpredictable, disequilibrating and non-equilibrating processes. There is no tendency for expectations to cohere in these processes. They are "non-expectable," the results of events that could not have been expected.

The degree of predictability of any event is related, then, to the extent to which it tends to exhibit repeatable, typical, or recognizable characteristics. Many routine events fall within the "very predictable" range. However, in the realm of productive activity, in modern economies, many events fall very definitely outside of this range. Methods of production, consumer goods, and services embody and depend on new knowledge to a high degree and their emergence is intimately related to and crucially dependent on the divergence of expectations.

Predictability in one sphere is thus the necessary ingredient for coping with its absence (novelty) in another sphere. The amazingly wide range of products and the persistent improvement in methods of production (in terms of reducing opportunity costs) are the results of a multitude of unintentional experimentations. Of the outcomes that we observe in the market system, we cannot say that they are the most "efficient" or the "best" of any that we could have had, and they are not an equilibrium in any Hayekian sense. But to the extent that we judge them to be better than many alternatives, to the extent that we judge progress to be occurring in that our lives are made more convenient and more exciting, we must recognize these outcomes to be the beneficial result of the kaleidic changes of the modern world.

Prices in Disequilibrium

The prices that economic agents observe and to which they respond are not equilibrium prices. That is, they are not prices that reflect an underlying compatibility of the plans of the various economic actors in the market. If expectations *were* consistent across individuals, in the sense that they were all destined to be fulfilled, then prices would reflect the unanimous judgments of individuals of the values of the goods traded; they would also accurately reflect the tradeoffs involved in trading one good for another, or refusing to do so. In this sense the prices would lend a degree of objective expression to the subjective, non-comparable valuations of individuals. While subjective valuations are not observable and there is no way of knowing subjective value scales, in an equilibrium situation prices provide hard information about what individuals are prepared to do and what various goods and services are "worth" to them. In this context, the exercises of modern welfare economics, employed in the service of normative investigations of alternative policy scenarios or institutional structures, make some sense. It is possible then to use price as a "proxy" for a measure of "utility" reflecting social losses and gains in some indirect sense.

In a disequilibrium situation, however, this is obviously no longer possible. If expectations across individuals differ and are inconsistent, then prices can no longer be used to reflect a unanimous judgment of value. The theorems of welfare economics no longer apply and, as is widely acknowledged, albeit ignored, notions of "economic efficiency" have no unambiguous meaning. One might wonder, then, what it is that prices actually do in disequilibrium.

It should be clear that a price is a social institution. When a price is established between a buyer and a seller there is a shared understanding of what it is and what it means. In the first instance, the price is an expression simply of the "terms of trade"; you give me this and I will give you that. It is a general shorthand description for expected action, action that involves hypothetical, yet-to-be-expressed details. For example, an advertised general price is an offer to do business that says: I will trade an unspecified amount of this for so many dollars per unit. And although the quantities acceptable may not be unlimited, there is usually understood to be an acceptable trading range. So price is, first, a statement of mutual expectations and obligations involving real things.

Second, prices enable individual calculation. Prices make budgets possible. In this regard the role of prices in monetary economies depends crucially on the existence of money as a universal medium of exchange and therefore unit of calculation (and one presumes, if exchanges are recorded, a unit of account; this is discussed further in Chapter 10 below). Since money is universal purchasing power it facilitates production and exchange over time. Prices play a pivotal role in these production and exchange activities. Without market prices, calculation would not be possible (Mises 1981). There would be no way for an individual to estimate what someone might be willing to exchange for various items. The prices involved in any budget calculation are either an expression of past transactions that actually occurred or they are expected prices of hypothetical trades that might occur in the future. It depends on whether one is doing accounting (attempting a judgment of past action) or budgeting for future action. That is, past prices express past trading achievements, while expected prices express perceived potential future trading achievements. Either way, and connecting the two, prices (third) enable trading decisions. If expected prices bore no relationship to the actual prices that materialized, they would serve no purpose. Indeed there must be a close relationship, close enough to yield a positive net value to the traders involved on both sides of the market, if there is to be a continuing market. So enduring trade in something is evidence that expectations have not been disappointed to the extent that trading is no longer worth while. (On the inertia of prices, see Mises 1971:108–123.)

Changes in prices (actual and/or expected) thus induce budgetary adjustments. They enhance or restrict the value of a budget and produce the familiar individual demand and supply responses. And price discrepancies (if noticed) provoke arbitrage activities that, if unimpeded, would continue until they were removed, until one price only were established. But price discrepancies are often in the eyes of the (entrepreneurial) beholder, the more so when such discrepancies refer to a comparison between present and future prices. Some arbitrage (for example, production) "opportunities" may be inconsistent with others and may not succeed. Once again, then, we affirm the impossibility of deriving the necessity of converging expectations and prices in the market process.

An individual budget has meaning only in terms of the prices that the trader faces (now and in the future) and his subjective scale of values. So, just as with other institutions, the institution of price *qua* price must exhibit some permanence if it is to serve its purpose. Individuals understand what a price, any price, is; they understand prices as a phenomenon. Individual prices are instances of price as an institution. And although they do not reflect equilibrium values, because they are contextually meaningful thcy motivate and facilitate economic activity.

Conclusion: Predictability Together with Disequilibrium

Hayek's notion of equilibrium as perfect plan coordination is limited because plans can never be completely specified. Thus complete plan coordination *ex ante* is not even logically possible. In a way, perhaps ironically, Hayek's own extensive work on the importance of tacit knowledge and the inherent limits of perception and articulation (for example 1945, 1967) point in this direction.

Thus we may conclude our examination of equilibrium by saying that the market process in general is not equilibrating. There is no tendency for *expectations in general* to become more coordinated. Expectations operate at many different levels, however. And at most of these levels, for most types of things there is a tendency towards coherence. We tend to cohere around certain rules of conduct, standards, categories, and other institutional phenomena, and most of our expectations are thus fulfilled. We have predictability together with disequilibrium where the latter refers to the characteristics of the market process. Divergent expectations lead, through rivalrous activity, to the emergence of new products and methods of production. In this process, the production and use of specific capital goods and the acquisition of the knowledge that enables us to produce and use such goods, play a crucial role. We turn now to a closer examination of this.

PART II

CAPITAL, INTEREST, AND PROFITS

In Part II I consider some of the more traditional areas of capital theory. Chapter 4 discusses the nature of capital. It is a curious fact about the concept of capital in economics that economists still disagree about what it is. A brief historical overview suggests that this probably has something to do with the evolution of the concept in the context of economic evolution more broadly. The transition from a predominantly agricultural economy to a predominantly industrial one, and then to an increasingly "information-based" one, has occasioned changes in the way in which economists and others have thought about production, and therefore about capital. Sometimes concepts appropriate for one context have been transplanted to another with unfortunate consequences. We begin with a look at Adam Smith's corn economy, and note its influence on Ricardo and those who followed him. We contrast the Ricardian approach with that of Carl Menger and the Austrian School. The most space is devoted to Böhm-Bawerk, arguably the most influential capital theorist of all. In Chapter 5 I look briefly at modern capital theory in the production function literature and the work of the Cambridge neo-Ricardians. We will find, surprisingly, that *both* are in the Ricardian spirit.

In Chapter 6 I examine the recent work on capital theory of John Hicks. Hicks struggled his whole professional life to reconcile various approaches to capital theory. In his last extended attempt he provides a very interesting and useful framework for thinking about capital values in and out of equilibrium.

In Chapter 7 I turn to a discussion of the nature of interest as a phenomenon. The nature of capital is bound up with the fact that production occurs over time. So the question of the relative valuations of useful outputs at different points of time arises. Does time itself exert an influence in determining the relative value of things? Indeed, we find that the fact that people are not indifferent to the date at which they obtain useful things is the essential explanation for the existence of the discounting of the future which is the basis of all capital valuations. This allows us to distinguish interest, which is an expression of this time discount (time preference), from profit.

Profit is seen to be the result of uncertainty. It is the reward for being right in an uncertain world, for discovering an "opportunity" that others had overlooked. Traditionally it has been approached by examining a world in which it would not exist, a world devoid of uncertainty. In such a world all incomes are certain and can be the basis of known contractual relationships. Such incomes are composed in the aggregate only of the payments for the services of the original factors of production, land and labor, which are wages and rent, and of "pure" interest. When we move from such an economy to the real world we can then understand that profit is what is left over after these "contractual" payments have been made. Profit is thus clearly distinguished from interest and rent (on physical capital).

I conclude with some observations connecting the capital processes (the processes of production) to planning processes more generally and as explored in the previous chapter. This lays an important basis for our discussion of disequilibrium theories of capital in Part III.

CHAPTER 4

Capital in Historical Perspective

Introduction: The History of Capital Theory is Relevant

Considerations involving capital are as old as economics itself. And, perhaps more than any other field in economics, current capital theory bears the stamp of its history. Modern discussions are very heavily influenced by the categories developed by capital theorists since Adam Smith, and by the contexts in which they wrote. The history of capital theory is a history of complex, often esoteric, intellectual battles. And more often than not, these theoretical debates about abstruse technical issues mask the underlying ideological differences that are the real issues. But there is one thing that many of the protagonists have in common: their adherence to a framework in which equilibrium, in some significant sense, prevails. In this chapter we shall examine some aspects of the various approaches to capital that have characterized the history of capital theory. In doing so we shall seek (a) to clarify the significance, or lack thereof, of the insights gained from the high points in the development of capital theory, (b) to remove the ambiguity that has surrounded key terms like "profit," "rent," and "interest," and (c) to clear the way for a consideration of capital in situations of disequilibrium where, it will be seen, many of the traditional issues are rendered moot.

The Questions

Market economies are sometimes referred to as "capitalist" economies, suggesting the presence of a phenomenon called "capital" that is in some way responsible for the character of the economy and for its mode of production in particular. At a general level we may want to say that capital is "that which makes production possible." Its origins can be traced to the idea of a fund of purchasing power (owned by "capitalists") which, when made available, allows for indirect methods of production, methods that involve production (or "capital") goods. This can be explained further as follows.

All production can be traced logically to the input of labor services and natural resources, what we may call *original inputs*. These inputs can be used to produce *useful outputs* or they may be used to produce *other inputs*. These other inputs, which are produced means of production, are thus logically called capital goods. They facilitate production. And since producing useful outputs using capital goods necessarily takes more time than producing outputs using only original inputs (from the vantage point of a moment in time when the capital goods are not yet produced), the capitalists' fund is very important in allowing these (advantageous) indirect methods to be adopted. (Defenders of the market system, against those who seek justification for the earnings of these apparently "unproductive," "non-working" capitalists, have often pointed to the necessity to reward the capitalists for parting with their wealth in order to facilitate these "roundabout" methods of production. Capitalists who own the capital goods directly may be thought of as lending the money to themselves.)

Capital, then, originates from the idea of a fund of money that facilitates the time-consuming use of production goods. But is it the fund or the goods, or both, that facilitate production? Can it be said that while the capitalists' fund facilitates the use of production goods under social arrangements where such goods are privately owned, it is the production goods and not the fund that are truly productive? If so, it seems logical to differentiate between a capital fund, which is just an accident of particular historical social arrangements, and capital proper which refers to the technologically necessary instruments of production. It seems natural from this perspective to think of capital as a "factor of production" along with the original "factors of production" —labor and land. In modern economics it is thus this physical capital that is now implied when no qualifiers are used. It must be recognized, though, that individual capital goods can accomplish nothing on their own. It is together with other capital goods and with labor and land that they may be seen to be (jointly) productive. How, then, are we to account separately for the contributions of the individual capital goods to the value that they help to produce? And if "capital in general" is to be thought of as a factor of production, it seems necessary that a relationship should be established between the notion of "capital in the aggregate" and the individual capital goods involved in the production process. The latter are diverse and heterogeneous in nature and it is not immediately obvious how one should proceed to add them together. A logical method is in terms of their values, their prices. But, as we shall see, it is only in equilibrium that such prices have the meaning that we seek, and even then will not be free of contentious ambiguity.

Thus investigations in capital theory often return repeatedly to the same fundamental questions:

- What is capital?
- Is it a separate factor of production?
- Is it a fund?
- Or is it a physical stock?
- How is capital to be measured?
- What is the nature of the earnings of capital?
- How is this related to interest?
- How are capital's earnings determined and justified?
- What determines capital's earnings in relation to earnings in general, that is, how does capital feature in the distribution of income and wealth generally?

These questions are related to the historical development of capital theory. We illustrate this with a brief impressionistic historical outline.[1]

Adam Smith's Corn Economy

Adam Smith was interested in the causes of economic progress. There is a natural and important connection between capital and economic growth and development. Growth theory had obviously not yet become the technical abstract specialization that it is today. Yet there is a "model" implicit in his work (Hicks 1965:36–42; Kregel 1976:20–23;

---

[1]This is obviously not meant as a detailed or complete history of thought in capital theory. Such a project would require a separate, and probably much longer, work. What follows here is simply a highlighting of certain ideas in their historical context.

Lachmann 1996:130–132).[2] Smith's world was still largely an agrarian society, but his implicit model survived the circumstances of his time. As we shall see, Ricardo in particular tried to extend Smith's insights into a world to which it was much less suited. This had significant consequences for the development of capital theory. Most modern economists working in the area are influenced (whether they know it or not) by Ricardo's agenda.

We concentrate on those aspects of Smith's work that arise out of his way of looking at capital in a predominantly agricultural society (Lachmann 1996:130), although, of course, he was aware of, and said much about, the implications of the rapid industrialization that was occurring. An agrarian economy (we may designate it as a "corn economy") depends largely on harvests. Next year's harvest depends, to a large extent, on how much of this year's harvest is plowed back in seeds and, even more, on how much corn there is this year. This year's harvest has three possible uses: to keep the working population alive and perhaps growing, to feed the animals used in production, and to use as seed for production. Thus, this year's harvest may be seen as a type of *capital stock*. In a modern economy it is natural to see elements of the capital stock at any time that are not being used, as a result of obsolescence or incomplete adjustment to new conditions. In a corn economy, by contrast, all capital is used, is homogeneous, and is turned over regularly once a year. So we have an initial harvest, a working population of certain size, and the possibility of a harvest next year that is dependent on labor and its productivity. It is not clear what Smith thought about the determination of wage rates. It is easiest to assume that he took it to be determined by subsistence or convention (ibid.:131).

We may formalize Smith's model in a rather simple way (Hicks 1965:36–42, Lachmann 1996:130–142). There is a crucial relationship between this year's harvest and next year's harvest. This year's output Y_t—our capital stock for this year—is divided up into seed corn, fodder, and food production. In the simplest formulation, the whole of the corn that the laborers uses for their (and their animals') consumption

---

[2]This "model," described below, is derived by Hicks from Smith's *Wealth of Nations*, (1982) book II, ch. III, "Of the Accumulation of Capital, or of Productive and Unproductive Labor."

plus their planting may as well be counted as their "wage." The capital stock then comprises a "wage fund" necessary to keep society going until the arrival of the next harvest. Then if N is the number of laborers, the (average) wage rate $w = Y_t/N$ or:

$$Y_t = Nw \, ; \, w = \text{real wages per worker}$$

Growth in the corn economy will thus depend on the number of workers N and on productivity p, the amount of corn produced (on average) by each worker.

$$Y_{t+1} = pN = pY_t/w \text{ or } Y_{t+1}/Y_t = p/w$$

Thus the rate of growth is equal to $p/w - 1$. This growth rate varies inversely with the wage rate and directly with average productivity. If p rises faster than population, the wage rate can rise.

This model neglects to account for all sections of the economy, for example, the towns and the landowners. If we assume that $k < 1$ of any year's output is set aside each year to feed the non-agrarian classes, then the wage rate must be $kY_t/N = w$. The capital stock is now not Y_t but rather $kY_t = K_t = Nw$. So $Y_{t+1} = (p/w)K_t = k(p/w)Y_t$, and the rate of growth is $k(p/w) - 1$. Obviously, as formulated, k is a measure of the "drag" on economic growth imposed by the "nonproductive" elements of society. This conclusion is a result of formulating output as consisting solely of corn and gives rise to some obvious objections. This aspect of Smith's model is of less concern to us at this point, however, than at some others.

Smith did not think of p, w, and k as constants. Economic growth means that the wage fund grows ahead of population. Smith believed that p would increase over time as a result of the division of labor, thus causing a rise in w. Thus p and w would grow together, though not necessarily at the same rate. Economic growth and capital accumulation in turn made the division of labor possible.

> The annual produce of the land and labor of any nation can be increased in its value by no other means, but by increasing either the number of its productive laborers, or the productive powers of those laborers who had before been employed. The number of productive laborers, it is evident, can never be much

increased, but in consequence of an increase of capital, or of the funds destined for maintaining them. The productive powers of the same number of laborers cannot be increased, but in consequence either of some addition and improvement to those machines and instruments which facilitate and abridge labor; or of a more proper division and distribution of employment. In either case the additional capital is almost always required. It is by means of an additional capital only that the undertaker of any work can either provide his workmen with better machinery, or make a more proper distribution of employment among them.[3] (Smith 1982:343)

Thus Smith regarded saving as necessary for the achievement of economic growth, and the earning of profit consequent not simply upon the accumulation of capital but significantly upon the fruits of the division of labor. In modern terms, Smith sees accumulation and technical progress as being tied together. And although he seems to identify a type of diminishing returns, this is clearly not in the form of a declining rate of return to investment in a given mode of production, but rather refers to the eventual possible exhaustion of investment opportunities for extending the division of labor (that is, for the *discovery* and introduction of new and improved production methods) and this leads naturally to reliance on foreign markets.

Smith's corn economy is obviously a special case that raises a number of questions. It is not clear, for example, whether he thinks of machines, buildings, etc., as capital and how their accumulation is to be treated.[4] However, it is an instructive special case. In this economy, since capital is homogeneous and is identical to output, there is no problem concerning the valuation (absolutely or relatively) of either. Thus the rate of yield or of growth can likewise be measured unambiguously. It is a one-commodity, subsistence fund economy in equilibrium where the capital stock uniformly lasts one period. Durability

---

[3]"It is worth emphasizing ... that Smith's concern with economic growth takes us back in a sense to the oldest part of the edifice, namely his treatment of the division of labor, the point being that the increasing size of the market gives greater scope to this institution, thus enhancing the possibilities for expansion, which are further stimulated by technical change in the shape of the flow of invention" (general introduction in Smith 1982:31).

[4]But see Ahiakpor (1997).

of capital thus plays no role. There is no question about the appropriate composition or durability of the capital stock (although Smith was aware of the changing shape of productive equipment) and past mistakes have limited influence. There are no individual differences in expectations regarding the type of product to be expected nor the date at which it is to arrive (although of course there may be some short-term uncertainty regarding the harvest). Thus, although production takes time, time does not feature in the valuation of capital and output, except in so far as future output may be discounted.[5] Neither labor units nor time units need to be used to value the capital stock. When we turn to Ricardo we see how special these conditions really are.

Ricardo's Uniform Rate of Profit

> In the more industrialized economy of 1815 it was no longer tolerable, even as an approximation, to assume that all capital was circulating capital; nor that, even in a metaphysical sense, all capital was "corn." The self-containedness of the single period was nevertheless so powerful an instrument, and so much depended upon it, that Herculean efforts had to be made to retain it. What Ricardo did, in his efforts to retain it, can now be understood (thanks to Mr. Sraffa).... Homogeneity was to be retained by reducing capital to its labor content (the *labor theory of value*); fixed capital was to be reduced to circulating by consideration of periods of production (in the manner to be worked out more fully, decades later, by Jevons and Böhm-Bawerk). But all the power of these devices ... could not save the self-containedness. It is apparent from Ricardo's own work that even in his hands the static method is already confining itself to its proper place—to the comparison of static equilibria, even of stationary states; it cannot extend to the analysis of a dynamic process. In the light of the subsequent developments there is nothing surprising about that. (Hicks 1965:47)

As mentioned, Smith's model was essentially a subsistence fund theory. There is a stock of food to maintain workers from one harvest to the next. What capital does for the owner is to facilitate the employment of

---

[5] Smith's discussion of interest (book II, ch. IV) makes it clear that he considers interest to be something different from profits. We shall return to this question below.

a certain number of workers for the production of a certain output. All economic considerations are such that one never has to look beyond this one-year horizon. This makes the application of the static method possible and largely excludes the consideration of expectations.

Ricardo had to face problems that Smith was able to avoid. Once machinery played a large part in the economy, Smith's assumption of a homogeneous capital stock was no longer defensible. The labor theory of value served to bring *all* economic goods within a common denominator. Ricardo used the "labor hour" as a unit of measurement; labor time is the common standard of comparison. Machines, corn, and cattle all cost labor and are seen to be comparable in those terms. If we have a stock of circulating capital (for example, a stock of corn), we can ask how many hours of labor it took to produce it and get a value for the input. But if we have a machine lasting fifteen years, although we can say its production took labor hours, the total input is not used up in one year and enters successively into the output of fifteen years. Ricardo deals with this by regarding fixed capital, like machinery, as circulating capital that circulates more slowly. Some part of the machine gets used up in each of the fifteen years. Fundamentally there is no difference. All capital stocks rotate, it is only a matter of degree. It thus becomes possible to calculate the value of the inputs of any capital item that matures in any given year and to compare it with the value of its output in that year, thus being able to calculate a rate of return.

Ricardo's main concern was with the distribution of income between the various categories of inputs and their owners. It was in order to give an account of the earnings of capital that he had to find some way to reduce the heterogeneous capital items to some common measure. His basic argument concerns the tendency for rates of return on various capital investments to become equal. This tendency provides a mechanism for determining flows of capital to various types of production. In long-run equilibrium a capitalistic economy establishes *a uniform rate of profit*. This is what explains the distribution of wealth. In equilibrium all capital ventures earn the same rate of profit. Ricardo thus started the now common practice of using what would be the state of affairs in a hypothetical situation of long-run equilibrium, a situation that is an end state of an indefinite number of interactions in an essentially unchanging environment, as if it were the everyday state of affairs. This is the equilibrium method of explanation. We speak of *the* rate of profit on capital as though it were a parameter.

Ricardo's concerns reflected his preoccupation with the future of capitalistic economies. The event of the Napoleonic blockade and the consequent rise in food prices led him to wonder about the long-term trend of an economy in which the population was rising. How would the population get fed? He seemed to accept Malthus's idea that the population would grow in such a way as to keep the wage rate at the bare level of subsistence. But if the population was growing, this would lead to the use of land of progressively inferior fertility. So with the wage rate fixed at subsistence level and the margin of production being extended to inferior land, the earnings (rent) of the landowners on the infra-marginal land would tend to rise. This means that the rate of profit is bound to fall. Pushed to its logical conclusion, the rate of profit would fall to zero, at which point capital accumulation would stop. A stationary state would have been reached. There could be no such thing as permanent growth. The only possible exception to this result is in "improvements in machinery connected with the production of necessaries," "discoveries in the science of agriculture," and international trade (Ricardo 1973:120; Kregel 1976:24).

These exceptions notwithstanding, Ricardo's emphasis and his legacy are his method of concentration on the hypothetical long run. It is this that prompts Lachmann to label both the Cambridge England neo-Ricardians and the neoclassical growth theorists as Ricardians (Lachmann 1973). They share the method of comparative static equilibrium analysis that derives from Ricardo and his interest in accounting for the "laws" of distribution. In this way the focus is clearly on the mechanisms of social development and away from aspects of human action and decision. If human planning features at all in the capital accumulation process, it is in a mechanical and implied way. Action is relied on implicitly to bring about the equilibrium that is assumed. If some capital venture were to become unprofitable, capital would be withdrawn and invested elsewhere. But where capital is durable, it can only be withdrawn very slowly. Thus we must assume that no changes occur while capital is in the (long) process of being shifted from areas of low profitability to areas of high profitability. And we are not permitted to ask how it is known which are the areas of low and high profitability. Somehow the economy is envisioned to grope its way soon enough to a configuration of capital items on which the rate of profit is uniform and the maximum possible. Reflecting on the discussion of the previous chapter, we realize that in a world of continuous unexpected change, flows of capital will not be able to keep up, and equalization will never occur. Prices of the various capital goods will be such that the original labor value invested in them has no enduring meaning and the whole Ricardian basis would seem to be of dubious relevance. Relevance rather than realism is the key, and evidently relevance is often "in the eye of the beholder." Ricardo's long-run equilibrium method, we shall see, continues to command many adherents.

In his discussion of the distinction between circulating and fixed capital, Ricardo was forced to consider the role of time in production. His labor theory of value contains the elements of what was to become a particular approach to dealing with the time dimension in capital theory. In a world of heterogeneous capital items, time is of the essence. A very different approach to dealing with it was provided by Carl Menger.

Menger's Time Structure of Production

Menger's pioneering approach is responsible for our thinking of capital in terms of a *time structure*, reflecting the structure of capital goods employed in the production process. There is no attempt in Menger to reduce the variety of goods and services available at various dates to a single dimension. At any moment in time some goods are useful for immediate consumption, and some are only useful in so far as they contribute to the *production* of goods available for immediate consumption. And since production takes time, a time element is already implicit in the contemplation of a set of economic goods at any single moment in time.

Menger thus characterizes production as a sequential process in which *goods of higher order* (capital goods) become transformed into *goods of lower order* (consumption goods). Capital goods are varied in nature but can be classified by where they fit, along a time continuum, into the production process. The lowest or first-order goods are, as noted above, consumption goods. The lowest-order capital goods are second order. The next highest are third order, and so on. With this model, he makes clear that the element of time is inseparable from the concept of capital. Any theory that treats the process of production as instantaneous necessarily misrepresents reality in an important way.

> The transformation of goods of higher order into goods of lower order takes place, as does every other process of change, in time. The times at which men will obtain command of goods of first order from the goods of higher order in their present possession will be more distant the higher the order of these goods.
> (Menger 1976:152)

And the rewards to saving result only if more time-consuming methods of production are adopted.

> [B]y making progress in the employment of goods of higher orders for the satisfaction of their needs, economizing men can most assuredly increase the consumption goods available to them accordingly—but *only* on condition that they lengthen the periods of time over which their activity is to extend in the same degree that they progress to goods of higher order.
> (Menger 1976:153, italics added)

The higher-order goods that people come to own must allow greater production if there is to be progress. That is, they must (in combination with other goods) be able to produce a greater volume of consumption goods in the future or, in other words, they must be able to extend consumption further into the future. It is interesting to note that, while Böhm-Bawerk's later discussion of the greater productivity of more "roundabout" methods of production is clearly drawn from Menger, the latter was clear that there is nothing mechanical about the relationship between saving (diverting consumption from the present to the future) and productivity. Saving may be *necessary* but it is not *sufficient* for economic progress. He envisaged the time-consuming creation of specific capital goods to be a necessary condition for achieving economic progress.

Menger first introduces these ideas in connection with processes in nature. People find the fruits of nature valuable. But at an early stage in the development of civilization they learn that they can do more than simply "gather those goods of lowest order that happen to be offered by nature" (Menger 1976:75). By intervening in the natural processes, individuals can have an effect on the quantity and quality of the subsequent yield.

> To understand the objectives of the "producers" is to understand that the earlier a producer intervenes, the greater are the opportunities to tailor the production process to suit his own purposes. This provides an intuitive basis for the notion that the more "roundabout processes" tend to have a greater yield in value terms. (Garrison 1985:165)

It is important to realize the role of subjective value in Menger's capital theory. The value attributed to any capital good is *prospective*, not backward looking as with Ricardo. "There is no necessary and direct connection between the value of a good and whether or in what quantities, labor and other goods of higher order were applied to its production" (Menger 1976:146). At any point in time there is a capital structure characterized by capital goods of various orders whose value is determined by the values attributed by consumers to the consumption goods they are expected to produce. "The value of goods of higher order is always and without exception determined by the prospective value of the goods of lower order in whose production they serve" (Menger 1976:150). These values manifest in the market as prices. As long as these prices remain (and are expected to remain) constant and as long as there are no technical changes in methods of production, the capital structure will remain constant. But if there should be a permanent change in the price of even one consumption good, this will almost always imply the need to change the capital structure in some way. Changes and substitutions will occur in response to the perceived changes in prospective output values.

The level and pattern of the employment of resources (including labor) and their earnings is determined and thus depends on *the strong link between the structure of consumption and the structure of production*. Changes in the demand for one (or some) consumption good(s) (*relative to others*) cause changes in the evaluation and use of *particular* capital goods, and in employment. The implication in Menger is that the market can accomplish this smoothly.

Time is inevitably involved in the notion of capital. Since the value of higher-order (capital) goods depends on the prospective value of the consumer goods they are expected to produce, the elapse of time, and with it the arrival of unexpected events, implies that some production plans are bound to be disappointed and thus the value of specific capital goods will be affected. The economic consequences of human error are implicit in Menger's view of capital.

Menger and Ricardo thus present contrasting and really irreconcilable visions. Adopting Menger's perspective, one cannot lose sight of the variety of goods and services and individual activities and choices. There is no suggestion of a uniform rate of profit. And yet there is an inescapable order within the variety provided by our understanding of the purposes of these individuals. "The process of transforming goods of higher order into goods of lower order, ... must always be planned and conducted, with some economic purpose in view, by an economizing individual" (Menger 1976:159–160). We see here the need to consider aspects of intertemporal planning discussed above in Chapter 3. No such need was suggested in our analysis of Ricardo's approach.

Böhm-Bawerk: Interest and the Average Period of Production

Introduction

Böhm-Bawerk is probably the economist most often cited in connection with the development of capital theory. He is thought of as the "father" of Austrian capital theory and credited with being the first to introduce the element of time and its implications clearly into considerations of capital (Hennings 1987d:233). This conception neglects the contribution of Menger. Böhm-Bawerk's work on capital was a conscious extension of Menger's. His departures from Menger are not seen universally as being an advance.[6] As we shall see, some of the later Austrians had reason to regret aspects of Böhm-Bawerk's work on capital and, even more so, the interpretations to which it gave rise. Whereas Menger produced hardly more than twenty-odd

---

[6]This statement relates to Böhm-Bawerk's work on capital. His work on interest theory was clearly an advance and marks the beginning of the pure time preference theory of interest to be dealt with below.

pages on capital theory (in spite of which it may be said that he laid the groundwork for a comprehensive theory of capital), Böhm-Bawerk produced three large volumes and some shorter works. It was a major part of his life's work. It is to be expected, then, that the scope for various and differing interpretations might be quite large. Austrian, Ricardian, and neoclassical capital theorists all find much with which they can agree in Böhm-Bawerk, albeit much also to disagree with. A reading of Böhm-Bawerk reveals an uneasy amalgam of the ideas of Menger and Ricardo. Capital theorists in general have chosen to emphasize the Ricardian elements.[7] The Mengerian elements might just as easily have been emphasized, had capital theory developed differently. As it is, modern capital theory, with its reliance on "production function" reasoning, can, with some justification, be traced back to Böhm-Bawerk (along with Wicksteed and some others). Much of the ambiguity surrounding the assessment of his contributions relates to his use of a theoretical device designed to provide a physical measure of the capital stock—the average period of production.

The Advantages and Disadvantages of Capitalistic Production

Böhm-Bawerk's characterization of a capital-using economy is very similar to Menger's. Production is a process involving time. Original factors are transformed, with the aid of produced means of production, into consumption goods. Like Menger, he too conceived of capital goods as being related to one another in terms of the stage of the

---

[7]"However much he denied any adherence to classical cost theories of value, his view of production and the role of capital and time bear the mark of the Ricardian tradition" (Hennings 1987a:104; also Hennings 1987c). See also Hennings (1987b:114–115) and Hennings (1997:ch. 8). Yet consider this same theorist's capsule assessment:

> A leading member of the Austrian School, he was one of the main propagators of *neoclassical* economic theory and did much to help it attain its dominance over classical economic theory. His name is primarily associated with the Austrian theory of capital and a particular theory of interest. But his prime achievement is the formulation of an intertemporal theory of value.   (Hennings 1987a:97, italics added)

Says Kregel (1976:28–29), "Böhm-Bawerk's role in the Austrian theory was to combine the Ricardian approach to capital in terms of labor and time with the 'new' marginal approach to pricing through utility."

production process that they occupy. And, like Menger, he conceived an increase in capital to involve a change in the *time structure of production* (not his term) in some way. It is not simply an augmenting of each type of capital good at each level of maturity (each stage of production), but a change in the internal structural relationships. Like Menger, he held that capital goods derived their value from their usefulness in the production of consumption goods; their value was to be derived from the value to consumers of the goods they produced. All durable capital goods are valued by the present value of their services using a subjective rate of discount (to be discussed below, see Hennings 1997:132). He emphasized the heterogeneity and specificity of individual capital goods and denied that they could be aggregated into some physical measure of the capital stock. Hennings quotes Böhm-Bawerk as follows:

> A nation's capital is the sum of heterogeneous concrete capital goods. To aggregate them one needs a common denominator. This common denominator cannot be found in the number of capital goods ... nor their length or width or volume or weight or any other physical unit of measurement.... The only measuring rod that does not lead to contradictions ... is the value [of these capital goods].   (Hennings 1997:132, his translation of Böhm-Bawerk 1959)

Böhm-Bawerk denies that capital goods are individually or intrinsically productive and insisted that the production processes that they make possible are the sources of any increases in value that arise. But since these processes can be characterized by a series of stages of production successively further back from the ultimate consumption goods in which they culminate, he perceived a connection between the number of such stages and the amount of value added. That is, there is a strong intuition connecting the length of production, indicated by the number of stages involved (the degree of "roundaboutness"), and the degree of productiveness that results.

> There are two concomitants of the adoption of the capitalist methods of production.... One is advantageous, the other disadvantageous. We are already familiar with the advantage. With an equal expenditure of the two originary productive forces,

labor and valuable forces of nature, it is possible by well chosen roundabout capitalist methods to produce more or better goods than would have been possible by the direct noncapitalist method. It is a truism well corroborated by empirical evidence.
(Böhm-Bawerk 1959: Book II, 82–83, footnote references crediting Lauderdale and Jevons omitted)

> [O]ne thing that can be stated with a reasonable degree of certainty is the proposition … that as a general rule a wisely selected extension of the roundabout way of production does result in an increase in the magnitude of the product. It can be confidently maintained that there is no area of production which could not materially increase its product over the result obtained by its present method. (ibid.:84–85)

Böhm-Bawerk felt that a more "time-consuming" process of production would not be chosen unless it was more productive in this sense, unless it added sufficiently more value to compensate for the longer "waiting" required. "The disadvantage which attends the capitalist method of production consists in a *sacrifice of time*. Capitalist roundaboutness is productive but time consuming. It yields better consumption goods, but not until a later time" (ibid.:82). Thus by wisely selecting more roundabout methods of production, increases in value can be obtained and these have to be weighed against the "cost" of waiting. In addition, however, it is apparent that the returns to greater degrees of roundaboutness must eventually diminish. In summary:

> All consumption goods which man produces come into existence through the cooperation of human powers with the forces of nature, which are in part of economic character, in part free natural powers. Man can produce the consumption goods he desires through those elemental productive powers. He does so either directly, or indirectly through the agency of intermediate products which are called capital goods. The indirect method entails a sacrifice of time but gains the advantage of an increase in the quantity of the product. Successive prolongations of the roundabout method of production yield further quantitative increases though in diminishing proportions.
> (ibid.:88)

Roundaboutness and the Average Period of Production

Böhm-Bawerk's lengthy exposition is generally imprecise. His discussions can be read as suggesting informal general properties of real capitalist economies. Capital accumulation involves judicious changes in the time structure of production that furnish greater output value. And output value is increased not only by augmenting existing products, but also by producing "better goods." Both output and input undergo "qualitative" change as opposed to simply quantitatively augmenting existing processes (even though he seems to be assuming a given technology). And this interpretation is strengthened by his connecting the fruits of roundabout production to the division of labor.

> Our modern system of specialized occupations does, of course, give the intrinsically unified process of production the extrinsic appearance of a heterogeneous mass of apparently independent units. But the theorist who makes any pretensions to understanding the extrinsic workings of the production process in all its vital relationships must not be deceived by appearances. His mind must restore the unity of the production process which has had its true picture obscured by the division of labor.
> (ibid.:85)

Yet, perhaps in order to deal with a variety of criticisms, for example as to the precise meaning of roundaboutness, in the very next paragraph Böhm-Bawerk now attempts to make his observations more formal and precise. An attempt to capture the degree of roundaboutness by measuring a period of production from the original factors to the emergent consumption good would be impossible and misleading in the modern world with its vast array of inherited capital goods. One could not, as it were, trace production back "to the moment when the first finger is stirred in the making of the first intermediate product that was later used in the production of the good in question, and as continuing until its final completion" (ibid.:86). And so he introduces the *average* period of production.

> It is more important, as well as correct, to consider the *average* time interval occurring between each expenditure of originary productive forces and the final completion of the ultimate consumption good. A production method evinces a higher or lower

degree of capitalist character, according to whether, *on the average*, there is a longer or shorter period of waiting for the remuneration of the expenditure of the originary productive forces, labor and uses of land. (ibid.:86)

And he proceeds to define arithmetically the average period of production, which we may succinctly express as follows:

$$T = \frac{\sum_{t=1}^{n}(n-t)l_t}{\sum_{t=1}^{n} l_t} = n - \left(\sum_{t=1}^{n} \frac{t\,l_t}{N}\right)$$

where T is the average period of production for a production process lasting n calendar periods; t, going from 1 to n, is an index of each sub-period; l_t is the amount of labor expended in sub-period t and $N = \sum_{t=1}^{n} l_t$ is the unweighted labor sum (the total amount of labor time expended). Thus T is a weighted average that measures the time on average that a unit of labor l is "locked up" in the production process. The weights $(n - t)$ are the distances from final output. T depends positively on n, the calendar length of the project, and on the relation of the time pattern of labor applied (the points in time t at which labor inputs occur) to the total amount of labor invested N.[8] Since this formula is in units of time it may be added across various processes to yield an overall measure of roundaboutness. In this way Böhm-Bawerk hoped to have solved the problem of measuring roundaboutness.

> It is highly probable ... that some fraction of a working day will have been expended centuries ago. But because of its minuteness it would be a magnitude which would influence the average so little, that it can almost always simply and safely be disregarded. (ibid.:87)

And he seemed to place a high reliance on this formulation.

> Wherever I have spoken in this or preceding chapters of a prolonging of the roundabout method of production, and of the

---

[8] In the special case where there is an even flow on inputs so that the same amount of labor time, l_0, is applied in each period, $\sum_{t=1}^{n}(n-t)l_t = (1/2)n(n+1)l_0$ and $\sum_{t=1}^{n} l_t = nl_0$ and therefore $T = n/2 + 1/2$ or simply $n/2$ (when n is large enough so that the 1/2 can be ignored, or when T is expressed in continuous time where it is absent). So,

> degree of capitalist character, I would have it understood that I mean this in the sense just set forth [the average period of production] ... [T]he measure must be the mean duration of the process, and that mean must be computed by averaging units, each of which represents a period of time.... For want of a better term, I shall use "average period of production" to distinguish it from the absolute production period. (ibid.:87)

In this way Böhm-Bawerk's lengthy, intuitive discussion of the nature of capitalist production as an increasing reliance on produced means of production in specialized production processes became associated with this rather specific and limited formula. Though in actuality a small part of his work as a whole, and arguably an aberration in his breadth of vision, it became the focus for many prolonged and energetic debates in capital theory.

Criticizing the Average Period of Production

Some obvious observations can immediately be made. The formula is crucially dependent on being able to identify the stages of production. It is assumed that the process begins at stage 1 and ends at stage n. In this way any kind of "looping" (coal is used in the production of iron and vice versa), where the output of one stage becomes available as an input of an earlier stage, is ruled out. Second, if the output is a flow (as it usually is), then we must also have some way to connect inputs that occur at time periods $n - t$ with precisely that output that arrives at time period n and separate them from those that need to be connected to outputs occurring at time periods $n + j$ where j is an index of time periods occurring after n. In other words, if the production process is a *flow input–flow output* process, a set of inputs are used to produce jointly a set of outputs occurring over time and the measuring of T becomes more problematic. Similarly, we must be able to identify the amount of labor time l that is used. This obviously presumes that it is possible to reduce any labor heterogeneity to comparable terms, like efficiency units, and then to measure the number of such units supplied per period of time. Also, as it is formalized, the services of land are

---

when inputs occur at the same rate over time, each unit is "locked up" on average for half the length of the production period.

omitted, although verbally they are definitely considered to be part of the process. Böhm-Bawerk adds parenthetically, "Let us ignore the cooperating uses of land, just for the sake of simplicity" (ibid.:86). Including the services of land, while mathematically simple, would raise the practical prospect of accounting for the varying productivities of each unit of land used per period of time.[9]

Traditionally Böhm-Bawerk's average period of production construct, though widely criticized, has been popularly used (particularly in mathematical models, where it is easily converted to a continuous time formulation (see Faber 1979; Orosel 1987)) as a purely labor-time formulation, with land neglected. Thus it has come to seem that *time itself* plays a role in the creation of value, and not the contingent activities (of humans or nature) that must necessarily occur *in time* if value is to be created. Or alternatively it could, ironically, be read as an expression of the labor theory of value, as suggesting that the essence of any value is the *labor time* that went into it. The average period of production construct thus gave rise to a vision of production quite out of character with Böhm-Bawerk's vision. His general characterization of a capital-using economy is in no way dependent on being able to measure, practically or conceptually, the degree of roundaboutness by the average period of production or any other measure. But, in using it in the way that he did, Böhm-Bawerk (inadvertently) encouraged the interpreting of his work as suggesting a type of mechanical production function, in which production time could be used as a measure of capital itself, and, therefore, of "capital intensity." The pivotal ingredient for the internal consistency of this approach is the presence or absence of (Hayekian) equilibrium. This can be seen by considering the criticism leveled by Clark (and in slightly different form a generation later by Knight against Hayek).

---

[9]It should also be clear that this formula does not allow for a unique or monotonic expression of "roundaboutness." In other words, (a) this measure may yield a number that is consistent with an infinite number of input patterns, different amounts of labor time occurring sooner or later in the process, and (b) when considerations involving interest are included, this measure may not rise or fall uniformly in any ranking of roundaboutness as we add labor-time units at various points; it may change direction (in its ranking) at some points under certain conditions if we change the inputs at various points in the production process. These types of considerations played an important role in later criticisms of any attempt to measure capital in physical terms in the Cambridge debates which we will examine below.

Böhm-Bawerk had attempted to incorporate Menger's vision of time in the production process using a quantifiable concept. Clark (1893) (and later Knight) attacked this concept as meaningless and indefensible, and, in the process, suggested a view of capital in which time as we know it seemed to play no real part at all. We have seen that the average period of production can only be calculated when the production process is describable in a very particular way. A favorite example in the literature is the case of wood production from a forest in which a fixed number of young trees are planted while the same number of trees are cut down each period. It should be clear that it is possible to say that, since production and consumption go on steadily each period,[10] they are in effect simultaneous.[11] Production and consumption are synchronized and occur together all the time (Clark 1893:313, 1988:14–18; see also Hayek 1941:114–145, 181, 195). In this case, it *is* possible to calculate the period of production. It is the time that it takes, on average, for a tree to grow from a seedling into a mature tree ready to be cut. If we assume that this time is the same for each tree, we have an even clearer measure. Clark's criticism can be understood to say that this time period is irrelevant since the forest is, after all, a permanent source of wood. Since production and consumption are in effect simultaneous, the relevant period of production is zero. This is the kind of vision that one is offering in suggesting that capital should be thought of as a "permanent" fund

---

[10] In this case, as in many others, "production" consists in harnessing the processes of natural biological growth for economic purposes. These were the first, and in some ways are the most fundamental, capital processes. Consequently much economic theorizing about capital proceeds from these first cases to argue by extension and, more often, by analogy to other, more complex cases.

[11] In this example "consumption" is equated with the harvesting of trees. Of course, in reality, trees are inputs for further production processes that result in consumption at a later date; for example, the manufacture of pencils. The essential point, however, is that the woodlot example above provides a case of perfectly synchronized inputs and outputs that, in principle, could characterize other processes where inputs lead ultimately to consumption. Once such a process is completely established and becomes "permanent," an endless and unchanging succession of inputs and outputs results, making it appear that production and consumption are indeed simultaneous. As explained in the text, however, this way of looking at the world is superficially valid only as long as there are no changes in the patterns of consumption and production. At any point of time, in any real capital-using economy, the capital structure that exists will be only partially adapted to the ever changing pattern of consumption.

yielding a flow of income. A "capitalist" economy is then one in which capital plays this role.

According to Knight (1936), the period of production, as applied to the economy as a whole, is always infinite or always zero, depending on the perspective that one adopts. In the former case, there is no such thing as an origin to the period of production. The infrastructure of capital goods dates back to Adam and Eve. There must always have been production with the help of some capital goods, and part of gross output was always used to maintain current capital goods and produce others. Output is a continuous flow that never ends. All social production is continuous. In the second case (where $T = 0$), time intervals are seen as irrelevant. In other words, we can either think of the production process as stretching back from the beginnings of human history and forward into the unending future, or we can think of the production process as essentially timeless, since production occurs simultaneously with consumption. Thus, Clark and Knight argued that it is quite wrong to say that there are time intervals in production. Consumption and investment take place *at the same time*—the two are concurrent, simultaneous. The whole thing is a misconception.

It is clear, however, that this view is valid only for an economy that has reached a state of stationary equilibrium—a situation in which the capital stock has been built up, is suitably maintained, and yields a continuous income (net of maintenance cost). It is a world where unexpected change is absent and all production techniques are unambiguously known. This implies that all production plans are consistent with one another. In terms of the forest example, the forest is already grown and yielding a steady output when our analysis begins. It tells us nothing about the decisions to grow the forest in the first place, when questions relating to the "period of production" must have been important. Production and consumption only appear to be simultaneous to the observer who does not care about the production plans that gave rise to the production process in the first place. One plants seedlings today not in order to cut trees today but in order to cut trees some years from now. One cuts trees today only because one planted seedlings some years ago. One cannot ignore the time element. Where the capital structure and the array of consumption goods is continually changing, production and consumption frequently do not even appear to be simultaneous. Even where we have a simultaneous and perfectly synchronized production process, considerations of the time structure and the decisions related to it must still enter. "The posited simultaneity of inputs and outputs literally leaves no time for an equilibrating process to take [or have taken] place" (Garrison 1985:129).

Clark's (and after him Knight's) emphasis on the technical and logical aspects of "period of production" concepts had the effect of making capital debates appear to be about abstract technical issues rather than about real economic issues. To concentrate on Böhm-Bawerk's (and later Hayek's) way of measuring production periods was to divert attention away from his (and Menger's) vision of the capital structure as involving time in the *decisions made by producers*. It is these decisions that are the roots of the changes in the capital structure. The period of production that is relevant is that which is perceived by every producer individually in the process of making a decision. Time enters into decisions through producers' subjective evaluations of the constraints and possibilities. The period of production as an objective construct is inherently problematic, but this is irrelevant for understanding the importance of time, of the fact that different consumption goods are or were available at different times. The capital structure implies a time structure of production. Böhm-Bawerk, following Menger, understood this even though the Ricardian aspects of his work pointed in a different direction.

Böhm-Bawerk as Neoclassical and Ricardian

Modern reformulations of Böhm-Bawerk, focusing on his average period of production, have shown how a connection can be made between his "model" and a classical and neoclassical approach (Dorfman 1959; see also Lachmann 1996:135–140). If a measure exists for the capital stock and the rate of flow of output, then the average period of production can be measured as K/f, where K is the capital stock and f is the output emerging from the production process in each period. (Alternatively, if the average period of production, T, is known or can be computed by reducing all inputs to labor time, the value of the capital stock, K, can be calculated as we shall see below). Dorfman uses the example of a reservoir in a stationary situation, where the inflow equals the outflow, implying a constant water level. Clearly the quantity of water can be expressed in terms of time. For example, with 100 million gallons of water, 2 million per day flowing in and out, this would imply that the average drop of water was in the reservoir for five days. The ratio of stock to outflow is 5, which is the period of retention of each drop. The same basic logic can then be applied to the capital stock.

In terms of the labor theory of value, f will be equal to the value of the labor expended to produce it. Using the same notation introduced for Smith's corn model above, we have $f = Nw$, and the average period of production $T = K/Nw$ or

$$K/N = Tw$$

According to Lutz, interpreting Böhm-Bawerk, "An increase in capital per worker in the process of production [is] identical with the adoption of a longer, more roundabout method" (Lutz 1967:9). So, in modern terminology, the capital–labor ratio is very simply related to the average period of production and the wage rate. In a neoclassical framework, where capital and labor can be continuously substituted for one another, changes in r and T must be in opposite directions for any level of output. K is a direct function of T (T is a proxy for K), and r (the rate of profit on K) diminishes with K. So $K/N = \Phi(w/r)$, with the first derivative positive. Implicit in this approach is a "production function" where output Q is a diminishing function of the average period of production T, $Q = \varphi(T)$ (see Hayek 1941:140–141, 189, 208). So Böhm-Bawerk can be seen as part of the neoclassical tradition leading directly to modern growth theory, to be explored below. (See also Hennings 1997:144–148.)

Alternatively in a *classical* world, with a given capital stock and a given number of workers, if the wage rate rises, the average period of production will fall. If w falls, it becomes possible to extend the period of production. Given the subsistence fund K and given the technique of production, the shorter the period, the less productive it is. As long as K and N increase proportionately nothing will change. T and w will not be affected. But if K, for example, increases relatively to N, T or w or both will rise. Thus capital accumulation puts upward pressure on the level of wages and the average period of production. In this way, Böhm-Bawerk can be seen to have added a new dimension, a time dimension, to Ricardo's theory of distribution. If T is taken to be constant (as with Smith and Ricardo), a datum of the constant technique of production, then the classical conclusion of an inverse variation between the wage and profit rates and the earnings of labor and capital follows.

Further Considerations: Value, Labor, and Equilibrium

Consideration of Böhm-Bawerk's work as reducible to symbolic, quantitative representation illuminates some further interesting aspects of period-of-production analysis. Although he previously denied that this was possible, Böhm-Bawerk has been interpreted as proposing the average period of production construct in order to provide a *purely physical* measure of capital. As we have noted, this involves finessing the qualitative aspects of labor and land. But it also ignores the heterogeneity of outputs. Essentially it assumes either that the mix of outputs is fixed, or that production techniques for the different commodities are identical and fixed, or that only one output is produced. Whichever it is, since these assumptions violate the essence of an economy where exchange plays a role in determining value, these considerations suggest (1) the impossibility of a purely physical measure of capital, (2) the lack of validity of the labor theory of value, and (3) the limitations of equilibrium analysis.

1. *The impossibility of a purely physical measure of capital.* Actually, at an early stage Böhm-Bawerk's critics pointed out that, even in his simple case of one output and one input (labor), it is impossible to obtain a purely physical measure when the role of implicit interest is considered. Böhm-Bawerk purportedly showed that if output is produced by homogeneous labor time over a period of time in a continuous and unchanging fashion, then the accumulated value of that output can be calculated as a weighted average of that labor time. Implicit in this is the idea that capital acts as a subsistence fund which has the appropriate time structure to feed the necessary labor. That is, the "right" amount of subsistence is available at exactly the right time to sustain the labor necessary at each moment in time. Now, if there are alternative uses for this subsistence fund, we must conceive

of it earning at least a return equal to its next best use. That is to say, the subsistence fund can be imagined to be earning interest over time. When this interest is calculated as simple interest, accruing only once every period, it can be easily shown that it cancels out of the formula for *T*, but when it is accrued continuously, as compound interest, as it should be, then the formula for *T* depends on the rate of interest (see, for example, Lutz 1967:20–21).[12] Since Böhm-Bawerk used the size of the capital stock as a determinant of the rate of interest, showing that the former depended on the latter seemed to involve catching Böhm-Bawerk in a hopeless circularity. The unsurprising truth is that the search for a purely physical measure of the capital stock was hopeless from the beginning. This was to be belabored later by the Cambridge (England) capital theorists who pointed to the fact that (in part) the distribution of wealth determined the relative prices of outputs, and particularly determined the level of wages relative to profits. So if the rate of profit equals the rate of interest which enters into the value of the capital stock, then the latter is not independent of the distribution of wealth. Thus the same physical quantities of various capital goods will not have a unique value. And, according to the Cambridge neo-Ricardians, since capital thus cannot be measured in purely physical terms, the notion of its marginal product is meaningless and its earnings are thus left unexplained. We shall consider this further in due course.

2. *The lack of validity of the labor theory of value.* This question, having been dealt with adequately in the literature, need not detain us too long (see, for example, Hausman 1981:17–20). Significant for our purposes is the role of time. If two processes of production have identical labor inputs at identical moments in time, but one must be allowed some extra time to "mature" (like glue drying, or wine aging), how

---

[12]This can be easily seen as follows. If l units of productive inputs are applied in the first and the second periods and if only simple interest is considered, then we may use the equation $2l(1+Tr) = l(1+2r)+l(1+r)$ where r is the rate of interest to solve for the unknown average period of production T. This gives 1.5 units, which is the same value as yielded by Böhm-Bawerk's formula, $(1+2l)/2l$. Using compound interest, however, the equation changes to $2l(1+r)^T = l(1+r)^2 + l(1+r)$. If we solve this for T we get $T = (\ln(2+3r+r^2)-\ln 2)/\ln(1+r)$ which contains the rate of interest, r (Lutz 1967:20–21).

can we say that nevertheless they have the same value? If resources other than labor, for example, physical space, are needed over time, and these resources have alternative uses, then the extra time taken will mean that the output requiring more "pure time" will command a higher value in the market if it is to be produced. Time itself does nothing, but production that occurs over time (naturally or with the aid of original non-labor resources) has a value unaccounted for by the labor theory of value. This criticism could perhaps be deflected by a reformulation in which all original inputs are "suitably" valued. As such it amounts to offering a "cost of production" theory of value and goes to the heart not only of issues of prime concern to capital, but also of issues of the entire corpus of economic theory. For our purposes we merely note that "cost of production" can only be said to "determine" value in some sense when equilibrium exists, that is, when the value of the output in the market is (as expected) exactly equal to all the payments to the inputs. There can be no capital gains and losses. This brings us then to our third observation.

3. *The limitations of equilibrium analysis.* The symbolic representation of Böhm-Bawerkian analysis and the criticisms that surround it only make sense in an equilibrium context. By this we mean a context in which production occurs in a continuous and unchanging fashion over time. There can be no disappointments regarding the production process. Production plans must be explicit and must dovetail. If this were not the case—if producers, for example, had different conceptions of what constituted the "correct" method of production—we could not speak sensibly of an average period of production to be computed from a consideration of input requirements. At the very least there would be as many such average periods as there were opinions. Similarly, and even more relevant, there can be no innovations in production methods that render resources obsolete (in whole or in part). Every such innovation changes the pattern of inputs and the average period of production implicit in the equilibrium situation appropriate to it. We may wonder what relevance this retains in a world in which a large part of the process of capital accumulation is associated with technological innovation. This is something that will occupy us at some length.

Conclusion: The Many Faces of Austrian (Böhm-Bawerkian) Capital Theory

Austrian capital theory has become synonymous in the literature with Böhm-Bawerkian capital theory. Ricardians, neoclassicals, and modern Austrians find much with which they can agree and from which they can draw in Böhm-Bawerk. But they are not the same things. Both the Ricardians and neoclassicals focus on some of the technical questions that surround Böhm-Bawerk's empirical insights on the greater productivity of roundabout methods of production. And they interpret these within an equilibrium framework. The modern Austrian (market process) theorists, following Mises, Hayek, Lachmann, Kirzner, and Rothbard (and also Fetter), focus on some of Böhm-Bawerk's less formal pronouncements and draw some crucial insights from them. In particular these involve the role of time in production and the nature of profits and interest. We shall examine this below. But first we must take note of some developments arising out of these various interpretations of Böhm-Bawerk, notably growth theory and neo-Ricardian distribution theory.

CHAPTER 5

Modern Capital Theory

Wicksell and others attempted to defend and extend Böhm-Bawerk's approach (Lutz 1967; Ebeling 1997). With the advent of the Keynesian revolution, however, interest in capital theory waned. It revived slowly in the post-war period. In retrospect we may identify two main lines of development. One is the familiar neoclassical approach, in which capital simply came to be understood as an amorphous stock of production potential equal to K as an argument in a production function. The other is the resurgence, emanating from the contributions of Joan Robinson (1956) and Pierro Sraffa (1960), of the Ricardian classical approach (the neo-Ricardian School), in which capital and labor are not continuously substitutable for each other, and the earnings of labor relative to capital (the prime focus of this literature) are seen to be determined by "social" rather than economic conditions. Modern capital theory controversy consists largely in the clash of these two perspectives. Ironically, as explained above, both of these approaches can be traced to the Ricardian aspects of Böhm-Bawerk's work.

The Production Function Approach

The Production Function as Metaphor

The production function is a metaphorical device (Lewin 1995:288–290). It is a mathematical shorthand expression for an input-output process.[1] Its use was motivated primarily by an attempt to account for the way

---

[1] "[T]he very idea of a 'production function' involves the astonishing analogy of the subject (the fabrication of things, about which it is appropriate to think in terms of ingenuity, discipline, and planning) with the modifier (a mathematical function, about which it is appropriate to think in terms of height, shape, and single valuedness)" (McCloskey 1985:79).

in which economies grow. It is the basis of modern growth theory and of growth accounting; of the attempt to answer the question: What factors account for the observed growth in the economy, and to what extent? As such it also answers the question: What explains the earnings of the various inputs and their owners? Aggregate output Q is seen to result invariably and inexorably from the application of aggregate inputs K and N. All three have been identified with various statistical aggregates. The classic treatment is Solow's seminal article.

$$Q = A(t) \cdot f(K, N) \qquad (5.1)$$

where the "multiplicative factor $A(t)$ measures the cumulated effect of shifts over time" (Solow 1956:402). The shifts in the production function to which he refers imply "technical change."

As with the formulations associated with Böhm-Bawerk's theory, it is possible to get carried away with the technical aspects of the production function and to spend time in detailed examination of its various possible forms (Cobb Douglas, CES, etc.) and their implications. A more charitable, and perhaps more enlightening, way to interpret the growth theory literature is as "an invitation to a conversation." The conversation is about the best way to describe "economic progress." This is clear from the very start. In the above formulation, Solow is unable to account for the growth observed in (measured) output by considering inputs of (measured) K and N alone. As a result he must look to something else to explain the "residual." In this case it is $A(t)$, the "technical change" parameter. So growth is a result of inputs of capital, labor, and technical progress. The subsequent conversation is basically about what this means and what these things (capital, labor, and technical progress) really are. The conversation has, indeed, been considerably broadened in recent years with a revival of growth theory which has concentrated on these questions. Because it has turned to an explanation of technical progress in terms of economically motivated decisions, rather than as an "exogenous" (unexplained) shift parameter, it has been called "endogenous growth theory" (for surveys see Grossman and Helpman 1990, 1994; Lucas 1990; Romer 1990, 1994; Solow 1994). In the process, the meaning and nature of the production function and its arguments (capital, labor, and technical change) have come under closer scrutiny. We can examine this further by taking a closer look at the implications of the production function approach.

Constant Returns to Scale and Endogenous Growth Theory

Essentially the production function depicts a process of *physical* transformation of inputs into outputs. To be of any practical use, the form of this transformation must be indicated. That is, it must be able to specify *how* the output varies in response to changes in the inputs. The notion of constant returns to scale (CRS) comes to mind. It seems logical that if all of the relevant inputs were doubled, the output should, as a result, double. And if CRS does prevail, it then follows that returns to any one input factor that can be continuously varied while the others are held constant will diminish. Thus the earnings of the factor inputs (and, by implication, of their owners) can be explained by assuming that they are paid in terms of the value of their declining marginal products.

CRS rests, as Romer (1990:98, 1994:12) has put it, on the notion of replication. If all of the relevant inputs are correctly identified, then it is possible, in principle, to replicate (therefore duplicate) the process.

> The most basic premise in our scientific reasoning about the physical world is that it is possible to replicate any sequence of events by replicating the relevant initial conditions. (*This is both a statement of faith and a definition of the relevant conditions.*) For production theory, this means that it is possible to double the output of any production process by doubling all of the rival inputs. (Romer 1990:98, italics added)

The notion of physical causation (determinism) is at the very basis of production theory. This notion is surely, as a principle, not open to dispute. It is almost tautological. If all the relevant conditions (including the necessary individual actions, following upon conscious decisions) that gave rise to ("caused") any situation, were to somehow be reinstated, then the very same situation would—almost by definition—arise again. This is held to be true without exception, except for the passage of time. In the physical sciences, when dealing with easily verifiable and classifiable events (like the full moon, the emergence of a homogeneous product from a production line), the number of relevant (initial) conditions is manageably small. Replication, identification, or production of the "same" event is thus quite simple. In the social sciences, however, everything depends on correctly identifying these relevant conditions. Although simple, well-understood, physical processes, like some production processes, are easily replicated, the transition from these to the aggregate economy level is extremely problematic.

At the very simplest level there is the insurmountable problem of aggregation of the diverse outputs and inputs and the correspondence of the aggregate statistical values to the theoretical symbols (supposedly in purely physical terms). Yet, as indicated above, it is perhaps not necessary to take these formulations so literally. Looking at the production function as a metaphorical device inviting conversation and speculation, the above considerations suggest that the conversation is about the "relevant initial conditions." This can be seen (and has been clear, for example, in application of the Hecksher–Ohlin theory of international trade for many years) by considering the relationship between factors of production and technical progress.

Consider a CRS production function in three arguments—land, labor, and capital (L, N, and K)—so that:

$$Q = f(K, N, L) \text{ and } \lambda Q = f(\lambda K, \lambda N, \lambda L) \tag{5.2}$$

where λ is a positive scalar. Call this a *complete production function*. It is complete in the sense that it includes every relevant and necessary input for the production of the product. For a complete production function it is possible to write:

$$gQ = s_1 gK + s_2 gN + s_3 gL \tag{5.3}$$

where g indicates the proportional rate of growth of the symbol and s_i ($i = 1, \ldots, 3$) is the "share" of the factor in (contribution to) the growth of the output gQ.[2] It must be true that $s_1 + s_2 + s_3 = 1$, so that the factor shares fully exhaust the product (according to Euler's law, if the factors are paid according to their shares, that is, according to their marginal products, their combined earnings would equal the total

---

[2] $s_i = \dfrac{d \ln Q}{d \ln F_i}$, where F_i is the factor in question.

product). Now if one were to mistakenly omit one of the arguments, say land, L, and write the function

$$Q = \theta(K, N) \tag{5.4}$$

then this function would have diminishing returns to scale. Call this a *partial production function*. It is inconceivable that any actually observed (measured) production function should not in some way be a partial production function. When we use a production function to make inferences from observed statistics, we are, no doubt, hoping that the partial function that we have postulated behaves, in some crucial respects, like a complete one. Doubling K and N would less than double Q since L is not doubled. Some "growth" would then be unaccounted for. If we attributed it to a shift parameter $A(t)$, as in the Solovian function,

$$Q = A(t) \cdot \theta(K, N) \tag{5.5}$$

then it would appear as though growth were in part due to some "exogenous" cause (technical progress), when in fact it is due to the productivity of L. The same exercise can be applied to a situation in which some input, call it H, acts on output Q by enhancing the productivity of N. Then a complete function,

$$Q = f(K, N, H) \tag{5.6}$$

that omits H, as in equation (5.4) above, will be "shifted" by "external" changes in H.

A related consideration is the question of nonrival inputs (for example Romer 1990:97, 1994:12). Nonrival inputs, of which there are many examples, "are valuable inputs in production that can be used simultaneously in more than one activity" (Romer 1990:97). Chemical processes, computer chip design, a mechanical drawing, a metallurgical (or other) formula, computer software, etc., are examples of nonrival inputs (ibid.) They may be excludable (appropriable) or not. If H is a set of nonrival inputs and R is a set of rival inputs (like K, N), then

$$Q = f(H, R) \tag{5.7}$$

has the properties that

$$f(\lambda H, \lambda R) > f(H, \lambda R) = \lambda f(H, R) \tag{5.8}$$

that is, there are increasing returns to scale because of the "external" benefits to the private accumulation of H. The $A(t)$ in Solow's basic equation (5.1) above can also be understood as the expression of nonrival inputs. Identifying and talking about them renders them "endogenous."

Growth Theory, Input Categorization, Knowledge, and Equilibrium

The implications of this discussion should be clear. First, tautologically, all production functions are CRS when specified correctly, that is *when all of the relevant arguments are included*. Thus technical progress can, in principle, be reduced to the discovery of a productive input, or to the accumulation of knowledge of how to use existing inputs, and so on. In principle, it is possible to always account for any output by a correct identification of all of the relevant inputs. Second, and more important, omission of any relevant input implies that CRS becomes much less likely. Solow has responded that CRS is not necessary.

> [T]he model can get along perfectly well without constant returns to scale. The occasional expression of belief to the contrary is just a misconception. The assumption of constant returns to scale is a considerable simplification, both because it saves a dimension by allowing the whole analysis to be conducted in terms of ratios and because it permits the further simplification that the basic market form is competitive. But it is not essential to the working of the model.
> (Solow 1994:48)

In other words, in the absence of CRS one can still use the notion of the production function to discuss the nature and causes of economic growth, but the content of the conversation will be somewhat different. Indeed this is what has happened.

Third, this discussion suggests that although one may go to great pains to include in one's measurements all of the relevant inputs, one may not be able to do so adequately because of the multiple dimensions (the unavoidable qualitative aspects) of the identified factors. So, to be more specific, when one includes labor as a factor of production and endeavors to measure it by counting the number of people working and while adjusting for the productivity of different types of labor, one may miss some vital "human capital." Further, we need not dwell on the difficulties of collapsing the multitude of capital items into a category called *K*. And with regard to land, the simple fact that "climate" plays a vital and yet elusive role in many productive processes illustrates the problem of the existence of *unique*, fixed factors. One is drawn back to the problem of aggregation and heterogeneity. The problem is to try to find a satisfying categorization of inputs and outputs such that economic growth (progress) is considered to be explained.

Two broad empirical observations feature in the literature as being important in stimulating economists to re-examine the traditional categorizations (Lucas 1990; Romer 1994). The first is the lack of convergence between rich and poor countries in economic performance. The second is the fact that human capital flows toward the wealthy economies in pursuit of higher returns. Consider a complete production function in two countries, identical in every respect. In the absence of barriers to factor mobility and competitive factor pricing (so that each factor earns a rent equal to its known marginal product), factor input ratios should tend to equality as capital flows to its highest earning location. This should result in capital flowing to the poorer countries where it is scarce, in turn producing a higher rate of growth in the poorer countries. The fact that this does not occur suggests that something is being left out of consideration. The same considerations apply to the flow of human capital. As Romer has put it, "If the same technology were available in all countries, human capital would not move from places where it is scarce to places where it is abundant and the same worker would not earn a higher wage after moving from the Philippines to the U.S." (Romer 1994:11).

Various explanations have been given. In one way or another they involve the broad notion of "differences in technology," which means, in terms of this framework, differences in the production functions or the availability of the inputs. But rather than stop there, growth theorists have tried to consider the forces behind the technology differences. Again Romer: "Technological advance comes from things that people do" (ibid.:12). Technical change, once considered beyond the scope of the discussion, has now emerged as an urgent research topic. It has finally become apparent that economic advance is the result of detailed and difficult, and frequently serendipitous, experimentation leading to dramatic but piecemeal innovations, and ways have been sought to incorporate this into the analysis of growth. The relationship of human capital to R & D expenditures and to public goods has been considered. In particular, it has been noted that innovation (of products and techniques) is inextricably bound up with the manufacturing and distribution process (learning by doing), so that one producer's experience may benefit another. There are external effects to the production process that manifest in the accumulation of "social" knowledge, which is a nonrival input. This suggests, among other things, that private incentives for "sufficient" investment in R & D may be lacking because of free-rider problems, but these conclusions have been tempered by the extent of our ignorance in this area (ibid.:19–20). (Our examination of the nature of knowledge and of innovation will suggest that the whole production function framework, as helpful as it may be as an organizer of ideas, is inadequate for this type of assessment.) The existence of external effects, as we have seen, may mean the presence of increasing returns to scale and increasing returns to single factors, like capital. In these circumstances, the accumulation of capital may be self-reinforcing, that is, it may not result in a decline in its marginal product. This is one way to "explain" the lack of convergence noted above.[3]

Limitations of the Production Function Framework

The limitations of the production function framework are related to its existence inside of an equilibrium world. *It is in equilibrium in that the production function is presumed to represent knowledge that is available not only to the theorist but also, in some way, to the economic agents of the model.* The outputs are assumed to follow in a technically known way from the application of the inputs, and the value of the

---

[3]The production function is used at both the "macro" and "micro" levels. It is the core concept in the neoclassical microeconomic theory of the firm. As such it has recently come under increasingly critical scrutiny. If the firm is portrayed as a complete CRS production function in a competitive market then one is at a loss to explain what limits its size and what makes it different from other firms. One is led naturally then to a discussion of scarce (inimitable) factor inputs that provide the firm with a (transient or permanent) competitive advantage. The nature of special knowledge, routines, capabilities, and the like feature heavily in this exciting literature. For a brief overview see Chapter 9 below.

outputs is likewise known, so that the inputs are paid the value of their marginal products. There is no room for or analysis of differences in individual valuations of inputs and outputs. (It will not do to assume that things are only known "probabilistically," since this presumes that a finite number of possible outcomes and their distribution is known.) There is no competition "as a discovery process." As noted, growth theorists have tried to extend this inherently static approach in an attempt to incorporate technological change and innovation. They have done this by considering R & D, for example, as another (in part nonrival) input, like H, with a known measurable marginal product. In so far as R & D leads to the discovery of "new" techniques and products, this is a contradiction in terms. We cannot have future knowledge in the present. We may have a general expectation (based on past experience) or a hope that expenditures on R & D will bear fruit, but we cannot know ahead of time exactly in what way. If we did, the R & D expenditures would be unnecessary. While the "new growth economics" has done much to bring these important aspects once again within the scope of economics, the traditional equilibrium framework it has used must be judged inadequate to account for these important phenomena.[4]

The production function approach to growth amounts to noting that certain things (inputs) *were* (historically) present that might account for the growth experience and arguably could feature similarly in future growth. It is a black box approach to the extent that it does not fully "explain" the connection, the process in time. In particular it

---

[4] Solow has perceptively and provocatively noted: "The idea of endogenous growth so captures the imagination that growth theorists just insert favorable assumptions in an unearned way; and then when they put in their thumb and pull out a plum they have inserted, there is a tendency to think that something has been proved." A theory of "easy endogenous growth" implies something like "[S]pend more resources on R & D, there will be more innovations per year, and the growth rate of A [in equation (5.1)] will be higher" (Solow 1994:53). It is Solow's judgment that "there is probably an irreducibly exogenous element in the research and development process, at least exogenous to the economy" (ibid.:51). As we shall indicate at some length, innovation, although it may be fostered or inhibited by the existence of certain institutional environments, cannot be "explained" in the same way that physical laws and outcomes can. In this sense it is exogenous or, as I prefer to say, autonomous. This is not meant to undervalue in any way the importance of the shift of focus that the new growth economics has occasioned.

ignores any "extra-economic" factors like the political and institutional environment or, more accurately, these are, at best, implicit in the analyses. (However, for an attempt to account explicitly for these phenomena while remaining within the production function framework, see Scully 1992.)

The production function is a black box also to the extent that it subsumes individual decision-making. As Kirzner has noted:

> A production function can be looked at "positively." As such it represents simply a set of technological relationships. On the other hand, a production function can be looked at as representing *opportunities*, from among which a human being is able to make a choice. Clearly an economics in which market events are seen as the results of deliberately planned actions, ought to view production possibilities, in this second way, as alternatives from among which planned courses of action may be constructed. (Kirzner 1966:45; see also Hayek 1941:147)

And in a footnote to this: "Current practice generally (and, as it seems to us, unfortunately) follows the 'technological' view. This is especially the case with respect to aggregate models ... this practice is especially unfortunate in the capital theory context" (Kirzner 1966:45).

The Neo-Ricardian Challenge

The production function has proven to be a very resilient metaphor. Even prior to the emergence of the "new growth economics," the production function approach was severely and, according to some, effectively, criticized by the neo-Ricardians. This debate between the Cambridges (England and United States) is well known and has been widely surveyed (Blaug 1974; Harcourt 1991; Harcourt and Laing 1971; Yeager 1976, just to mention a few). I will accordingly not attempt yet another comprehensive survey or evaluation here. Rather we will visit this approach only to take note of an episode in the history of capital that is instructive for what both sides of the debate took for granted; namely, equilibrium.

In many ways the challenge mounted by the neo-Ricardians revived familiar criticisms of the Böhm-Bawerkian attempt to measure capital. Growth theory is an implicit capital theory—it includes K as a factor of production, where K is some measure of the produced means of production. In addition, growth theory appears to address the related question of income distribution. Because capital, like any other input, is subject to diminishing returns, it will be accumulated up to the point where the value of its marginal product just repays the opportunity cost of its employment, conveniently expressed, for example, by the interest cost of the financing that facilitates it. In this way, the neoclassical (production function) approach supports the impression that thrift, by providing funds for investment, is a positive contributor to growth, in a measure directly related to the productivity of capital. This, incidentally, also provided a justification for the earnings of capital (owners of capital) which needed to be paid the value of its marginal product if it were to be wisely invested. The neo-Ricardians attacked these conclusions by attacking the very concept of capital employed. They marshaled new and varied examples to show (as we have seen in our examination of Böhm-Bawerk's theory) that capital as a measurable quantity cannot be conceived of as being independent of income distribution and prices. They showed, for example, that a measure of the *quantity* of capital used in any technique of production varied with the interest rate at which the inputs are accumulated. Thus the same *physical* items will have a different measure at different interest rates. It is not possible to separate the *value* and the *quantity* of capital. Moreover, while one technique may prove optimal at one interest rate and give way to another at a lower interest rate, a paradoxical re-switching may occur at an even lower interest rate, where the first technique again may become preferred. Thus, no matter how one ranked the techniques in terms of "capital intensity" (a crucial notion for the production function that relied on variations in the capital–labor ratio), one could not, in general, say that lower interest rates would induce more "capital-intensive" techniques of production to be adopted, and one was thus left without a theory to explain the earnings of capital. (It is also possible to show that there are cases, even without re-switching, where a fall in the interest rate results in a "less capital-intensive" technique, a phenomenon of "capital reversing.") The distribution of earnings between wages and profits appears to be arbitrarily exogenous to the economy.

This is a very quick overview of the neo-Ricardian approach. It does not capture the intricacies with which its proponents were able to fill many pages. At the end of the day they succeeded in convincing the neoclassicals with their technical virtuosity that, from a technical standpoint, truth was on their side. Indeed, a purely physical measure of capital is not to be had in a multicommodity world where incomes and prices may change. And, indeed, capital reversing and re-switching were theoretical possibilities. But, as Hicks put it, they looked like "being on the edge of the things that could happen" (Hicks 1973b:44). The neoclassicals retreated into the world of the practical and appealed to the use of the production function as a self-evidently useful metaphor (a parable; Samuelson 1962). In so far as the question of how one decides on the persuasiveness of this metaphor was left unanswered, the debate must be judged as having been inconclusive.

It is important to note, however, the rules of the game under which it proceeded. Neither side in the debate raises any questions relating to the availability or use of knowledge or expectations regarding production techniques. Both adopt the Ricardian assumption of a uniform rate of profit on capital invested equal to *the* rate of interest. This enables both sides to talk about capital earnings as interest or profits as though these were the same things. There is the implied presumption that all economic agents share knowledge about investment opportunities, so that capital markets are always at all times fully arbitraged. There is no room for differences and inconsistencies in plans and valuations. In fact the "re-switching" and "reversing" that occurs does not happen in time. It is a question of the comparison between alternative equilibria, between alternative steady states. As Yeager has remarked:

> It is loose but convenient to speak of interest rate movements and of switches between techniques. Strictly speaking, the discussion concerns not changes or events but alternative states of affairs. They might best be thought of as prevailing in separate economies identical in all respects except those necessarily associated with different interest rate levels.
>
> (Yeager 1976:313n.)

There is no analysis of transition from one equilibrium to another.

Thus, although the debate seemed to be about issues in real-world economies, the relevance of the models used is very questionable. The neoclassicals seemed to think that it was a question of the degree of substitutability between inputs, which the neo-Ricardians assumed to be low (their models involved discrete substitutability by "switching" from one fixed technique to another). Neither side wondered about the relevance of their framework to the market process as we know it.

There is a related point (see Kirzner 1996). The neo-Ricardian critique is dependent on the idea that interest is a return to capital. The neoclassical approach identifies interest as the surplus value generated by productive capital. This provides a justification for the incomes earned by capitalists who are merely enjoying the value of what their capital has created for consumers. The neoclassicals are then criticized because capital cannot be shown to be a factor of production whose price varies inversely with the quantity employed (owing to reswitching, reversing, etc.) Now there are two related problems with this critique, in addition to the question of relevance noted above. First, it should not be surprising that no measure of the capital stock that is independent of prices (the distribution of income) exists. Capital processes are composed of a variety of fundamentally incommensurable components applied over time. Changes in the rate at which values are capitalized and discounted are bound to yield ambiguous results. This, in itself, says nothing about the justification of the earnings of producers. But, second and more important, the neoclassicals are mistaken in their view that interest is the return to capital. We will show below that it is better understood as an intertemporal price ratio that expresses the phenomenon of time preference. If this is correct, then the earnings of producers are to be understood as something completely different. Producers as workers earn wages (or salaries) and as entrepreneurs, who add value by fulfilling consumers' hitherto unperceived needs, they earn profits. We shall thus have to look more closely at the nature of interest, profits, and wages. I do this in Chapter 7.

Summary Conclusion

In this brief historical overview we have seen how some of the recurring questions in capital theory have been answered. We have become aware of the role of time. Capital describes a process in time. The passage of time has implications for knowledge and expectations. Different theorists have attempted to wrestle with this in different ways. In Smith's corn economy, with a regular known cycle involving one homogenous product, it was hardly relevant. Ricardo tried to maintain the simplicity of the corn economy in a multicommodity world with durable capital (variable production cycles) by imagining the economy to settle down to some known state of affairs which is duplicated every period. Menger's approach avoided any explicit consideration of equilibrium and highlighted clearly the role of time in any conception of the production process. Böhm-Bawerk tried to combine Menger and Ricardo, but since they offered essentially irreconcilable views of the world, he ended up with more than one theory of his own which, not surprisingly, gave rise to a varied progeny. The production function approach as well as the approach of its most severe critics, the neo-Ricardians, are both, in an important sense, Ricardian theories.

One capital theorist who defies categorization is John Hicks. While working in the formalistic idiom of neoclassical economics he was always sympathetic to those aspects of the subject that defied formalization. He was also a grand synthesizer and his work thus reflects aspects of many traditions. In his last extensive work he developed a framework that proves extremely useful in understanding a variety of issues. This is examined in the next chapter.

CHAPTER 6

The Hicksian Marriage of Capital and Time

Reviving the Austrian Theory of Capital

John Hicks has written extensively on capital. In addition to his three very influential books which have capital in the title (1946, 1965, 1973b) he has published numerous articles. He was a scholar who returned many times in his life to the same questions, sometimes with different answers.[1] In *Value and Capital* (1946, first edition 1939) he critically considered Böhm-Bawerk's average period of production. His *Capital and Growth* (1965) was a series of exercises in growth theory. But, as with all of Hicks's work, this book contains much discussion of an informal nature. These extended discussions show that he was thinking carefully about the implications of time for the theory of capital. We see it in his introductory remarks on methodology, particularly his discussion of equilibrium; we see it in his survey models of Smith and Ricardo (summarized above) and we see it in his concern about how to portray the *transition* from one equilibrium steady state growth to another, the problem of the 'traverse.' And then in a series of contributions in the 1970s, including his book *Capital and Time* (1973b, also 1976), he became very concerned with time as a topic in economics. Along with this came a revived interest in the Austrian theory of capital.

Hicks called his new approach to capital a *neo-Austrian* approach. This label does not seem to have been auspicious for the acceptance

---

[This section uses material from Lewin (1997d).]

[1] "Capital (I am not the first to discover) is a very large subject, with many aspects; wherever one starts, it is hard to bring more than a few of them into view. It is just as if one were making pictures of a building; though it is the same building, it looks quite different from different angles. As I now realize, I have been walking round my subject, taking different views of it" (Hicks 1973b:v).

of his approach. The modern Austrians did not embrace it (Lachmann 1973), and the mathematical Böhm-Bawerkians (Faber 1979) criticized it for other reasons. In this chapter I re-examine this new approach. I find that it is quite revealing in a way that perhaps Hicks himself did not fully realize, and that much of what we have discussed above in the impressionistic historical overview comes together in Hicks's final treatment.

Hicks and Time

Hicks had an abiding interest in, and a fascination with, the implications for economics of the passage of time. His treatment is ambiguous, however. Hicks's attitude to time parallels in many ways his relationship to the Austrians (particularly of the market process variety). Few economists have been more influential. Yet few defy categorization as he did. He was at once Keynesian, neoclassical, and, in his verbal remarks if not in his formal models, he made important concessions to the Austrians. His critics thus had an easy target, being able to find numerous inconsistencies. From the one side he was criticized for being too formal and mechanistic. From the other he faced technical challenges to his formal models. He continually walked a tightrope.

We see this in his treatment of time. He believed in the importance of the "irreversibility of time." Time is not strictly analogous to space. Concerning this realization he says: "I have not always been faithful to it, but when I have departed from it I have found myself coming back to it" (1976:263). One cannot escape the fact that the future is not determined in the same way as the past is. "How easy it is [however] to forget, when we contemplate the past, that much of what is now past was then future." This has profound implications for the meaning of any time series.

> Action is always directed towards the future; but past actions when we contemplate them in their places in the stream of past events, lose their orientation toward the future which they undoubtedly possessed at the time when they were taken. We arrange past data in time-series, but our time series are not fully in time. The relation of year 9 to year 10 looks like its relation to year 8; but in year 9 year 10 was future while year 8 was past. The actions of year 9 were based, or could be based, upon knowledge of year 8; but not on knowledge of year 10, only on

> guesses about year 10. For in year 9 the knowledge that we have about year 10 *did not yet exist.* (ibid.:264, italics added)

One of the far-reaching implications of this concerns the theory of capital. Consider changes in the value of the capital stock.

> The value that is set upon the opening stock depends in part upon the value which is expected, at the beginning of the year, for the closing stock; but that was then the future, while at the end of the year it is already present (or past). There may be things which were included in the opening stock because, in the light of information then available, they seemed to be valuable; but at the end of the year it is clear that they are not valuable, so they have to be excluded. This may well mean that the net investment of year 1, calculated at the end of year 1, was over-valued—at least it seems to be over-valued from the standpoint of year 2. (ibid.:265)

We see here much with which Lachmann, for example, would agree (see Chapter 8). And similar statements are to be found throughout Hicks's work, particularly in this latter period. Yet when he reviewed Hicks's *Capital and Time* Lachmann focused critically on Hicks's more formal "out of time" analysis (Lachmann 1973). Lachmann all but ignores the potential of the first two chapters and much of Part III for a more subjectivist approach, one that incorporates aspects of the connection between time and knowledge that he had worked out.[2] In what follows in this chapter I examine the essentials of Hicks's conceptual

---

[2]It is clear that Hicks was sensitive to Lachmann's criticisms:

> Most of my critics have been ... equilibrists; but there is one, for whom I have the greatest respect, who has opened fire from the other flank. Professor Ludwig Lachmann ... is (like Professor Hayek) a chief survivor of what I distinguished as the Mengerian sect of the Austrian school. It is clear that his view of me is like Menger's view of Böhm-Bawerk. He cannot of course abide the steady state. Even the modest uses of it which I have made ... fill him with dismay. Even the explanations which I have now been giving (and which are meant, incidentally, to assure him that I am more on his side than on the other) will, I fear, fail to placate him. His ideal economics is not so far away from my own ideal economics, but I regard it as a target set up from heaven. We cannot hope to reach it; but we must just get as near as we can.
> (Hicks 1976:275, footnote omitted)

framework (from *Capital and Time*) and attempt to draw out some of the implications and insights that emerge when interpreted from a subjectivist (Mengerian) point of view. This framework is a convenient and efficient organizing device in which all of the various influences on the capital formation process come together.

A Simple Conceptual Framework

Hicks begins by noting the different kinds of capital and different kinds of capital processes in which they are found.

> There are different theories of capital because there are varieties of capital. The capital, the *real* capital, of any economy extends the whole way from very durable instruments—almost land, and some would say that land itself should be included—to goods that are *in the pipeline*, goods in process of production.
> (Hicks 1973a:97)

The old Austrian theory (of Menger and the Mengerian elements of Böhm-Bawerk) is a "goods-in-the-pipeline approach" while the production function approaches are of "a quasi-land, fixed capital" variety. A satisfactory theory of capital should be able to encompass both. Böhm-Bawerk's attempt to capture Menger's vision used a *flow-input–point-output* approach and Wicksell extended this to a *point-input–point-output* (aging wine) approach. These models are models of *time*. They characterize the production process *in terms of* time (or, as in the case of Wicksell, in terms of a capital quantity derived using time units—quantities of dated inputs). Hicks is concerned to provide a theory of capital that is *in* time. Such a theory would have to be a *flow-output* theory. "Goods that are produced by the use of fixed capital are *jointly* supplied. It is the same capital good which is the source of the whole stream of outputs—outputs at different dates" (ibid.:98; see also Hayek 1941:67). We have already discovered this problem in reviewing Ricardo's theory.

> If it were not for joint supply we could, on the whole, get on very well with a cost of production theory of value. So it is here. If it were not for the joint supply that is implied in the use of fixed capital, we could get on very well with the Böhm-Bawerkian model, in which we associated with every unit of

final output a sequence of previous inputs which have "led to" that output; so that the cost of the final output is representable as a sum of the costs of the associated inputs, accumulated for each by interest for the appropriate length of time. In an economy which uses fixed capital such imputation is not possible.

(ibid.:99)[3]

So Hicks proposes the abandonment of the "period of production" approach. There is no measure of roundaboutness.

> What we must not abandon are Böhm-Bawerk's (and Menger's) true insights—the things that are the strength of the Austrian approach. Production is a process in time ... the characteristic form of production is a sequence, in which inputs are followed by outputs. Capital is an expression of sequential production. Production has a time structure so capital has a time structure.
>
> (ibid.:100)

Thus, we define a *production process* as a stream of inputs, giving rise to a stream of outputs. A production process may be thought of also as a *technique* (for converting inputs into outputs) or a *project*. It may take many concrete forms, like the building of a factory, or the construction of a machine, or the exploration for oil, etc., followed by the flow of a particular output (or set of outputs). Many (most? all?) production processes can be characterized in this way. Inputs and outputs are to be thought of in terms of *value* (or *expected value*), so outputs could be negative, but it is hardly conceivable that outputs should precede inputs at the start. Hicks asks a fundamental motivating question: "What, in general, are the conditions that must be satisfied in order that the process should be *viable*?" (ibid.:100).

Considered in this way the question can be answered by the use of some simple and familiar arithmetic which, though simple, has some

---

[3]In a footnote to this Hicks notes:

> The point, it may be remarked ..., is well understood by the intelligent accountant. He is well aware that in the case of products that are jointly supplied, the allocation of overhead costs is arbitrary; and he is also aware that the depreciation allowances which he makes are arbitrary, for they similarly involve an allocation of common costs to the jointly produced outputs at different dates. (Hicks 1973a:99n.)

important implications. We start by looking at the situation faced by the *individual* decision-maker *ex ante*. So the input and output values are *prospects*. In this way we are attempting to uncover certain general principles that are implicit in *any* production plan.

Every process (or project) has a capital value (familiar as the net present value, NPV). This is the discounted flow of the sum of the net values yielded by the project over its life. Hicks shows that a necessary condition for the viability of any process as a whole is that its capital value should be positive (or at least non-negative) *at every stage in its life* (Hicks 1973a:17, 1973b:100). In other words the NPV should be positive whatever the date for which we make the calculation. The capitalized value of the output flow must always be at least as great as the capitalized value of the flow of inputs. If this were not the case then the process would be abandoned at the point at which the NPV ceased to be positive. At every stage in the life of the project the question of its continuation may be raised. At each point this is essentially an investment decision. So the project will not be continued if the value of what remains (the remainder) at any date, and *contemplated from any date*, is not positive (non-negative). Contemplated at the date of inception, it is possible to calculate a capital value at each imagined future date in the life of the project. What we are saying here is that each and every such capital value, as contemplated by the decision-maker, must be non-negative. If even one of them were negative, that would indicate that the project should terminate at that date. In fact that defines the termination date.

While this general principle (we may call it the positive remainder principle) must be true as an implication of rational planning, as of the point in time of the decision, it may of course happen that in the execution of the project the capital value at some point before planned termination unexpectedly becomes negative. This does not imply that the project should be immediately abandoned (although in retrospect it would seem that it should not have been started). The principle of the irrelevance of sunk costs applies and one would have to consider it as a new project where the "costs" of abandonment (long-term contractual costs, for example) have to be compared against the "costs" of continuing (Hayek 1941:89). Similarly, the capital values at any point may, during the execution of the project, turn out to be unexpectedly high. Thus we may define a successful plan as one whose capital values turn out as expected (or better).

Of course present-value criteria are well known and are implied in all discussions of capital. What Hicks makes explicit here is the way in which present-value appraisals change over time, specifically over the life of the project. He addresses the *intertemporal value structure* of a project, the logic within a single human plan concerning the relationship of the capital values at various contemplated dates to one another. So when Lachmann asks "What can we say about the firm's production plan in general and the pattern of use prescribed to its capital combination in it?" and answers, "We might say of course that the firm will act in such a manner as to maximize the present value of its expected future income stream, but such a description of the equilibrium of the firm is of very little use to us" (Lachmann 1986:64), he may be underestimating the usefulness of thinking in terms of the influences on the (present) capital value of any plan.

Each plan (or capital project) will have an implicit yield, better known as the internal rate of return (IRR). If the capitalization process is conducted using this rate then the initial value will be zero; it is the rate that causes the NPV at the inception date to be zero. If the same rate, the IRR, is used to calculate the capital values at all other dates, they will become positive, rise to a peak (or perhaps a series of peaks) and eventually fall again to zero at the termination point. Hicks also shows that for projects defined in this way the IRR is unique (Hicks 1973b:22, but see the discussion below following the next section). The foregoing can be greatly clarified with some basic algebra.

Formalization

We denote input values and output values at time t (contemplated at time 0) as a_t and b_t. Also,

$$a_t = \sum_i w_{it} \alpha_{it}$$

where w_{it} is the price and α_{it} is the quantity of input i at time t, assuming a set of ($i = 1, \ldots, m$) inputs.[4] For convenience we will suppress the i

---

[4] One may think here of a production function like $Q_t = f(\alpha_{1t}, \alpha_{2t}, \ldots, \alpha_{mt})$ at each point in time t. The meaning of the α_{it} will depend on the context. Where we think of all factor inputs as reducible to the *original inputs* in a sort of "macro" context, then they are of the form of "labor" and "land." Considered as a component of an individual production plan the $\alpha_i t$ must include produced inputs, that is capital goods.

subscript, assuming only one type of input, and write $a_t = w_t \alpha_t$ without loss of generality (alternatively a and w may be thought of as vectors). Similarly, we write $b_t = p_t \beta_t$, where p is the price and β the quantity of the output.[5] For convenience we define $q_t = b_t - a_t$ as the net output value at any date t. We denote the capital value at time t by k_t.

$$k_t = q_t + q_{t+1}R^{-1} + q_{t+2}R^{-2} + \ldots + q_n R^{-(n-t)}$$
$$= q_t + R^{-1}k_{t+1} = (b_t - a_t) + R^{-1}k_{t+1} \quad (6.1)$$

where $R = 1 + r$, and r is the per period rate of interest, or more accurately, rate of discount. This says that the capital value at the *beginning* of any sub-period t (k_t), which is the discounted value of all of the remaining net outputs, can also be calculated as the net value of the output of that period ($q_t = b_t - a_t$) plus the capital value of the remainder, for sub-periods after t ($R^{-1}k_{t+1}$). And this holds for any value of t.

Hicks now offers what he calls the "Fundamental Theorem": it is always true that a fall in the rate of interest (rate of discount) will raise the capital value of any project throughout (that is, as calculated at any date t), while a rise will lower it. The proof follows from equation (6.1) and it is instructive to reproduce it here at some length.

> [S]uppose that the q's are unchanged but that r falls, so that the discount factor rises. We see at once ... that k_t is bound to rise, provided that k_{t+1} is positive; and provided that k_{t+1} is not reduced by the fall in interest. But a similar argument applies to k_{t+1}. Thus we may go on repeating, up to the end of the process, where $k_n = q_n$. Thus k_n is unaffected by the fall in r; so k_{n-1} must be raised, and therefore k_{n-2} must be raised; and so on, back to k_t. So long as all the k_t's are positive (as we have seen that they must be, in order that the process should be viable), every k_t (0 to $n-1$) must be raised by the fall in the rate of interest.
>
> ... We have taken it for granted that the duration of the process remains at ($n+1$) weeks [sub-periods], even though the rate of interest falls. But it is immediately clear that even if the duration is variable, it cannot be shortened. For since we have

---

[5] For a multiproduct firm, $b_t = \sum_j p_{jt} \beta_{jt}$, where there are $j=1, \ldots, z$ outputs. As with a_t, b_t may be conceived of as the vector product of the vectors p_{jt} and β_{jt}.

> shown that with unchanged duration, every k_t ($t < n$) will be *raised*, it must still be advantageous to go on for at least the same duration, at a lower rate of interest. All that is possible is that the process may be lengthened.
>
> But the process will only be lengthened if k_{n+1} (which was zero at the higher rate of interest) becomes positive at the lower. That can happen, if the lengthening requires some net input (repairs, for instance, which only become profitable when the rate of interest falls). If it happens, however, all earlier k_t must be raised, *a fortiori*. So the Theorem continues to hold when duration is variable. (Hicks 1973b:20–21)

This characterization of a capital plan thus shows, in the first instance, how the planner's appraisal will be affected by changes in the discount rate applied. But it is equally clear that this appraisal will depend on all of the other conditions that characterize the project. For example, if the prices of the inputs w_t were to rise (or be expected to rise) the capital values would fall. Similarly a rise (expected rise) in the price of the product would raise all k_t. Changes in technology may affect these prices, by affecting processes elsewhere in the economy, or they may change the pattern of inputs, a_t, required.

The value of r for which $k_0 = 0$ is the IRR. This can be thought of as the yield of the project. It represents the minimum that would have to be earned on any alternative project if this one were to be abandoned in its favor. If "wages" w_t were to rise (uniformly) all of the k_t would be reduced. This implies that the yield of the project, its IRR, would fall. Thus for a given project (or set of projects) there is a trade-off between changes in w and r, other things constant. This is the sense in which the neo-Ricardians perceive the existence of a "factor price frontier" defining different equilibrium distributions of income between the factors of production. Considering hypothetical changes in w and changes in r necessary to "compensate" for these changes (by keeping $k_0 = 0$), one can imagine situations in which one technique, while dominant at a given level of r, loses its dominance as r falls and then regains it again as r continues to fall with rises in w. The significance of this is far from clear, however, given that any pattern of inputs a_t is, in principle, possible. Also, there is no unambiguous way in which we can decide which project, or technique, is more "capital intensive" (see the discussion in Chapter 5).

Moreover, it is important to note that in the context we have developed above, *r cannot be taken to be the price or rate of earnings (profits) of capital.* The variable *r* is the rate of discount applied to the overall earnings of the project at different dates. In fact the identification of *w* as "wages" is a terminological simplification that in no way assumes that all of the inputs are reducible to labor. Included among the a_t inputs are produced means of production. The variable w_t really refers to wages *and rents* on capital goods. The neo-Ricardian framework thus (from our perspective) seems to be predicated on an untenable view of the nature of the earnings of capital. We shall return to this below.

Looking Forward and Looking Backward

It should be emphasized that the view of the production process presented above is a forward-looking one. All of the values are prospective. We may even think of each project as a *capital prospect*. As such there is an unavoidable, but often suppressed, speculative element to it. There is at least one other possible way to look at production processes in time, that is, *retrospectively,* as a *result* of *capital invested.* From equation (6.1),

$$k_0 = q_0 + q_1 R^{-1} + q_2 R^{-2} + \ldots + q_{t-1} R^{-(t-1)} + k_t R^{-t} \qquad (6.2)$$

for any value *t* between 0 and *n*. Using the IRR in R, $k_0 = 0$, so,

$$k_t = (-q_0)R^t + (-q_1)R^{t-1} + \ldots + (-q^{t-1})R \qquad (6.3)$$

Looked at this way, k_t is the sum of the net inputs, $-q_t = a_t - b_t$, from 0 to $t - 1$, *accumulated* by interest up to period *t*. This captures the idea of inputs maturing at a rate equal to the IRR and emerging as a final output.

For plans that are successful, in the sense that the capital values k_t turn out to be exactly equal to what they were expected to be, when *discounted or accumulated* using the IRR, it should be clear that the two ways of looking at capital (prospective and retrospective) are exactly equivalent, they describe an ongoing and, in an essential sense, unchanging process. This is what the assumption of a steady state buys us, namely that the process—all processes—look the same at all points of time and *for* all points of time. In the steady state, since all plans are successful in this sense, the interest rate on loans must be equal to the (known) yield on projects, and the latter must be uniform (for any given investment period) across projects. We are back to a Ricardian world.

We note in passing that the neoclassical production function approach is a steady-state approach in this sense. Equation (5.1) can be written:

$$Q_t = A_t(t) \cdot f(K_t, N_t) \tag{5.1'}$$

inserting time subscripts to indicate an ongoing process in time, or

$$Q_t = A_{t-1}(t) \cdot f(K_{t-1}, N_{t-1})$$

if we allow for time lags.

We thus have an identical series of inputs (proportional to the stocks of factor of production) and outputs in every period t. Changes in the inputs will cause changes in the outputs once and for all. The process looks the same from all points of time.

Hicks is critical of the steady state:

> I am very skeptical of the importance of such "steady state" theory. The real world (perhaps fortunately) is not, and never is, in a steady state.... A "steady state" theory is out of time; but an Austrian theory is in time. (Hicks 1973b:109)

And he goes on to explain that a theory that is in time would have to take note of history, would have to include inherited history, including the inevitably less than optimal capital stock, as a "cause" of subsequent events.

For a theory that is in time, perspective matters—things look very different from different points of time. Most specifically, any process having a yield that is greater than the market rate of interest on loans, which it would have to have to be undertaken in the first place, would have the property that the capital value measured forward (prospectively) will be greater than the backward (retrospective) measure. And this will be true even at point 0 where $k_0 = 0$ measured forward. This is a basic implication of rational planning. If a process is successfully being carried out, and if its yield is greater than the interest rate, *a capital gain will accrue at each stage of the process*. Surely this is the real meaning of profit. The existence of profit, in this sense, absolutely depends on a disequilibrium between the yield and the interest rate. And this can persist only if there is no steady state, if there is no uniform (zero by this definition) rate of profit. The existence of profits implies different (varying) expectations.

Technical progress will imply that the yield on new processes (embodying the new knowledge) will be above old processes (those processes that do not). Old processes will, if there is enough time, be replaced by new ones. The capital stock, the stock of tangible things, will, at any point of time, reflect the accumulated results of past gains in knowledge. Although this is inimical to the steady state, everything that has been said above regarding the characterization of projects, techniques, and processes that make up capital, remains valid.

Social accounting, however, can only be done consistently in a steady state. Out of the steady state (a limiting case of which is the Ricardian stationary state) it is strictly impossible to derive aggregate values for capital and therefore for output (since the value of output depends on the value attributed to capital maintenance). Hicks explains this and then proceeds to assume a steady state in order to explore aspects of social accounting and transitions between such states. This, no doubt, is the reason for his less than warm reception at the hands of modern Austrians. Nevertheless, his simple arithmetic framework reveals a lot, even for those who believe that the market process should be analyzed as a disequilibrium phenomenon. Hicks's framework summarizes nicely the various influences on the individual valuations of any capital projects, including the valuations of any components of that process, like the individual capital goods, and alerts us to be cautious in concluding too readily what the effects of changes in interest rates, wage rates, product prices, or technologies might be. Similarly, it can accommodate consideration of qualitative changes such as the discovery of a new input or product. Ultimately everything can be analyzed in terms of the effect on the valuation of the particular project under consideration. For the economy as a whole, the variables in the framework, rather than being parameters, will be interrelated. An increase in the demand for a particular product, for example, will have implications for the prices of the inputs into its production. But the precise effects will depend on the patterns of complementarity and possibilities for substitution that characterize the production process. There is no simple law of derived demand for the economy as a whole (Hayek 1941:appendix 3; many of the questions considered by Hayek 1941 can be analyzed much more succinctly within Hicks's framework). We shall be able to make further use of Hicks's approach.

Conclusion: Capital Planning

Hicks's framework presented above is a convenient way to think about capital. It is fully consistent with a modern Austrian approach as developed, for example, by Lachmann and Kirzner. According to this approach, capital must be thought of in terms of intertemporal plans. We must make a distinction between capital goods and capital as an abstract category. The latter refers to the *value* to be attributed to a particular plan or set of production plans. The profits or losses to be attributed to a production plan are the result of changes (or the absence thereof) in the capital values attributed to it over time. These appreciations (or depreciations) in value are, in turn, the result of (are derived from) changes in consumers' evaluation of final production.

The meaning and the value of any particular capital good derives from its position in a particular production plan. "The identification of a 'resource' as distinct from other physical things, cannot be made without reference to human purposes" (Kirzner 1966:38). All capital goods are, in effect, an expression of "unfinished plans" (ibid.:ch. 1). As such, these capital goods can be valued by what they add to the value of the plan. The value of any income source is derived from the income it is expected to produce, so the value of any capital good is familiarly thought of as being equal to the discounted value of the estimated income it adds to any production plan — the discounted value of its marginal product.

All production plans are affected by, among other things, changes in the rate of discount that is pertinent to the plan. A fall in the discount rate will increase its value, a rise will decrease it. Thus if rates of discount are affected generally by macroeconomic changes, notably changes in interest rates, these may be expected to have a general effect on the expected value of existing and planned capital projects. In particular, those projects with the longest time horizon will be most affected. (This is well known and expressed in the proposition that the elasticity of present value is higher, the higher the time horizon.) It is important to remember that the discount rate is only one of the variables that affects the capital values of any and all projects. Hicks's approach has the virtue of providing us with a particularly clear framework in which the various influences may be revealed. So we might write a general capital value (vector) function as

$$k_t = k_t(w, \alpha, p, \beta, r, n)$$

indicating that r is only one of the determinants of k_t; r is perhaps especially important because of its macroeconomic significance as the indicator of the relationship between present and future prices of consumption goods. However, the structure of prices and wages in general may affect the project (through p and w) and technology obviously matters (α and β). Hicks's approach gives a comprehensive picture.

Appendix: The Meaning of the Internal Rate of Return

The rate of return on any investment is a concept that is widely used and has high intuitive appeal. We pause here to consider it a little more carefully. We shall see that it is not quite as straightforward as it appears on the surface, and that many aspects of its meaning are, and must be, imposed on it by the decision-maker.

Hicks presents arguments for the existence and uniqueness of the IRR. Any viable process must be viable for $r = 0$, "if its inputs and outputs are undiscounted, its k_0 must either be zero (in which case $r = 0$ is its internal rate of return) or it must be positive. But in the latter case, if the rate of interest rises … k_0 steadily diminishes, and must finally be reduced to zero—save in one special case … when $b_0 - a_0$ is positive (or zero)" which is a case of "production without capital." If $b_0 - a_0$ is negative, and k_1 is positive (as it must be if k_0 is not to be negative), it is inevitable that

$$k_0 = b_0 - a_0 + R^{-1}k_1$$

should ultimately be reduced to zero by a rise in the rate of interest. So an IRR exists. The IRR is unique because the Fundamental Theorem applies as much to k_0 as to any other k_t. "If we start from a rate of interest which is such that k_0 is zero (the other k's being positive), any reduction in the rate of interest must increase k_0. So k_0 cannot be zero again at any lower rate of interest" (Hicks 1973a:140 and 140n.)

It seems that Hicks obtains this result because of the way that he defines a project as a series of positive yields over time (for each period except the first). Thus a negative yield (positive outlay) can be used to demarcate the start of a new project. From a more general perspective the IRR need not be unique.

$$k_0 = q_0 + q_1 R^{-1} + q_2 R^{-2} + \ldots + q_n R^{-n} = 0$$

$$= \sum_{t=0}^{n} q_t R^{-t} = 0 \text{ (looking forward from 0 to } n\text{)}$$

thus

$$R^n k_t = \sum_{t=0}^{n} q_t R^{n-t} = \sum_{t=0}^{n} q_{n-t} R^t = 0$$

or

$$0 = q_n + q_{n-1} R + q_{n-2} R^2 + \ldots + q_0 R^n \text{ (looking backward hypothetically from } n\text{)}$$

The last line can be written:

$$0 = Q_n + Q_{n-1} r + Q_{n-2} r^2 + \ldots + Q_0 r^n \quad (6.4)$$

Where the Q_t are linear combinations of the q_t and r, and, it will be remembered, $R = (1 + r)$. Equation (6.4) is an nth order polynomial, with the roots equal to the IRR(s). Generally there will be more than one root: the number of roots will be equal to the number of changes in sign of the coefficients (Q_t) at most (I owe this approach to the lecture notes of Professor L. Sjaastad of the University of Chicago). Since Hicks has assumed one change in sign, there is only one IRR.

The use of an IRR is, at bottom, a matter of convention. It depends not only on how one divides up a project over time, but also on assuming that the "internal" yield is the same for each subperiod. It seems intuitively clear, however, that the individual planner must have in mind some benchmark against which to test (subjectively) the attractiveness of a project in comparison, for example, with investing in the market. Each planner will define his own boundaries.

CHAPTER 7

The Nature of Interest and Profits

Introduction

The above discussion clarifies, I hope, the nature of capital and some of the issues that surround its characterization. It will be remembered that the rate of discount featured in considering the capital value of any plan. This is sometimes also referred to in the literature as the rate of interest or the rate of profit. The question arises then as to the nature of interest as a phenomenon, and the relationship between interest and profit. As basic as this is, it remains a source of confusion in economics. Once again, the role of time is central. What is the connection between interest and time? Many theorists have seen interest as being determined by the technological characteristics of production, by "productivity," in relation to the willingness of consumers to abstain from consumption, to save. In the conventional wisdom, interest is the result of "productivity" and "thrift." While there is a sense in which this is true, a closer and deeper examination reveals that, in a more fundamental sense, the phenomenon of interest *per se* has nothing to do with productivity. Rather, interest is the result of the essential nature of time and the way that we experience it. This viewpoint is sometimes called a pure time preference theory (PTPT) of interest. And interest is to be clearly distinguished from profit which, as we have tried to show, is the result of changes in capital values that reflect the implementation of successful capital investments in an uncertain world, where expectations differ.

In this chapter I re-examine and re-evaluate the PTPT of interest. While I endorse it in the main, it seems to me that some of its proponents have perhaps fostered confusion by the way in which they have presented it. I then turn to a discussion of profit.

The Pure Time Preference Theory of Interest

The Interest Problem and its Resolution in Terms of PTPT Restated

The PTPT is notable for its obscurity (from the viewpoint of modern rival theories)[1] and for its resilience. Interest in it has recently resurfaced as part of the development of Böhm-Bawerkian capital theory (see Faber 1979; Pellengahr 1986a,b, 1996) and has been periodically revisited in the process of the development of Austrian market process theory (Yeager 1979; Garrison 1979a,b, 1988), and most recently by Kirzner (1993). Murray Rothbard is well known for his defense of the PTPT (see for example Garrison 1988) derived from Mises. We begin here with a brief restatement.

If an income source (a capital asset) is known to yield a steady income for a finite period of time, why does the price of the source not equal the sum total of the incomes earned over the life of the asset? So, to be more specific, a "machine" may be assumed to yield a net income of $100 a year for ten years and then be replaced by a new model.[2] Why can the machine not be sold for $1,000? This is a simple way of formulating the generic problem. If the value of an income source is derived from the value of the income it yields, why is the source not

---

[In this section I use material from Lewin (1997b).]

[1] At the very heart of the terminological thicket is the use of the word "interest" in at least two different contexts. The same word is used for a description of the rates earned and paid on money loans in actual real-world economies and for a description of the value premium of present over future goods in a hypothetical world devoid of uncertainty and change, although in the case of the latter, qualifiers like "originary," "pure," "neutral," and "natural" are sometimes added (notwithstanding that these qualifiers are used as well by different theorists to mean different things). See, for example, Rothbard (1975:17–18). On the one hand the phenomenon of "interest" is something with which we are all, in our everyday lives, very familiar. On the other hand, if we study economics we are told by PTPT theorists that "interest," while ubiquitous and crucial to the functioning of any market economy, is nothing we can actually observe because it is hopelessly mingled with profits and losses, inflation (price) premiums, and uncertainty premiums (Mises 1966:253; Rothbard 1970:321).

[2] We leave aside the question of how we know that the "machine" is the source of the income. Strictly speaking, we should say that the use of the machine together with other production goods *adds* $100 to income each year. In familiar terms the marginal product of the machine is valued at $100 per year. This will be explored further below.

valued at the sum total of the income yielded over its life? Surely, at any price below $1,000 someone could buy the machine and earn an income in excess of the price paid, a surplus. Why is this surplus not competed away?

The answer provides the identification, and indeed the definition, of interest as a phenomenon. *One hundred dollars today is not valued the same as $100 a year from now.* They are economically different goods. In terms of the consumer's subjective preference ranking, the marginal utility of $100 today is greater than the marginal utility *today* of $100 a year from now. This is *time preference* whose expression is interest.[3]

We may note some assumptions and implications. The income at various dates must be *that which would be valued the same at the same date*. The only differentiating factor is time (although it may be admitted that the passage of time itself cannot be without significance, of which more below)—*it is a pure time preference*. Second, it is important to keep all notions of interest rates, such as we observe in the loan market, out of the picture. To admit them into the individual's choice theoretic context would be to fall prey to an all too common circularity. We cannot explain interest rates in terms of individual time preferences if we assume an interest rate already to exist. This is no different in principle from realizing that individuals' preference rankings exist "prior" to and independently of the prices of the items they are ranking. Time preference is a subjective phenomenon like individual preference rankings and as such is unobservable. But it is nevertheless quite real and exists even in the real world of uncertainty and inflation and is reflected (together with risk and uncertainty) in market interest rates, just as other prices express other aspects of individual preferences (interest rates being derived from a ratio of intertemporal prices). Third, it is apparent that interest does not depend in any way on the productivity of capital. It does not even depend on the existence

---

[3]Specifically, using a neoclassical approach, we may say that the interest rate is the ratio of the marginal utilities minus 1. Symbolically $MU_t/MU_{t+1} = 1 + \tau$ where τ equals the rate of time preference. Or, more generally, $MU_t/MU_{t+n} = 1 + \tau_n$, where τ_n is the rate of time preference for time horizon n. Marginal utilities are understood to be as of time t. So MU_{t+n} is the marginal utility of the prospect in question to be enjoyed at time $t + n$ but contemplated at time t.

of productive assets (whose combined value is identified as capital). Indeed the price of a capital asset, its capital value, would fully reflect the (discounted) *value* (by its owner and as expectedly evaluated by consumers) of its product, so that a more productive asset would cost more. The *rental return* to capital is conceptually quite distinct from interest. Interest is not the return on capital. Interest would exist in a pure exchange economy as long as there was a positive time preference. A positive time preference is a necessary and sufficient condition for the existence of interest. In fact, in this context, interest and time preference are virtually synonymous. Interest is thus "explained" by the propensity of individuals to discount the future. And, since interest, by definition and by intuition, would not exist in the absence of this propensity, it makes sense to say that the phenomenon of interest is due to and only due to time preference. The "essence" of interest is time preference.

So far so good. It would seem that, stated in these terms or similar ones (for example Kirzner 1993; Garrison 1988), PTPT would be clear, if not unobjectionable, and objections would be in terms of arguing for other conceptual schemes. It is apparent, at least to this author, that the PTPT account of interest is not well understood, even by eminent theorists. It seems that a plausible explanation for this is the way in which the PTPT has been developed in the literature. It may be helpful to examine certain aspects of the development of the theory. The most influential theorists are probably Böhm-Bawerk (1959), Fetter (1977), Mises (1966), and Rothbard (1970).

Böhm-Bawerk, Fetter, Mises, and Rothbard

Böhm-Bawerk's exhaustive (and exhausting!) survey of interest theories establishes clearly the primacy of time preference. He effectively disposes of productivity accounts in explaining the phenomenon of interest. His account of time preference is much admired. But then in his later volume (1959), when he turns to an examination of *the determinants of time preference*, he advances three reasons for the existence of a positive rate of time preference. Two of these are "psychological" (impatience and myopia), while the third is "technological" (the "technical superiority" of present goods over future goods). What he meant by this third reason was the productivity of capital goods that represent the results of "roundabout" methods of production—because of productivity, present goods could be used to obtain a greater volume of future goods and so were demanded at a premium. In this way he involved himself in an unfortunate and celebrated contradiction.[4] To many later theorists it appeared as though Böhm-Bawerk had come to embrace a kind of Fisherian eclecticism, one that established the duality of time preference and productivity in the determination of interest rates. In fact much of the recent mathematical work on "modern Austrian capital theory" seems to reflect this (Faber 1979, 1986). In a way the contradiction became obscured because the question changed. PTPT was never really about the determination of market interest *rates*; it was about explaining interest as a phenomenon (Kirzner 1993:183ff.). As we shall see, the fact that productivity may play a role in the former in no way diminishes its irrelevance for the latter.

Frank Fetter's reputation as being unique among economists in his clear grasp of the PTPT owes a great deal to Rothbard (Rothbard 1977). But, according to Rothbard, while Fetter articulated a valid criticism of Böhm-Bawerk's inconsistency, at the same time he failed to grasp certain important aspects that were valid in Böhm-Bawerk's theory.[5] It was left to Mises to establish a valid theory using what was valuable from Böhm-Bawerk and Fetter and putting it in his own unique framework.

> The leading economist adopting Fetter's pure time preference view of interest was Ludwig von Mises ... Mises amended the theory, in two important ways. First, he rid the concept of its moralistic tone which had been continued by Böhm-Bawerk ... Mises made clear that a positive time preference rate is an essential attribute of human nature. Secondly, and as a corollary, whereas Fetter believed that people could have either positive or negative rates of time preference, *Mises demonstrated that a positive rate is deducible from the fact of human action*, since by the very nature of a goal or an end people wish to achieve that goal as soon as possible. (Rothbard 1987:421, italics added)

---

[4] See, however, Maclachlan (1993:39–40) for a slightly different interpretation.

[5] So, for example, among other things, he "never fully realized the importance [of distinguishing] between land (the original producer's good) and capital goods (created or produced producer's goods)" (Rothbard 1977:6).

So, according to Rothbard, Mises has *the* definitive PTPT of interest. Rothbard claims (a) that Mises has demonstrated "that a positive rate is deducible from the fact of human action, since by the very nature of a goal or an end people wish to achieve that goal as soon as possible" and therefore (b) that time preference can never be negative.

It is these claims that render the PTPT of interest obscure. A closer examination of Mises' work and Rothbard's reveals that they are not so easily established. Mises and Rothbard wanted to establish (positive) time preference as a pure (nonempirical) category, like action; something that was impossible to deny. But because of its link to time and because of the connection of time to uncertainty (the gaining of new knowledge), the attempt to do so involved Mises (and by extension Rothbard) in a logical contradiction—that is, he assumed the absence of uncertainty in order to "prove" the necessity of time preference as an implication of action, when action in a world without uncertainty is, by his own definition, impossible (Lewin 1997b). The distinction between assumption and empirical judgment also seems to be blurred by Mises' difficulty in establishing a clear definition of time preference (see also Pellengahr 1996).

The PTPT of Interest Reformulated

This is a difficult and controversial subject. No doubt others will interpret Mises differently and this is not the place for a lengthy defense of my own view (which is available in Lewin 1997b). Instead I will simply offer a reformulated account of the PTPT of interest, one that does not claim time preference as a "pure" category. Fetter's and Böhm-Bawerk's "empirical" approaches look much better from this perspective.

Time preference is difficult to define. The prospects being compared over time must in some sense be the same things *but for the passage of time*. What, then, makes them the "same things"? Are they the same goods? In this case the definition of a good is problematic—ice cream in summer versus ice cream in winter are not the same good. But then, are we talking about more "ultimate" goods, like "satisfaction obtained from eating ice cream"? If so, we are comparing a present satisfaction with the contemplation of an identical satisfaction in the future. How are we to calibrate these? An alternative way to express time preference, one that is purged of any "hedonic" elements, is as follows:

> Comparing the purchase of (a) a prospect that is ranked 1 today with (b) a prospect that would be ranked 1 today if it were available today but is only available tomorrow; since (as indicated by the ranking) (a) is preferred to (b), time preference exists.

A key point can be made: *time preference is strongly intuitively connected to the presence and type of uncertainty in the world.* Consider the simple experiment that one often uses in teaching the concept of time preference. The teacher takes out a ten-dollar bill and asks the class which they would prefer: (1) the ten dollars right now or (2) the same ten dollars this time next week. He adds that the students may not earn any interest on the ten dollars. Of course, everyone opts for (1). Then the teacher changes option (2) to (2'), ten dollars plus i this time next week. At some level of i, (2') will just be preferred (or the students will be indifferent between the two). This is then used as an indication of, and as a measurement of, time preference. Now if you change the choice a little by adding the assumption that the prospect of ten dollars next week is a certain prospect—the teacher is a perfectly safe bet, while the students' ability to keep the ten dollars safe over the course of the week is less than certain (for example, we could imagine a dangerous society in which predatory behavior regularly threatens people's savings) then (2) could very well be preferred to (1). Alternatively, if we assume that (2) and (1) are equally and completely certain, then a priori it does not seem to be possible to say that one will be preferred to the other. The knee-jerk preference of (1) over (2) seems to be crucially bound up with the fact that the students automatically realize that the passage of time brings with it unexpected events and that "a bird in the hand is worth two in the bush." Resorting to constructs that banish the essential nature of time seems to hinder rather than help in understanding time preference.

It should be noted that among some writers sympathetic to the time preference approach there is no assumption that it need always be positive or that it is a logical rather than an "empirical" phenomenon. We have already noted Fetters' contribution. In Kirzner's recent article he implicitly expresses doubts about Mises' treatment, when he says,

"This theory solves the interest problem by appeal to widespread *possibly universal* positive time preference" (Kirzner 1993:171, italics added), and again: "PTPT accounts for this phenomenon [value productivity] by reference to widespread *possibly universal* preference for the earlier, rather than the later, achievement of goals" (ibid.:192, italics added). In considering why (market) interest rates cannot be negative, Lachmann explains:

> The ultimate reason for this lies in the simple fact that stocks of goods can be carried forward in time, but not backwards. If present prices of future goods are higher than those of present goods, it is possible to convert the latter into the former unless the good is perishable or the cost of storing excessive; while future goods cannot be converted into present goods unless there are ample stocks not otherwise needed which their holders are ready to reduce for a consideration. And as there are always a number of goods for which the cost of storage would be small, money being one of them, a negative rate of interest would be eliminated by a high demand for present goods which are easy to store and a large supply of easily storable future goods, at least as long as the stocks carried are covered by forward sales.
> (Lachmann 1978:78)

So, given that the passage of time is what it is, and given that (in our society) generally some goods can be transferred to the future intact (notably money), we would expect time preference and interest rates to be positive.

Conclusion: Interest is not Profit

Every production plan involves capital values. These depend crucially on the rate of discount used to obtain them. This rate of discount is an expression of a positive time preference, although it may be affected by other things. Time preference is its essential explanation. Since capital involves time it also involves time preference. Observed interest rates which, depending on the context, are sometimes used to obtain capital values, do not measure the return to capital. Capital is in this respect no different from any other input. The contribution of any and all inputs will be similarly discounted in any production plan. Payment to the inputs would tend to reflect their opportunity costs. Thus any surplus remaining after the payment to the inputs of "wages" and "rents" is profit. We now take a closer look at this.

The Nature of Profit

Profits In and Out of Equilibrium

One way to examine the nature of profit is to examine a hypothetical situation in which it would be absent. This has been the basis of a number of similar approaches in neoclassical as well as Austrian economics: in the former, the steady state and its extreme, the stationary state; in the latter the "evenly rotating economy."

In an economy in which there was no uncertainty (if one could imagine such a world) there would be no profit. All production plans in such a world would be successful in the sense explained above. All capital values k_t would look the same from all points of view and to all individuals. In such a world the rate of discount would equal the uniform internal rate of return on all capital projects and this in turn would equal the rate of interest for the time period in question. This is the world of general equilibrium. If we assume no growth, no capital accumulation, it is a stationary general equilibrium and also an evenly rotating economy (ERE) (see Rothbard 1970:274ff.). In this kind of world it is possible to do some simple social accounting.

The structure of production will be constant and will reflect the best use of the generally known productive techniques. This is the state to which we are to imagine the economy will tend to move in the absence of any change. There are no profits and losses. The prices of capital goods—reflecting the value of their discounted marginal products—are fully captured by the prices of the original "primary" factors used to produce them. And there are only two such primary factors of production—(ground) land and (raw) labor. Everything else in the economy is ultimately produced using these two primary factors, either directly—at the highest stage—or indirectly, combining with already produced capital goods to add value to the next stage. All other incomes can be analytically "swept back" to those of the original factors. The incomes of land and labor are incomes in the nature of a rent, and in the ERE only labor and land earn pure rent.

A rent is the unit price of the service yielded by a long-lived asset. In the case of a nondurable good it is equal to its price. In the ERE the rent on a particular physical asset will equal its discounted marginal value product (DMVP). Thus all durable assets that have a value in production (and can be bought and sold) have capitalized values that will determine their prices. For a perpetual income stream the capitalized value will be equal to the rent divided by the discount rate. Since all rents, except those paid to land and labor, "balance out"—since the prices paid for capital inputs by a producer of capital goods at any stage of production must be offset against the prices of the goods produced—the only "pure" capitalized values are for land and labor. Since labor cannot be bought and sold in a free society—it can only be rented—the only pure capitalized value that would be observed is that of land.

Thus, in this world, there is a crucial distinction to be made between capital, land, and labor, since capital earns no net (pure) income and the distinction between land and labor has to do with the lack of a market for the latter—a matter we take up briefly below (and in detail in Chapter 11). To reiterate, capital goods refers to produced means of production, whereas land refers to the nonproduced resources of nature. This distinction is likely to trouble the modern reader who might find it difficult to imagine any productive land that has not been altered in some way in the interests of productive activity. Also the fact that at a certain time in the distant past unspoiled land entered into the production of a particular consumption good is, from an economic point of view, irrelevant. Economic agents take the world as they find it and look forward when making decisions—they inherit a variety of capital goods whose value depends not on their history but on their future usefulness. For both of these reasons the distinction between capital and land needs to be carefully formulated. Whether a piece of land is "originally" pure land is in fact economically immaterial, so long as whatever alterations have been made are permanent—or rather so long as these alterations do not have to be reproduced or replaced. "Permanence" is not really the key.

> The key question is whether a resource has to be *produced*, in which case it earns only *gross* rents. If it does not or cannot, it earns *net* rents as well. Resources that are being depleted

> obviously *cannot* be replaced and are therefore *land*, not capital goods. (Rothbard 1970:460 n. 15)

So land is any nonhuman resource that cannot be "produced" or "reproduced." And capital goods are produced means of production that require (allow) maintenance or reproduction. As such, they include the structures on land, agricultural land, and valuable human-made features of the landscape that need to be maintained. Land, then, includes less than what we are accustomed in common usage to mean, one important element being "location." "[This] concept of land ..., then, is entirely different from the popular concept of land" (ibid.:415; see also Hayek 1941:ch. V).

An ERE at any time, then, will have as productive factors land, labor, and capital in the sense discussed. Land does not refer to the resources of nature in their pristine originality, but rather to any non-reproducible resources that may happen to exist at the time that the economy arrived at the stationary state of the ERE. (Rothbard is aware that the ERE cannot abide depletable resources—that would otherwise qualify as land—and bemoans this as an unfortunate shortcoming of an otherwise useful construct.) In this economy, the only net incomes earned will be the wages of labor, the rents of land, and pure interest. The value of the final product will be accounted for by the contributions of land (in the restricted sense explained), labor, and interest. So in this discussion, profits and losses (which are conceptually completely distinct from interest) have the necessary function to correct the ubiquitous malinvestments and misallocations that occur outside of the particular (zero profit) ERE to which the economy is assumed to be tending. "Profits are an index that maladjustments are being met and combated by the profit-making entrepreneurs" (ibid.:468, italics removed). And in a continually growing economy, land may earn an income in terms of an increasing capitalized value.

Theory and Reality

This approach is useful in sorting out some common but fundamental confusions, like the difference between interest and profit, and is strong, for example, on the explanation of the concept of rent. Careful readers come away with a much better understanding of fundamental categories like interest, wages, rent, and profit. They are thus able to demystify much of capital theory. Profit is seen as a disequilibrium phenomenon, a result of fluctuations in capital values in response to diverse entrepreneurial visions and actions. It is not interest, it is not rent, and it is not a return to any single factor of production, unless entrepreneurship be regarded as a factor (something that is hard to defend). We shall return to this. Once we leave the certain world of the ERE (or any steady state), however, it is useful to consider wages, interest, and rent as categorically separate from profits along the same lines as discussed above, in that they are *contractual* in nature, being the result of the fulfillment of (implicitly or explicitly) contractual arrangements between employers and employees or borrowers and lenders. Profits are familiarly understood, then, as the *residual noncontractual payment* to the equity holders in the production process. This is a valuable insight suggested from ERE steady-state type reasoning and, of course, also conforms to the vision of the modern property rights approach to the firm. (See Chapter 9.)

PART III

CAPITAL IN A DYNAMIC WORLD

I have, to this point, explored aspects of the history of capital theory, and the nature of interest, profit, and rent. One should distinguish between capital goods and capital as an abstract category. The latter refers to the *value* to be attributed to a particular plan or set of production plans. The profits or losses to be attributed to a production plan are the result of changes (or the absence thereof) in the capital values attributed to it over time. These appreciations (or depreciations) in value are, in turn, the result of (are derived from) changes in consumers' evaluation of final production.

The meaning and the value of any particular capital good derives from its position in a particular production plan. Production plans are like any other human plans (as discussed in Part I). They are defined by particular purposes and they are informed by particular kinds of knowledge. Every production plan must envisage a combination of resources—a capital combination. Capital goods and labor and land work together to fulfill the plan. This combination must be made by someone with the knowledge of how to do it. This involves knowledge of the natural world, technological knowledge (knowledge type 1), and knowledge of social habits and institutions (for example, if individuals have to be coordinated and motivated—knowledge type 2). It may also involve specific expectations (knowledge type 3) concerning individual behavior (can we rely on a particular worker?) or nature (will the weather be favorable?). But it seems reasonable to assume that often most of the knowledge involved in the *implementation* of the production plan is heavily weighted in favor of knowledge types 1 and 2. There are notable and important exceptions: those production plans that depend heavily on the "speculative" actions of others—for example, on the supply of a yet to be discovered source of raw materials, etc. — or those production plans that depend heavily on the implementation of innovative (untried) productive techniques and the results of research programs (as in the search for a new chemical substance or medical drug). In general, production plan implementation rests heavily on typical events and, perhaps to a lesser extent, on specific ones. In addition to successfully coordinating the inputs, the successful implementation of any production plan rests, however, on the successful sale of its output. And it is this aspect that is most likely to be dependent on the particular producer's expectations (knowledge type 3).

In a world in which the production and sale of outputs was part of a plan that was assumed to be consistent with all other related plans, so that there were no disappointments in production schedules or, most notably, in the sale of output, the value of the resources that were part of the plan would clearly be certain. And if everyone shared in the knowledge of the value of the output and the contribution of each input, then, in some sense, these values would be reflected in prices of the inputs. In such a situation of perfect plan coordination, a meaningful capital aggregate could then be obtained.[1] It should be clear, however, that such a construction abstracts not only from time, but also from those aspects of a capital-using economic process that are responsible for its dynamic, innovative character.

If it is true, by contrast, that production plans typically rest on expectations of the sale of particular outputs, sometimes of new products, sometimes involving new production techniques, then we should not reasonably expect such plans to be consistent and coordinated with all other plans in the economy. In particular, capitalistic production involves rivalrous activity that clearly implies the pitting of one entrepreneurial vision against another. In such a world the value of productive resources, indeed the value of productive ventures as a whole, cannot be known to all and cannot be added together. Many will depend on mutually exclusive outcomes. These outcomes might be simple market shares in the case of similar but differentiated (brand named) products or they may be the progressive adoption of particular

---

[1] It is not clear that prices would exist in a world of perfect certainty such as that postulated here. In such a world everyone would know ahead of time who should have which resources, etc. But resources could unambiguously be imputed values which may be thought of as "prices."

standards like Windows versus Unix or VHS versus Beta. For example, we can imagine two video stores, one renting VHS cassettes, the other Beta cassettes, reasonably basing their expansion plans on inconsistent expectations, each betting on the growing adoption of their particular standard.

Production plans, considered as a whole, are typically in disequilibrium—are based, at least in part, on inconsistent expectations, not regarding the "rules of the game" but regarding the viability of the product or the productive technique. There is no way to derive an aggregate measure of capital in this situation. The net present values as (assumed to be) computed by each individual planner are based on inconsistent futures. However, this absence of equilibrium in no way precludes action—no more so than the absence of knowledge of the outcome of a football game prevents the players from playing. All action occurs within an institutional environment that includes the knowledge of the actors, and, as we have seen, much of this knowledge does imply a consistency of expectations.

In Part II I impressionistically traced the development of capital theory from Adam Smith through Ricardo to modern times. I drew a distinction between the Ricardian and Mengerian traditions. In Part III I turn to a discussion of some non-Ricardian approaches to capital theory and related topics. Some of these may be seen to derive from Menger (Hayek, Lachmann), while others (essentially complementary to the Mengerian line) may be termed "post-Marshallian" (Penrose, Richardson, Teece, Williamson, Loasby, Langlois, and others). What these approaches have in common for our purposes, is a process approach to the accumulation of capital. Capital decisions are seen as occurring within an evolving economic environment and are embedded within individual production plans. The success or failure of these plans is inevitably linked to the organization of production. This leads, therefore, to a discussion of the nature of economic organization more generally, particularly to the economics of the firm. Indeed we shall see that capital theory cannot be separated from a consideration of the economics of business organization.

CHAPTER 8

Modern Mengerian Capital Theory

Introduction

Our considerations in Part II suggest the following conclusions from which we shall proceed in this part.

1. *Capital theory historically involved misleading physical analogies.* Examples are:

   (a) Biological analogies: reproductive processes in which "growth" occurs automatically (the Crusonia plant, the woodlot); incubation periods, where capital processes are likened to physical ones that depend primarily on the passage of time (although implicitly it is *what happens* in time that matters) like aging wine.

   (b) Notions of interest that are linked with physical or biological accretion: the idea that interest is that implicit increase in value that occurs continuously and inexorably over the production period.

An approach to capital theory disconnected from its unhelpful historical baggage must realize that the production process is a process of *value enhancement* over (in) time. It may involve physical processes (transformations) but its essential characteristic and driving force is the creation of value, the regrouping of physical resources into more valuable combinations as a result of deliberate production decisions (not to imply that all or even most of these decisions are "successful"). We shall be concerned to discover how production decisions are made. We realize also that interest is a phenomenon that is crucially distinct from productivity (although we need not deny that the *rate* of interest may be influenced by productivity, often in non-obvious ways).

2. *We can dispense with "time period of production" approaches to capital.* While we cannot but note and emphasize the importance of the connection between time and production, and the intuitive validity

of the idea that in order to reap the fruits of more productive specializations we have to adopt production methods that are more "roundabout" (more complex, more indirect), nevertheless we cannot capture this idea in the form of any simple notion of "period of production." Nor need we do so.

In this regard we shall find a number of modern theorists leading the way. The Austrian tradition emanating from Menger in the work of Mises, Rothbard, Hayek, Kirzner, and Lachmann has provided important insights. We shall focus here primarily on the work of Lachmann but we must take note briefly of the important work of Hayek on capital theory, if only for the subsequent work which it inspired. We will then turn to a discussion from another tradition, that emanating from Alfred Marshall. A group of theorists who have been referred to as "post-Marshallian" (Foss 1994, 1995, 1996a,b) has done considerable work on the economics of the firm which bears a clear connection to considerations of capital structure. One of the contributions of this part will be to illustrate the connections between these two literature strands and how one can inform the other.

Hayek and the Fundamental Questions of Capital Theory

In his work on capital Hayek stands, in a sense, between the Böhm-Bawerkian–Ricardian approach and the Mengerian and post-Marshallian approach. His work on capital theory dating from the early 1930s and culminating in the publication of *The Pure Theory of Capital* (1941), was prompted by a concern with the business cycle. In *Monetary Theory and the Trade Cycle* (1933) and *Prices and Production* (1935b) he developed what came to be known as the Austrian (Mises–Hayek) theory of the business cycle. This is essentially a monetary theory of fluctuations, but one that emphasizes a (monetarily induced) "distortion" of the capital stock. Hayek thus naturally drew from the work of Böhm-Bawerk and the relation between the capital stock and time. In so doing he simplified and glossed over many of the subtleties and complications relating to capital aggregation. In his subsequent work, in the environment of the gathering momentum of the Keynesian revolution, he sought to clarify and develop the capital theoretic underpinnings to this work, which he saw as the viable alternative to the flawed and superficial Keynesian approach (see the collection of articles in *Profits, Interest and Investment* (1939)). Finally, his writing of the *Pure Theory* reflects his initial determination to lay out fully the fundamentals of capital theory and to make plain why he maintained that an understanding of capital was vital to a valid approach to (macro)economic policy.[1] In the actual implementation of the project he became aware of the enormity of the task he had set himself, and the finished product, though intricate and involved (by far his most difficult work in economics), was seen by him as an unfinished compromise (as is very clear from his remarks on pages vii–ix of the preface). (Hayek had planned a second volume that would have applied the *Pure Theory* analysis to trade cycles.)

The basic approach of the book is an equilibrium approach along the lines of (the "Ricardian") Böhm-Bawerk, Wicksell, and Jevons (all of whom he credits as having anticipated in all essential ways what he has to say). But, in his voluminous side comments and general discussions, he makes it very clear that he understands the limitations of this (equilibrium) approach, and points the way to a more "dynamic" disequilibrium treatment. Thus this work contains not only a fairly early working out of what was later to become a research area of neoclassical economics under the rubric of intertemporal equilibrium theory, but also a wealth of important observations on the meaning of capital maintenance in a dynamic, changing world and other important insights that served as raw material for Lachmann's later work on capital theory. It is the latter contributions in which we will be interested.

Whereas the classical (Ricardian) theory of capital (as we saw in Part II) had become concerned with explaining the determination of the rate of profit earned on an abstract category of resources (or a fund) known as capital, the Mengerian approach suggested paying attention to the *structure* of capital. Hayek's sympathies lie clearly with the latter.

> Our main concern will be to discuss in general terms what type of equipment it will be most profitable to create under various conditions, and how the equipment existing at any moment will be used, rather than explain the factors which determined the value of a given stock of production equipment and the income that will be derived from it. (Hayek 1941:3)[2]

---

[1] This interpretation of Hayek's work on capital theory is my own.

[2] It is a problem for the reader that, having stated this general objective, Hayek then turns to a protracted examination of capital under equilibrium conditions reminiscent of the classical approach, and never really fulfills his originally stated objective. It has been suggested (by Hayek, among others) that Lachmann did just that (see Lewin 1997a).

Hayek's *compositive* sympathies are clearly stated:

> The problems that are raised by any attempt to analyze the dynamics of production are mainly problems connected with the interrelationships between the different parts of the elaborate structure of productive equipment which man has built to serve his needs. But all the essential differences between these parts were obscured by the general endeavor to subsume them under one comprehensive definition of the stock of capital. The fact that this stock of capital is not an amorphous mass[3] but possesses a definite structure, that it is organized in a definite way, and that its *composition of essentially different items* is much more important than its aggregate "quantity," was systematically disregarded. (ibid.:6, italics added)

---

[3]In this approach it is clear that both Lachmann and Hayek benefit from Schumpeter's pronouncements. In his lectures on capital theory Lachmann states:

> Schumpeter has a succinct statement of the compositive school approach. Whenever we are talking about a given situation—meaning given tastes, resources and technology—resources must exist in a certain stock of *inherited* goods, i.e., goods provided in the past. They are simply there, like land. These resources are limited in the way that they can be used. The stock of existing goods constitutes a constraint on human action going forward. The stock of capital *is neither homogeneous, nor is it an amorphous heap*. Its components complement one another. Some goods must be available for the operation of others. The nature of the composition of the stock is vital—it constitutes a given "structure." (Lachmann 1996:126–127, see also 144)

This is an allusion to the words of Schumpeter. In a section entitled "The Structure of Physical Capital," Schumpeter seems to anticipate much that is relevant to Lachmann's (and Hayek's) viewpoint.

> The initial stock of goods is neither homogeneous nor an amorphous heap. Its various parts complement each other in a way that we readily understand as soon as we hear of buildings, equipment, raw materials, and consumers' goods. Some of these parts must be available before we can operate others; and various sequences or lags between economic actions impose themselves and further restrict our choices; and they do this in ways that differ greatly according to the composition of the stock we have to work with. We express this by saying that the stock of goods existing at any instant of time is a *structured quantity or a quantity that displays structural relations within itself*, that shape, in part, the subsequent course of the economic process.
> (Schumpeter 1954:631–632, italics in original)

Hayek explains the problems associated with any attempt to aggregate the capital stock in value terms or in terms of units of labor or time and intends to work systematically towards a theory in which this is not necessary. He begins, however, with a discussion of how an economy directed by a central dictator might make decisions regarding the formation and use of capital goods in an economy devoid of change. This, of course, abstracts from any issues related to the relative evaluation of consumption goods, since the only valuations that matter are the dictator's. Thus the solution is essentially the same as the classical one. There is, by assumption, no disequilibrium problem; heterogeneity is seen not to matter. Of course, Hayek does this as a foil, a relief against which to illuminate the real-world problems of heterogeneity and change. His method is first to get the abstract problem right. Unfortunately, but understandably, much of the literature that refers to this work concentrates on these equilibrium exercises, rather than on the original focus that Hayek sought to maintain, that is, of inquiring into the decisions governing the use of the various capital resources at our disposal.[4]

The Problem of Imputation

Essentially Hayek was concerned with the question: how are resources made and used? Or, more accurately, *how are these decisions made?* That is, we seek to understand the decision-making process which leads to the adoption of certain types of capital equipment in combination with others. Obviously, decision-makers have to form a judgment as to the worth of any capital combination and its various components; they have to *impute* a value to the capital goods they have or are considering acquiring or producing. This is clear from Menger's notion (developed further by Wieser, who seems to have invented the term "imputation")[5] that the value of any resource is derived from the value

---

[4]In the final section of the book (pt IV) Hayek turns to some dynamic considerations. While this section is very useful, particularly in its treatment of fundamental issues concerning saving and investment, it does not really deal with capital and could be seen perhaps as an extended and effective (but largely ignored) reply to Keynes.

[5]The imputation question was an important issue for the "second" generation of Austrian economists (the interwar period) and may have been responsible for a less than accurate understanding of Mises' contribution to the socialist calculation debate on the part of some Austrian economists. See Kirzner (1994b:vol. II: 20; also chs 15 and 19 thereof).

of the final output for which it is responsible. But, as we have noted in previous chapters, the question remains as to how we are to decide which unit of output is attributable to which unit of input. In the neoclassical literature this problem is solved by assuming that production methods can be varied continuously in such a way that the marginal contributions (products) of each unit of input can be easily discovered. This is also Hayek's assumption in his discussion of a centrally directed economy. This way of dealing with the problem abstracts from the most interesting questions in capital theory, questions that turn out to be relevant to considerations of economic organization.

It would seem, however, that there is a necessity to invoke some notion of marginal (value) product. The producer must have in mind some opportunity cost when assigning a resource in one particular way rather than another and thus must also have in mind the supposed contribution that its (marginal) assignment makes. As we shall make clear, however, in a world of uncertainty and change, there is an inescapable element of judgment and speculation involved in this. Different decision-makers will see things differently and will (implicitly) impute different values to the capital resources at their disposal from what others would. These differences produce the capital valuation process that is part of the market process and which renders economic calculation possible.

The economist's description of the imputation process, where the decision-maker has recourse to the value marginal product schedule, is an idealized construct. The process of actual decision-making must mirror in an implicit way this idealization. But it does so by using certain simplifying conventions (for example, based on accounting practices) that form part of an institutional structure rendering the decision manageable (tractable). And in so far as these conventions reflect a widespread sharing of forms of appraisal, they supply the decision-maker with knowledge (type 2) of "how to do it" (as distinct from what to decide—type 3). We shall return to this.

Lachmann's Conceptual Framework

The Structure of Capital

Perhaps the most important development of Hayek's original project is to be found in Lachmann's capital theory. In 1956, Lachmann, who

---

[This section uses material from Lewin (1997a).]

had been a student and colleague of Hayek's at the London School of Economics, published *Capital and its Structure* (Lachmann 1978).[6] This work was really the culmination of his earlier work on capital, the most complete of which was his 1947 article (see Lachmann 1938, 1939, 1941, 1944, 1947, 1948; see also Lewin 1997a).

According to Lachmann:

> The generic concept of capital without which economists cannot do their work has no measurable counterpart among material objects; it reflects the entrepreneurial appraisal of such objects. Beer barrels and blast furnaces, harbor installations and hotel room furniture are capital not by virtue of their physical properties but by virtue of their economic functions. Something is capital because the market, the consensus of entrepreneurial minds, regards it as capable of yielding an income.... [But] the stock of capital used by society does not present a picture of chaos. Its arrangement is not arbitrary. There is some order to it. (Lachmann 1978:xv)

The value of the capital stock, being dependent on individual expectations and evaluations (time preferences included), is not an objectively observable phenomenon or necessarily even a meaningful concept. Only in equilibrium, where all individuals' expectations were consistent one with the other, would such a value have any meaning. Lachmann chooses to develop his analysis in a *disequilibrium* framework. In other words, Lachmann considered the notion of a capital stock (which made sense in an equilibrium context) to be untenable and unhelpful in a disequilibrium world. He thus offers a theory of the *capital structure* rather than the *capital stock*.

Lachmann thus emphasizes the *heterogeneity* of the capital stock. The fact that capital goods are physically very dissimilar is significant precisely because of the existence of disequilibrium. Physical heterogeneity could be reduced to value homogeneity if the values

---

[6] As mentioned above, there is some evidence to suggest that both Hayek and Lachmann saw Lachmann's work as a continuation of Hayek's project. When asked about the *Pure Theory* Hayek once remarked, "I think the most useful conclusions drawn from what I did are really in Lachmann's book on capital" (Kresge and Wenar 1994:142). Also, it is clear that Lachmann's inspiration was Hayek's work on capital (of which *The Pure Theory* was the culmination). In his 1948 article he refers to Hayek (1937a) and says, "The ideas set forth by Professor Hayek have been the main inspiration of this paper" (Lachmann 1948).

of the various capital goods could be simply added together. Where disequilibrium means that individuals have different and *frequently inconsistent* expectations, one cannot simply add together individual valuations. The physical heterogeneity is not the essence of the matter. Different physical goods that perform the same economic function could be counted as the same good. It is the difference in *economic function* that matters. For the most part different capital goods look different because they are designed to perform different functions. But the same capital good could perform different functions under different circumstances. Heterogeneity in use is the key.

Although the capital stock is heterogeneous, it is not an amorphous heap. The various components of the capital stock stand in sensible relationship to one another because they perform specific functions together. That is to say, they are used in various *capital combinations*. If we understand the logic of capital combinations, we give meaning to the capital stock and, in this way, we are able to design appropriate economic policies or, even more importantly, avoid inappropriate ones (for example Lachmann 1978:123).

Complementarity and Substitutability

Understanding capital combinations entails an understanding of the concepts of *complementarity* and *substitutability*. In neoclassical microeconomics, these concepts are developed within a market equilibrium production function framework. Production goods are substitutes or complements for one another to the degree to which, and in the manner in which, their marginal products are related. The marginal products of complements are positively related while those of substitutes are negatively related. What is envisaged is a situation in which production goods are combined in a technological relationship of known and well-understood inputs and outputs. The values of all possible outputs are known with certainty (or with probabilistic certainty), and from this it is possible to calculate the values of the marginal products under all conceivable circumstances. Hence, we have the picture of a given budget line (or hyperplane), formable out of the given *equilibrium* prices of the production goods and the quantities used, confronting a given isoquant. Substitution is then simply a matter of moving around the isoquant in two-dimensional or multidimensional space. Substitution occurs because of a change in the price of a production good. There is no analysis of any events that occur in disequilibrium, i.e., of events that occur between the time that a price change occurs, is perceived, is acted upon, and results in the establishment of a new equilibrium. The same sort of analysis is applied to changes in technology, which are analyzed as changes in the positions or shapes of the isoquants.

As a mental picture of a single production plan at a point of time, the isoquant diagrams (or algebras) may be enlightening. They summarize a certain "logic of choice." But they have little to do with Lachmann's conception of what substitution and technical progress mean in reality. His concepts pertain to a world in which perceived prices are actual (disequilibrium) prices, in the sense that they reflect inconsistent expectations and in which changes that occur cause protracted visible adjustments. Capital goods are complements if they contribute together to a given *production plan*. A production plan is defined by the pursuit of a given set of ends to which the production goods are the means. As long as the plan is being successfully fulfilled, *all* of the production goods stand in complementary relationship to one another. They are part of the same plan. (It is not inconsistent to say that their perceived marginal products are positively related, in the sense that their joint outputs depend on each others' performance. An increased availability—reduction in price—of any one input raises the potential outputs of the plan attributable jointly to all of the inputs and may increase the (joint) demand for all of them.) The complementarity relationships within the plan may be quite intricate and may involve different stages of production and distribution. Substitution occurs when a production plan fails (in whole or in part). When some element of the plan fails, a contingency adjustment must be sought.[7] Thus some resources must be substituted for others. This is the role, for example, of spare parts or excess inventory. Thus, complementarity and substitutability are properties of different states of the world. The same good can be a complement in one situation and a substitute in another.

---

[7] It is easy to see how his approach relates to the analysis of the individual planning process suggested in Chapter 2, that is, that plans depend on different kinds of knowledge, and are multilayered and necessarily vague.

Lachmann uses the example of a delivery company (Lachmann 1947:199; and Lachmann 1978:56). The company possesses a number of delivery vans. Each one is a complement to the others in that they cooperate to fulfill an overall production plan. That plan encompasses the routine completion of a number of different delivery routes. As long as the plan is being fulfilled, this relationship prevails, but if one of the vans should break down, one or more of the others may be diverted in order to compensate for the unexpected loss of the use of one of the productive resources. To that extent and in that situation they are substitutes. Substitutability can only be gauged to the extent that a certain set of contingency events can be visualized. There may be some events, such as those caused by significant technological changes, that, not having been predictable, render some production plans valueless. The resources associated with them will have to be incorporated into some other production plan or else scrapped—they will have been rendered unemployable. This is a natural result of economic progress which is driven primarily by the trial-and-error discovery of new and superior outputs and techniques of production.

What determines the fate of any capital good in the face of change is the extent to which it can be fitted into any other capital combination without loss in value. Capital goods are *regrouped*. Those that lose their value completely are scrapped. That is, capital goods, though heterogeneous and diverse, are often capable of performing a number of different economic functions. Lachmann calls this property *multiple specificity*.

The Capital Structure is Composed of Complementary Heterogeneous Items

Lachmann's world is consciously similar to Schumpeter's world (Schumpeter 1961) of "creative destruction," except that for Lachmann the innovating entrepreneur is not disrupting some preexisting general equilibrium. His world is one in which a continuous evolutionary process of changing patterns of capital complementarity is occurring. At any point in time, different entrepreneurs will have different and frequently incompatible production plans. Over time the market process will validate some and invalidate others. Lachmann sees the market process as tending to integrate the *capital structure*, in other words, rendering plans more consistent, although he is careful to add (as we saw in Chapter 2) that the forces of equilibrium may be overwhelmed by the forces of change.

The concept of the capital structure (to be explained further below) is built out of the notion of capital complementarity. A production plan is a construction of the human mind. As such it exhibits a necessary internal consistency. From the point of view of *the individual planner*, it might be said that the plan is always in equilibrium. The plan is always in equilibrium in the sense that every planner, being rational, may always be counted on to do the best that he can, given all the relevant constraints, where such constraints include the time available to adjust to any unexpected changes. That is to say, at any given point of time any individual planner is in equilibrium with respect to the world as he sees it at that point of time. All productive resources employed in that plan stand in complementary relationships to one another. *Between* any two points of time, during which unexpected changes will necessarily have occurred, resource substitutions will have been made in an attempt to adjust to the changes. Complementarity is a condition of plan equilibrium (stability); substitutability is a condition of plan disequilibrium (change).

The notion of the capital structure does encompass a sort of economy-wide equilibrium as an ideal type. At the individual level, disparate elements of the production plan are brought into consistency by the planner. These elements are all present in a single human mind. There is no such mechanism guaranteeing consistency between different production plans. The market process does, however, tend to eliminate inconsistencies between plans in so far as not all of them can succeed. In this way plans that are consistent with (complementary to) one another tend to prevail over those that are not.[8] So whereas the

---

[8]This would seem to imply that the production plans of individual firms are identical with the plans of one or other individual in that firm. This is not necessarily the case, however. Firms must find a way to harmonize the different visions of its various planners. Presumably the larger the firm, the more difficult this is. But those firms that do so more successfully and adopt successful supra-plans will tend to survive. The market process works its way into the firm in this way. In this way Lachmann's work on capital is relevant for and related to the post-Marshallian theories of the firm that we shall examine below.

individual planner ensures the complementarity of all of the resources within a production plan, the market process tends towards a situation of overall *plan complementarity*. This is what constitutes the capital structure. The heterogeneous assortment of capital goods stands at any time in a kind of ordered structure defined by their functions and by the relationships that the various plans have to one another. The latter is a result not of any supra-plan, but of the market process. A capital structure in which this tendency were complete, in which every capital good and every production plan were complementary to every other, would be a completely *integrated* capital structure. In summary:

> In a homogeneous aggregate each unit is a perfect substitute for every other unit, as drops of water are in a lake. Once we abandon the notion of capital as homogeneous, we should therefore be prepared to find less substitutability and more complementarity. There now emerges at the opposite pole, a conception of capital as a *structure*, in which each capital good has a definite function and in which all such goods are complements. It goes without saying that these two concepts of capital, one as a homogeneous fund, each unit being a perfect substitute for every other unit, the other as a complex structure, in which each unit is a complement to every other unit, are to be regarded as *ideal types*, pure equilibrium concepts neither of which can be found in actual experience. (Lachmann 1947:199)

Lachmann chose to describe the world in terms of a capital *structure* rather than a capital *stock*. This choice reflects a judgment that to obscure capital complementarity through aggregation would result in an inaccurate and misleading picture of the role of capital in the economy. This can be seen in his account of how the market process works.

The Market Process and the Production Process

At any moment in time individual planners hold inconsistent expectations. This means that the passage of time must disappoint some of them. Some production plans must fail (in part or in whole) while others, of course, may succeed beyond their expectations. This is reflected, according to Lachmann, in two crucial ways—in capital re-evaluations (*capital gains and losses*) and in *changes in cash balances*. Whereas the "wealth effects" of neoclassical economics are usually assumed to be small enough to be neglected, the capital gains and losses of

Lachmann's world are the most important forces driving changes in the capital structure. These market evaluations of the prospects of success or failure of the firm and its capital combination are reflected in the financial assets associated with the firm. The financial assets (for example, debt and equity) form a superstructure over the capital assets of the company and constitute its *asset structure*. They are claims to the physical assets of the company and as such reflect their value (or others' opinions of their value). Thus, there is an economy-wide *financial structure* (composed of the individual asset structures) that is related to and reflects the capital structure of the economy. The capital structure and the capital combinations of which it is composed are in turn related to the plan structure. At each of these levels—plans, physical assets, and financial assets—various institutions exist that help define the various structures. A vitally important institution in the financial structure is the stock market. On the stock market assets are valued and revalued every day in accordance with companies' performances. The stock market reflects a daily balance of expectations concerning the earning prospects of companies. It is probably fair to say that Lachmann considered the stock market to be the most important institution of the market economy (he did *not* share Keynes's view that it was basically random in nature (Lachmann 1978:68–71)) and the one, more than any other, that differentiated it from socialized economies—the institution that, together with others in a private financial capital market, was responsible for facilitating the adoption of those capital combinations that contribute to economic progress (Lachmann 1992).

> Capital gains and losses provide entrepreneurs with feedback from the market. Ventures that continue to sustain capital losses will eventually have to regroup or stop operating. In this way the financial structure and the capital structure interact to produce a continuing reshaping of the latter.
> (Lachmann 1978:94)

Cash Balances as Excess Capacity and Constraint

A more immediate form of feedback comes in the form of changes in the cash balances of the company. The company holds cash as a form of "excess capacity" in order to preserve flexibility. In a sense, cash is the most substitutable of the company's capital assets. Thus changes in cash balances, like changes in inventory, provide an important indicator of the results of the operation over a period of time. A persistent negative cash flow is the ultimate long-term discipline and often also the first indicator of a problem.[9] Lachmann sees the traditional neoclassical portfolio approach to cash balance and financial asset holding as misleading. While it is true that production plans must include decisions about financial asset mix (the optimum manner of financing), to assume that *observed* cash and asset portfolios reflect optimal choices is to lose sight of the feedback process discussed above. That is to say, empirically observed changes in cash holdings and asset values reflect not only intended outcomes but they also reflect results that are *unintended* (mistakes or surprises—good and bad). In the portfolio equilibrium view, the portfolio reflects the results of portfolio selection based on underlying preferences and shared knowledge. In Lachmann's (disequilibrium) market process view, the portfolio value reflects portfolio results which are often different from what was intended and cannot be assumed to reflect accurately the preferences and intentions of the planners. Rather it is a barometer of the viability of the overall plan.

> Capital gains and losses.... [E]ssentially ... reflect in one sphere events, or the expectation of events, the occurrence of which in another sphere is indicated, and knowledge of which is transmitted, by changes in money flows.
>
> (Lachmann 1978:95)

Capital Accumulation Ordinarily Involves a Changing Capital Structure

Perhaps the most important general implication of a disequilibrium approach to capital is the proposition that *all capital accumulation entails a changing capital structure.* This follows from the observation that most technical change is embodied in new (improved) capital goods and/or involves the production of new consumption goods. Capital accumulation that accompanies economic growth as we know it is not simply the addition of the same kinds of capital goods doing the

---

[9]Of course, negative cash flows occur routinely and are planned for in start-up businesses, some of whom go on to become corporate giants. It seems as though a distinction between planned and unplanned might be useful here.

same things. Lachmann's view of capital accumulation and economic progress is in many ways very prophetic of the revolutionary kind of economic change that has characterized the twentieth century, including the last quarter of the century. It is, in this view, impossible to separate the phenomena of technical progress and capital accumulation; capital accumulation always proceeds hand in hand with technical change. By the same token, failed production plans imply "holes" in the capital structure that signal investment opportunities for others. An approach to economic growth that visualizes capital as a homogeneous aggregate to which investment expenditure adds in an indiscriminate way, so that a government policy adding directly to investment expenditure is, in essence, no different from an increase in private entrepreneurial investment expenditure, is not only untenable but also has far-reaching consequences. The capital structure will be *irreversibly* different in these two cases. It is very likely that government expenditure "crowds out" not only private sector expenditure but also private-sector-induced technical progress. The shape of the capital structure will be different and, because capital assets are heterogeneous, specific, and durable, will remain different from what it would otherwise have been. It takes a lot of faith in the abilities and objectives of the government agents involved to imagine that no sacrifice in entrepreneurial discovery is involved.[10]

The Disequilibrium Method is Particularly Applicable in a World of Rapid Changes

> The world around us abounds with problems to which a structural theory of capital of the type outlined in this book is germane. It is hoped that a number of them will attract the attention of economists.
>
> (Lachmann 1978:xi)

The choice of how to characterize capital is dependent on the kind of world in which one lives. In a world in which unexpected changes occur relatively rarely and in which methods of production, distribution,

---

[10]Lachmann's capital theory framework blends nicely with Kirzner's views on entrepreneurship and Hayek's views on information to yield some very specific insights on "investment policy."

and interaction are very stable (Adam Smith's corn economy), it might make sense to characterize capital as an equilibrium stock, a fund of more or less agreed-upon value. But in a world in which change is rapid and unpredictable, Lachmann's characterization of capital as a structure of heterogeneous items becomes even more appropriate. In particular, with regard to the effect of change on incomes, employment, and lifestyles, Lachmann's changing capital structure gives insights that are not available from an equilibrium approach.

It is generally agreed that we are living in an age of profound changes. It is not the fact of changes in technology that is revolutionary, it is the speed with which it is occurring that is new. The pace of change is not only quicker, it is accelerating. At the same time, however, our ability to absorb and adjust to change has increased many-fold.

Underlying virtually all of the major developments of this century is the revolutionary change in the way in which we generate and use information—hence the phrase "information age." In some respects this is only the latest in a line of similar revolutions like the original emergence of language and the development of writing, accounting, and printing. The latest, and to date most profound, development in this line of developments is electronic communication, of which the telephone, the computer, and the video and audio recorder are all part. Electronic communication in all of these aspects is responsible for the developments of global markets, of desktop publishing, of fuel injectors for automobiles, of computer aided design of everything from microchips to airplanes, and so on.

To understand the phenomenon of accelerating change occurring together with our enhanced abilities to adapt to change we must realize that *the scope and pace of technological change itself is governed by our ability to generate and process relevant information.* This means that the current pace of technical change is dependent on past technical advances, particularly the ability to generate and process information. If technological change is seen as the result of many trial-and-error selections (of production processes, of product types, of modes of distribution, etc.) then the ability to generate and perceive more possibilities will result in a greater number of successes. It will, of course, also result in a greater number of failures. Lachmann's proposition that capital accumulation, proceeding as it does hand in hand with technological change, necessarily brings with it capital regrouping as a result of failed production plans, appears in this perspective to be particularly pertinent. "[E]conomic progress ... is a process which involves trial and error. In its course new knowledge is acquired gradually, often painfully, and always at some cost to somebody" (Lachmann 1978:18). Today new knowledge acquisition is not so gradual.

The Market Process has Discernible Phases: Imitation and Innovation

The market process is one of continual flux. The shaping and reshaping of the capital structure is driven by the changing shape of the mix of consumer products. This perspective led Lachmann to a characterization of market activities in terms of two distinct phases. "A competitive process taking place within the market for a good consists typically of two phases, and in it the factors of innovation and imitation may be isolated as iterative elements" (Lachmann 1986:15). The successful introducer of a new product or new brand of product gains temporary monopoly power. The spreading knowledge of this success attracts imitators. The learning curve for the latter is shorter. Prices tend to fall as margins are competed away. This brings further pressure for product differentiation and capital reshuffling (reorganization). The process is inseparable from technological change. Market share and firm size at any point of time thus have very little to do with monopoly power. They are both transitory states of a continuing innovation–imitation cycle. This view finds close application in the electronics industry and the development of personal computers, fax machines, copy machines, cameras, cellular phones, and so on. Notably the innovation–imitation cycle is shortening. This is another aspect of the rapidity and acceleration of change. From this perspective the classical doctrine of capital flows establishing a uniform rate of profit is found seriously wanting.

From Böhm-Bawerk to Lachmann and Back: The Division of Labor and the Division of Capital

An important aspect of the information revolution is that it allows for the formation and management of ever more complex capital structures. In his work on capital Lachmann proposed a reinterpretation of a controversial aspect of Böhm-Bawerk's theory, his famous proposition concerning the superior productivity of roundabout production (i.e., of production processes that are more indirect, that take more "production time") (Lachmann 1978: ch. V). Lachmann regarded Böhm-Bawerk's use of time as a unit of measurement for the capital stock as untenable and seriously misleading. He felt strongly, however, that Böhm-Bawerk's intuition about the sources of economic progress was correct. "[T]he intuitive genius of Böhm-Bawerk gave an answer [that], to be sure we cannot fully accept and which, moreover, is marred by an excessive degree of simplification, yet an answer we cannot afford to disregard" (Lachmann 1978:73). Therefore he suggests dispensing with the notion "period of production" and replacing it with the notion "degree of complexity." Whereas Böhm-Bawerk argued that the period of production increased with capital accumulation, Lachmann argues that capital accumulation results in the increasing complexity of the production process. In this way he hoped to have given a new and more appropriate meaning to the notion of increased roundaboutness. Lachmann argued that Böhm-Bawerk's ideas were closely related to those of Adam Smith (Lachmann 1978:79). Both were concerned about the sources of economic progress. Both lived in a world that was "neither a stationary nor a fully dynamic world" (1978:79). Our world is, however, a dynamic world, one in which technical progress is an outstanding feature. For Böhm-Bawerk, roundaboutness was not a form of technical progress. "Technical progress requires new forms of knowledge spreading through the economic system while Böhm-Bawerk assumes as given knowledge equally shared by all" (1978:79).

> For Adam Smith the division of labor was the most important source of progress. The same principle can be applied to capital. As capital accumulates there takes place a "division of capital," a specialization of individual capital items, which enables us to resist the law of diminishing returns. As capital becomes more plentiful its accumulation does not take the form of multiplication of existing items, but that of a change in the composition of capital combinations. Some items will not be increased at all while entirely new ones will appear on the stage.... The capital structure will thus change since the capital coefficients

change, almost certainly towards a higher degree of *complexity* i.e. more capital items will now be included in the combinations. The new items, which either did not exist or were not used before, will mostly be of an indivisible character. *Complementarity plus indivisibility* are the essence of the matter. It will not pay to install an indivisible good unless there are enough complementary capital goods to justify it. Until the quantity of goods in transit has reached a certain size it does not pay to build a railway. A poor society therefore often uses costlier (at the margin) means of transport than a wealthier one. The accumulation of capital does not merely provide us with the means to build power stations, it also provides us with the means to build factories to make them pay and enough coal to make them work. Economic progress requires a continuously changing composition of social capital. The new indivisibilities account for the increasing returns.

(Lachmann 1978:79–80, italics in original)[11]

Böhm-Bawerk's thesis about the higher productivity of roundabout production is an empirical generalization. It can be applied, reinterpreted, to our own world. We have achieved, and will continue to achieve, greater productivity, that is, the production of more and better consumption goods and services, by the continuing introduction of new indivisible production goods (which embody new production techniques). This can be cast in terms of Böhm-Bawerk's idea of "stages of maturity." Böhm-Bawerk argued that capital accumulation will take the form of an increase in the number of stages of production. "The richer a society the smaller will be the proportion of capital resources used in the later stages of production, the stages nearest to the consumption end, and vice versa" (Lachmann 1978:82). (We leave aside the question of identifying a "stage of production" concentrating on the intuitive meaning of Lachmann's point.) The increased number of stages is indicative of increased complexity, which, in turn, is indicative of increased productivity. Increased complexity implies "an ever more complex pattern of capital complementarity" (ibid.:85).

---

[11]In an important sense durability is an aspect of indivisibility. "While it might be technically possible, the cost of producing a one-blow hammer would be certain to exceed the value of this task" (Steele 1996:144). The profitability of producing a hammer thus depends on there being sufficient demand for its multiple uses.

> We conclude that the accumulation of capital renders possible a higher degree of the division of capital; that capital specialization as a rule takes the form of an increasing number of processing stages and a change in the composition of the raw material flow as well as of the capital combinations at each stage; that the changing pattern of this composition permits the use of new indivisible resources; that these indivisibilities account for increasing returns to capital; and that these increasing returns to the use of capital *are*, in essence, the "higher productivity of roundabout methods of production."
>
> (Lachmann 1978:84–85, italics in original)[12]

Finally, Lachmann contends that the increased complexity of the capital structure also implies an increased vulnerability.

> A household with six servants each of whom is a specialist and none of whom can be substituted for another, is more exposed to individual whims and the vagaries of sickness than one that depends on two or more "general maids." Thus an "expanding economy" is likely to encounter problems of increasing complexity ... [among which are] disproportionalities and the resulting maladjustment of the capital structure [which] may give rise to serious problems in economic progress.
>
> (Lachmann 1978:85)

Concluding Summary

Lachmann's capital theory seems to have been ahead of its time. It was mostly ignored. Yet, when considered in the light of recent developments in the theory of organizational structure, one finds a striking number of commonalities (without any reference to Lachmann, however).[13] Lachmann's capital theory can be seen as a kind of unintended

---

[12]The reference here to increasing returns is especially noteworthy in light of the current rediscovery of the phenomenon in the context of a variety of new initiatives in economics. These include the new focus on nonlinear economics (Day and Chen 1992), the economics of "lock in" (Arthur 1989, 1994), institutions and economics, and evolution and economics (Hodgson 1988, 1993). Economists are now beginning to place greater emphasis on the importance of particular historical events in explaining the emergence of technologies in a manner that Lachmann clearly foreshadowed in his capital theory. On the topic of increasing returns see Buchanan and Yoon (1994).

[13]At the time of this second edition, this has changed dramatically. The manage-

prelude to some of this work. In addition, these commonalities reflect back on Lachmann's work in giving a new, and arguably more complete, view of capital and its structure.

Lachmann establishes that the competitive process and capital accumulation are inextricably linked. Furthermore, capital accumulation (the progressive creation of capital value over time) necessarily implies an evolving capital structure, that is, a capital structure that is becoming more "complex." The degree of specialization and interdependence grows. He captures this interdependence by the notion of complementarity. Resources that depend on each other in joint production are complementary. In the face of unexpected changes such "joint ventures" (capital combinations) often have to be regrouped. Much depends, therefore, on the degree to which existing resources can be adapted to originally unintended uses, a property that Lachmann calls *multiple specificity*. The variations in the degree of specificity are reflected in the capital gains and losses experienced as a result of the changes that occur and are the crucial driving force of the market process.

Lachmann's theory is thus a theory of progress in which such progress is reflected in and achieved by a continuing specialization of economic activities, a growing *division of capital* to supplement (and complement) Adam Smith's division of labor; we have, in general, an increasing division of function. What is noticeably absent from the theory is an explanation, apart from a kind of "black box" reference to the market, of how this is accomplished. That is to say, we are not told how this progressing complexity is managed.[14] How, to use Hayek's famous phrase, is the necessary "division of knowledge" implied by the increasing division of function to be organized? Lachmann's theory subsumes, and does not explain, an organizing function, which he delegates to the entrepreneur. Lachmann would surely agree, however,

---

ment and organizational literature is now replete with references to Hayek, Kirzner and, most recently, Lachmann, most prominently in the growing area of entrepreneurial studies. See for example Chiles, Bluedorn, and Gupta (2007) for an appreciation of Lachmann's work. See also Chiles, Tuggle, McMullen, Bierman, and Greening (2010).

[14]He seems to imply that a progressive vertical disintegration takes place, thus suggesting an immanent theory of the size of the firm. In this way his theory is related to the literature on the dynamics of the firm to be discussed below.

that the evolving capital structure is necessarily part of an evolving organizational structure.

Since all production in the modern world is joint production involving capital combinations (that is, combinations of resources in general, including capital), production necessarily involves organizing or coordinating the various activities of the resources involved. How is this done? Who owns the resources and why? More specifically, relating to the imputation problem anticipated above, there is always a problem of how to share the fruits of any joint venture. All production activities are joint (cooperative) ventures, directly or indirectly, between individuals (workers, capital owners, entrepreneurs). So the question of organizational structure arises logically out of Lachmann's worldview.

CHAPTER 9

Capital and Business Organizations

> [I]n capitalist reality as distinguished from its textbook picture, [the] ... kind of competition which counts [is] the competition from the new commodity, the new technology, the new source of supply, the *new type of organization*.
> (Schumpeter 1947:84–85, italics added, quoted in Penrose 1995:114n.)

Böhm-Bawerk argued that economies progress by the progressive adoption of wisely chosen roundabout methods of production. Lachmann reinterpreted this to mean the evolution of abilities enabling the use of more and more complex production structures. How is it that Böhm-Bawerk's "wise choices" get made and that such abilities to use more complex methods evolve?

In this chapter I investigate the relationship between capital and business organizations. The classical approach to capital that developed out of the economics of Ricardo (whether in its neo-Ricardian or neoclassical variety) did not feature "capitalist" institutions in any way. And although Carl Menger was among the first, and most profound, of economists to analyze the diverse nature and function of institutions, he did not tie up his insights into the compositive nature of capital with the decision-making functions of business institutions. Hayek and Lachmann, working in the Mengerian tradition, elaborated on Menger's insights, but did not develop a theory of organizational structure to complement the theory of the capital structure examined in the previous chapter.

A large literature on the structure of business organizations has recently developed. It has been variously characterized as the new institutional economics (Langlois 1986b), transaction cost economics, evolutionary economics, and post-Marshallian economics.[1] In many ways it is most accurately thought of as an alternative to (critique of, extension of) the neoclassical theory of the firm. It is beyond our purpose to undertake here a review or evaluation of this literature. We examine, however, its implications for an understanding of how a "capitalist" economy works.

That there are indeed such implications is perhaps the explanation for the scarcity in modern economics of contributions that can be classified in the field of capital theory. The highly abstract debates, explored in Part I, take on an increasingly sterile appearance in the light of these mounting contributions on the periphery of mainstream economics relating to an understanding of the organizations that actually accumulate and use capital. This literature has only recently attempted a connection to the theory of capital more broadly. We begin by examining two pioneering contributions.

Capabilities and Capital

This new literature on business organizations is sometimes also referred to as the "capabilities" literature.[2] This is in reference to the conception of a firm as a repository of certain kinds of evolving abilities that are the key to understanding the "why" and "how" of the firm (Demsetz 1991). It is in order to organize the necessary capabilities in a reliable manner that the firm is seen to derive its purpose. So in a fundamental way, this literature grows out of the problem originally posed by Ronald Coase (1937) in his classic article probing the essential rationale of the firm (Williamson and Winter 1991). Using the market to purchase the necessary inputs (capabilities) is costly, involving transactions costs (the need to locate, identify, and bargain for inputs and construct and enforce contracts) which have to be balanced against the costs of internal ownership and direction of resources (the costs of training, monitoring,

---

[1] The invocation of Marshall's name is related not to his "neoclassical" theory of costs and supply, but rather to his insistence that biology and evolution are more enlightening in the business environment than are mechanics and physics, and to his many discussions of the role of institutional factors (like trade practices and agreements) in the "ordinary business of life."

[2] It is closely related to, and often overlaps with, contributions in "managerial economics" and corporate strategy and is sometimes referred to as the "resource-based view" of the firm. See, for example, Collis and Montgomery (1998). For an important pioneering article see Teece (1982).

and policing). The nature of these various costs have been the substance in much of the discussion of this literature. It is not surprising, as we shall emphasize below, that they involve considerations relating to the nature and acquisition of different types of knowledge.

A parallel source of origin of this "capabilities" literature, and the one from which it derived its name, is the pioneering work of G. B. Richardson (1990, 1972)[3] and Edith Penrose (1995). This approach is more concerned with the way in which firms function and grow than in explaining their existence, although the latter emerges by implication. So this second source has adopted a more dynamic, evolutionary approach and one that is more obviously related to the question of capital accumulation.

Capabilities and Equilibrium: G. B. Richardson

In common with Lachmann's approach to capital, Richardson's examination of investment in business institutions is an avowedly disequilibrium approach. In strikingly similar fashion to Lachmann (but apparently independently),[4] Richardson mounts a devastating critique (perhaps the finest to be found) of the relevance of the model of perfectly competitive equilibrium (1990:pt 1). There are, as we will see, other informative commonalties.

Richardson advocates

> the setting aside of the concept of perfect competition, both as an explanatory device and as an ideal, my aim being to demonstrate that, even as a hypothetical system, it has one quite fundamental flaw, the exposure of which will point the way in which constructive revision can most properly be made.
>
> (Richardson 1990:1)

This "fundamental flaw" is the inability of entrepreneurs (investors in capital) to get the necessary information, in or out of equilibrium. If they were in equilibrium, how would they know it, how would they know their actions were optimal? If they were out of equilibrium, how would they get the information necessary for them to take the actions that would produce a tendency toward equilibrium? (Recall our discussion in Chapter 3.)

---

[3]The term "capabilities" in this context was invented by Richardson.
[4]It seems that the common denominator is Hayek (1937a).

Given the manifest inconsistencies and implausibilities of the equilibrium model, Richardson sets himself the task of explaining how it is that investment activities actually proceed in a highly orderly fashion in which the activities of suppliers, manufacturers, and consumers are in great measure highly coordinated, even in the face of changes in the economic environment. He begins by distinguishing between two kinds of relevant investment information: *market information*—information about the activities of other market participants—customers, competitors, or suppliers—which obviously influences the profitability of investment; and *technical information*—information relating to the physical transformation possibilities. It is the availability of market information that Richardson sees as most problematic.

> It is evident an entrepreneur could rationally undertake an investment decision only if he had some minimum information about what other entrepreneurs would or would not do, if he were assured that competitive investment would not exceed and complementary investments would not fall short of, certain critical levels. (Richardson 1990:32)

Since "a general profit potential, which is known to all, and equally exploitable by all, is, for this reason, available to no one in particular" (ibid.:14), Richardson is concerned to determine how entrepreneurs obtain the minimum necessary information. Investors in capital projects need information about complementarities and about substitutes. We consider these in turn.

Complementarities occur at two levels. On one level they refer to necessary complementary activities required to complete the project. This includes the supply of materials by suppliers, the provision of services by contractors, and similar activities. And, obviously, these complementary activities must be available at the right time in the right sequence. We see here a manifestation of the time structure of production. At another level there are complementarities in consumption that will determine the profitability of any investment project taken in isolation.[5] The sale of radios will depend on the availability of electricity. (One may recall here Lachmann's discussion of indivisibilities and the scale and scope of investments, a theme echoed by many theorists

---

[5] Activities are complementary "in the sense that their combined profitability when undertaken simultaneously, exceeds the sum of the profits to be obtained from each of them if undertaken by itself" (Richardson 1990:72).

in this literature.) Computers must be sold in order for the production of printers and of software to be profitable (and vice versa). We see here a manifestation of a structure of consumption activities, which has its own logic in time and space and which will concern us later.

Richardson is grappling with the evolution of the capital structure "from the bottom up," as it were. Like Lachmann, he perceives this structure as held together by complementarities at various levels, notably levels internal and external to the firm.[6] But he is much more explicit regarding the microeconomics of the evolution of this capital structure. The capital structure exists within and is dependent on a broader decision-making structure that addresses the problem of how the minimum information necessary for the making of decisions is made available to the decision-makers. Richardson identifies a number of "helpful imperfections" that constitute this decision-making structure. Among competitors we find numerous types of trade agreements (defining aspects of "the rules of the game"), joint ventures, and tacit understandings that ensure that perceived opportunities are not squandered. Much evidence exists (Chandler 1977, 1990, 1992) to suggest that cartel formation, antitrust concerns to the contrary notwithstanding, were crucial stages in the emergence of modern capitalism.[7]

A different kind of "imperfection" exists that helps to ensure that responses by competitors to perceived profit opportunities do not

---

[6]"An entrepreneur will have to recognize that the profitability of his own investment will depend on the terms on which he can obtain inputs, and therefore indirectly on the volume of the investment which has been, or will be, undertaken elsewhere. Thus *the same kind of complementarity which exists between the application of different resources within the firm, exists also between the application of resources by different firms.* In the former case coordination, designed to ensure the best combination of complementary factors, is brought about directly by the entrepreneur in control; in the latter, it has to be achieved by different means" (Richardson 1990:73, italics added). And in considering the interdependence as well as the cost structures of different firms, he notes, "The whole economy one may presume, is united by bonds of this kind, the strength of which will vary widely according to circumstances" (ibid.:74).

[7]As I have suggested repeatedly, and shall have occasion to repeat again, these evolved devices are made necessary by the dynamic nature of the world in which investment decisions are taken. In a world in which no significant changes were taking place they would be (or would become) unnecessary. And indeed, in such a world, cartel and price fixing/market sharing agreements might indeed be a concern for eager policy-makers. But a world of persistent technological change invites and requires persistent organizational change and, in any case, is not conducive to such "anticompetitive" agreements enduring over time.

negate them (the opportunities). These fall into the category of factors limiting the ability of individual firms to expand in response to perceived opportunities. Unlike the neoclassical firm,[8] firms in a dynamic world are idiosyncratic, they possess unique (inimitable) and limited capabilities that they have developed over the course of their histories (not always in a conscious manner).[9] Richardson refers here to "economies of experience" that serve as natural and helpful barriers to entry (ibid.:60). Thus not every would-be investor is in a position to take advantage of a perceived opportunity at any point of time or within the relevant period (indeed *the very perception of the opportunity* may depend on particular capabilities). Emphasis is laid here on the importance of investments in specific and specialized assets, that is assets whose value is somewhat unique to the firm within which they are combined with other specific assets in a complementary relationship.

> The more specific the resources required for the manufacture of the product, and the smaller their elasticity of supply, the greater will be the likelihood that scarcities and bottlenecks will deter further expansion. Expansion in the capacity of some industry may be temporarily held up, that is to say, by delay in undertaking complementary investment elsewhere.
> (ibid.:61)

The information requirements implied by complementarities are similarly mitigated by information networks and specific capabilities. Every investment project can be conceived of as a conscious, if necessarily and deliberately vague (because of the need for adaptability), plan.

---

[8] It is interesting to note that in the neoclassical literature the production function does "double duty," serving as a tool of analysis for both the economy as a whole and for the individual firm. Given the assumption of CRS in readily identifiable inputs, this is not surprising, since there is nothing to limit the size of firm. In an important sense the economy is simply "the firm writ large."

[9] It is difficult to avoid the use of anthropomorphic language that suggests the firm possesses some sort of collective consciousness. I affirm strongly, however, that it is ultimately the individuals in the firm, at any point in time, in their various capacities that are the decision-makers and the perceivers of information and in whom the capabilities "of the firm" must ultimately reside. I hope to make clear in what way the organization (the firm) may manifest these capabilities in different individuals at any point of time yet provide for their carrying forward through time and across individuals.

> Every business can be regarded as having to formulate, with greater or lesser precision, an investment program consisting of a set of planned activities related through some process of production or transformation. It will be based on an assessment of the various technical and market conditions upon which the prices at which the firm will buy its inputs and sell its outputs will depend. As this assessment is likely to be in the form, not of certain knowledge, but of expectations of varying degrees of reliability, an entrepreneur will wish his program to be as flexible or adaptable as possible, in order that it can be modified to take account of changing and unexpected circumstances.
>
> (Richardson 1990:79)

That plan will usually include contracts of various terms and conditions, which will tend to reduce the degree of uncertainty attaching to the production plan, but only at the sacrifice of adaptability. In addition, the freedom of choice of the entrepreneur is further likely to be restricted by the fact that certain work is already in progress and certain specific inputs have already been purchased. One may assume that the entrepreneur will attempt to balance adaptability and uncertainty in a dynamic way as time unfolds. This uncertainty is of a "radical" or "structural" nature (Langlois and Robertson 1995); that is, it is not probabilistic uncertainty, but uncertainty about the very structure within which decisions will have to be made in the future. It includes "uncertainty about the particular factor combinations which, at some future date, it will prove most advantageous to adopt" (Richardson 1990:83). Richardson is thus emphasizing the "element of trial and error" present in every real-world production process. Thus we can say "there is no unique single way in which complementary investments come to be coordinated" (ibid.:84). And there is certainly no unique way that is known ahead of time to all producers, as suggested by a simple production function formulation. In terms of the market (or the economy) as a whole, then, the firm cannot be said to be in equilibrium. There is no overall plan consistency. "[D]ifferent people may form different expectations or beliefs on the basis of identical information" (ibid.: 188).

Richardson does not dwell on the necessary failures that must occur as a result of these inconsistencies—the trial-and-error process at the level of the market—and is more concerned to show how successful production decisions can be made. His analysis is rich and (although it was relatively neglected for some time) has laid the basis of a number of important contributions to our understanding of the workings of organizations and investment processes.

Penrose and the Growth of the Firm

Perhaps an equally important, and in very many ways complementary, pioneering work, is that of Edith Penrose (1995). Penrose's work is concerned with the dynamics of firms. What external and internal factors are responsible for the way in which firms develop over time, the activities they undertake (or contract with others to undertake), the techniques they adopt, the products they choose to produce and so on?[10] The firm is viewed as a specialized "pool of resources" (cf. capabilities)[11] whose nature (productive potential) changes over time in response to events internal and external to the firm. Penrose has a compelling bona fide theory of endogenous change.

With the passage of time, the knowledge possessed by the employees in any firm changes. This knowledge, which includes productive and organizational skills related to the firm's particular experience, is a productive resource specific, in some degree, to the firm. Thus, with time and experience, the firm accumulates productive capabilities that provide it with an important source of "excess capacity." For example, in the earlier stages of the production and introduction of a new product, employees are in the process of trial and error learning about the product. As they accumulate expertise, much of which is of an informal, noncommunicable nature, they will find that they need less effort to achieve the results. The accumulated skills will present the firm with a form of increasing returns and indivisibilities that cry out to be used and provide an irresistible internal impetus to expansion. Much of what was novel becomes "routine," leaving capacity for the development of new endeavors. This expansion occurs naturally into the production of new products and services that use similar skills (a point emphasized also by Richardson (1972)). Skills, however, are con-

---

[10] We note again the caveat about using language that suggests that the firm *per se* "chooses."

[11] Penrose refers to these as "competencies."

tinually changing. Since experience generates new knowledge, "the productive opportunity of a firm will change even in the absence of any change in external circumstances or in fundamental knowledge" (Penrose 1995:56; see also Loasby 1991:62).

Expansion may occur through merger and acquisition, which is a way to acquire specialized human capital, or through internal expansion. But, however it occurs, in a competitive, technologically progressive industry, a firm specializing in the production of given products can hope to maintain its position with respect to those products "only if it is able to develop an expertise in technology and marketing sufficient to enable it to keep up with and participate in the introduction of innovations affecting its products" (Penrose 1995:132).

> Expansion is also often necessary in a growing market because a firm's share in the market is sometimes itself an important competitive consideration. In some industries, for example in the production of certain types of durable consumer goods, consumer acceptance of the product is influenced by whether the producer can reasonably claim to be one of the "leading" producers. It is under these conditions that growth is often said and with good reason, to be a necessary condition of survival.
> (Penrose 1995:133)

This insight may be described as a "grow or die" hypothesis.

In common with Richardson, Penrose notes the importance of complementarities in consumption in sometimes influencing the nature of firm expansion, especially when similar skills are called for in production, marketing, or distribution. The same firms that make washers tend to make dryers. In the final analysis, however, it is the ability of the firm to maintain the productive value of its basic abilities, its human and physical resources, that determines its ability to survive. Capital investment takes place within a perceived decision-making structure, only part of which consists of the technical intertemporal imperatives of production. In a very real sense, prospective demand has to be "manufactured" through internal organization, market agreements, distribution arrangements, and marketing efforts, and these will have to be continually adapted.

> In the long run the profitability, survival, and growth of a firm does not depend so much on the efficiency with which it is able

> to organize the production of even a widely diversified range of products as it does on the ability of the firm to establish one or more wide and relatively impregnable "bases" from which it can adapt and extend its operation in an uncertain, changing, and competitive world. (Penrose 1995:137)

Each business is thus a kind of "research program" (Loasby 1991) in which products, processes, and methods of production and organization are continually being tried out.

Organizations in a Dynamic World

Joint Production is the Key

Penrose and Richardson laid the basis for much of the work that followed in exploring the nature of business organizations in a dynamic world—a world of incessant, unpredictable technological change. These organizations can be seen as evolved responses to the need to make decisions in such a world. It may be doubted that organizations such as the firm would have any enduring rationale or would survive in a world of stable equilibrium. Seen from the perspective of the evolving capital structure of the economy as a whole—the matrix of valuable, related productive capabilities—firms are incubators and filters through which these capabilities become available to the economy as a whole. The nature of the firm is thus relevant to the nature of the production processes. What is the rationale of the firm and what determines its boundaries and how they change over time?

A crucial feature of the firm, from our perspective—indeed in many ways its defining characteristic—is the fact of *joint production*. (We recall Hicks's (1973b) emphasis of "jointness" as the key defining characteristic of (the problem of) capital.) The fact that resources have to be combined in diverse and sometimes mysterious (not fully perceived) ways, in order to be productive, can be seen to be the central principle around which firms function. Firms are in the business of making, monitoring, and altering productive capital combinations (cf. Lachmann 1978). We must include in the "capital" of these capital combinations, the human capabilities (skills, perceptions, judgments, etc.) to which we referred above and which we shall examine further in Chapter 11.

The problem that the firm faces is quite simply the imputation problem. (The imputation problem contains within it other (sub)problems, like forecasting the level of sales. This will emerge from our discussions below.) When a number of resources cooperate jointly in the production of a common output, unless we are dealing with a fairly divisible, repeatable process, in which the levels of output and input can be varied along a broad continuum so as to isolate in an "objective" way the contribution at the margin of each input (physical and human), there is bound to be a substantial degree of indeterminateness about the relative input contributions.

We may contrast this with the neoclassical competitive model in which the productive processes are, in effect, standardized. The production function approach is one in which, by assumption, input and output can be easily connected, thus facilitating the identification of marginal product. Competition thus ensures that earnings of the factor owners will tend to equal the values of the marginal products, and this of course also militates in favor of the most efficient use of resources. Efficiency and fairness are bound together. It is also a world in which the capital values of the individual capital items that constitute the capital stock can be easily and conveniently calculated as the present value of the stream of value marginal products thus identified. And in this world the perception of capital in terms of aggregate economic values makes sense.

But in such a world there is no reason for the firm. All resources could be separately owned in a state of complete decentralization and could be brought together when necessary in order to fulfill profitable joint ventures. Since the marginal products are known to all, the matter can be handled by contracting with each of the factor owners. Labor could be seen to hire capital just as validly as the other way round.[12] It is natural, therefore, that, in seeking to explain the

---

[12]Joseph Salerno points out (following Mises) that, given that production takes time, it is natural that "capital" employs "labor" as it is the capitalist that saves and advances the resources with which labor must work. So property rights considerations can also be seen to be implied by the temporal nature of production. But surely this would be the case only in a world of uncertainty. In a world where everything was accurately foreseen, complete contracts could be written for the advancement and use of the capitalists' savings. No hierarchical relationship need be implied. An "employment" relationship seems to be the result of the need to adapt to open-ended futures, in which discretionary command (in order to adapt to unexpectable contingencies) must reside with one or other party, as discussed below in the text.

existence of the firm in a manner basically consistent with the perfectly competitive model, recourse should be had to the costs of contracting and exchanging—transactions costs.

Yet, as we shall see, when examining this approach in greater detail, the existence of the firm must lead to an abandonment of the essentials of the competitive model and to the embrace of the firm as a response to productive processes which have an irreducible degree of indeterminateness (and arbitrariness). The seminal article in which Coase (1937) sought an explanation for the existence of the firm, and which has been the seed of a voluminous and diverse literature on the firm and its nature and development, was at its base an appeal to problems presented by the incompleteness, *in some sense*, of information. Transactions costs are introduced as "frictions" in the otherwise smooth functioning of the economic system. As has been noted many times, however, "all transactions costs are at base information costs" (Langlois and Robertson 1995:30, referencing Dahlman 1979).

The Existence of the Firm and its Boundaries[13]

Following Alchian and Woodward (1988) and Langlois and Robertson (1995) we note that the transactions costs literature can be divided into at least two (apparently) distinct approaches. One emphasizes the costs of administration, direction, negotiation, and monitoring of the joint productive activities, while the other emphasizes more specifically the problems of assuring quality or performance of contractual obligations. Langlois and Robertson call the former the measurement cost view and the latter the asset specificity view.

---

[13] The dimension along which the boundaries of the firm are drawn may be an issue. The usual one is ownership. This is a legal distinction (Masten 1991). But it is not the only one. Another is control. For example, the owner of the firm does not own the labor that it employs. In what sense are the employees working "within" the firm? The usual answer is that there exist long-term contracts that effectively give the owner of the firm ownership over the outputs of the labor employed and control over their inputs. However, they do not always go together. Along the control dimension, control over resources may exist even in the absence of ownership, as in the case of joint ventures between two separate legal entities. Alternatively, divisions within firms may behave with a great deal of autonomy, effectively like separate firms. We shall retain the familiar dimension of ownership, realizing that the dividing line between the market and the firm is in many ways quite fuzzy.

The central notion of the measurement cost approach is connected to the indeterminateness of joint production. The difficulties in (inability to) isolate individual input contributions lead to a variety of important *organizing* problems, which the business *organization* is designed to solve. This approach focuses on the indivisibilities inherent in team production which may lead to shirking or fraud, which is costly to monitor and detect (Alchian and Demsetz 1972). An apparent implication of this is the suggestion that the residual claimant be the one to monitor and control since he has the most incentive to do so. This begs the question of who the residual claimant should be. Yoram Barzel (1982) has suggested it be the owner of the input whose contribution to the joint output is most difficult to measure. This is the input factor whose owner is most tempted by the potential fruits of moral hazard and, therefore, most in need of self-policing. This person then becomes the principal, leaving the inputs more easily measured to be owned by the agents. But this in turn rests on the presumption that we know, ahead of time, which contributions are easiest to measure and monitor. In some situations this may be obviously true, but surely not generally, suggesting that a certain degree of arbitrariness (noneconomic considerations) may be inevitable in determining the structure and boundaries of ownership.

The asset specificity approach, as its name implies, focuses on the information problems associated with the fact that joint production relies to a large extent on assets that are specific to their current employment. This is an (unconscious) application of Lachmann's concept of multiple specificity. An asset is specific when its opportunity cost is substantially below the value of its current contribution to production. In other words, the price that the asset could fetch in the market for employment in its next best use is substantially below (the discounted sum of) its current marginal value product(s).[14] It is producing a "rent" (surplus). The greater the specificity, the greater the "rent." This means that it (its owner) is both powerful and vulnerable,

---

[14]Of course, as I point out, an important aspect of using the firm to organize production is that marginal products are not easy to determine. Still, where an asset is specific in nature it is clear to all those involved in the production process that the value of its marginal contribution is substantially above its opportunity cost, even if a degree of arbitrariness attaches to the measurement of these values.

depending on which contingency one considers. On the one hand, the owner of a specific asset can engage in profitable opportunistic behavior, the more essential the asset is to the joint product, by threatening to "hold up" the production process unless the terms of the joint product agreement (contract) are altered in its favor. On the other hand, the other factor owners could behave opportunistically by threatening to cut out the specific factor, thus subjecting its owner to a capital loss directly proportional to the degree of specificity, unless the "rent" appropriation is altered in their favor. The outcome will thus depend on the (perceived) balance between these two risks and on the costs of enforcing (at law or otherwise) any prior existing explicit contracts. There is a large literature on these questions which includes discussions of specific historical examples, like General Motors and the Fisher Body Company (for overviews see Williamson and Winter 1991; Langlois and Robertson 1995).

Both of these approaches suggest that the firm is an organization whose purpose is to cope with the inevitable information problems of joint production. If information were completely available, albeit at a (known) cost, then all production could be handled in a series of spot and long-term contracts. "When contingencies can be adequately specified, or when the decisions of the cooperating parties don't affect one another, contracts are possible and integration [into firms] is unnecessary" (Langlois and Robertson 1995:28). As it is, contracts are necessarily and deliberately incomplete. There is no way to account completely for all of the possible contingencies. In the literature this is sometimes described by saying that agents are "boundedly rational" and/or that information is "impacted" (contains unfathomable implications). These are variations around the Hayek/Popper/Polanyi theme concerning the special characteristics of knowledge (and the information from which it derives), which we discussed above in Chapter 2. In this context the "knowledge problem" is very specifically related to the indeterminacies of team production, involving as it does complementarity, specificity, indivisibility, and change. Production not only involves complementary specific assets that are indivisible, but these relationships change over time. The importance of change is not always sufficiently emphasized and we shall return to it in a moment.

As suggested, one way to cope with the necessary incompleteness of the joint production contract is through the distinction between residual rights and specific (contractual) rights. All factor owners besides the residual claimant are paid a preagreed rate of earnings. The surplus over and above this is counted as profits (as suggested in our discussion on the nature of profits in Chapter 7 above). Profits then serve as the barometer by which a firm's performance is judged. The firm is owned by the residual claimant who contracts with other factor owners. The residual claimant must make a judgment as to which factors to own and which to buy (or rent).

Thus where one draws the line between "the firm" and "the market" depends on a variety of considerations that derive from the nature of joint production. The same indeterminacies and uncertainties of joint production that provide for opportunistic behavior also account for and provide clues to coping with the difficulties of framing, monitoring, and enforcing explicit contracts. As Langlois and Robertson (1995) suggest, however, these considerations are likely to be continually changing over time and thus the boundaries of the firm are unlikely to be static.[15]

Production and Change

Production is a *joint venture* and production *takes time.* These two characteristics account for many (perhaps all) of the interesting and problematic aspects of the production process. When we say that production is a joint venture, this includes not only the fact that production processes may involve combining inputs in close proximity or under centralized control, but the more general fact that, whether under centralized control or not, production is a process of value creation (when successful) that depends on a variety of complementary inputs. Production is characterized by an implicit (and evolving) input and output structure that transcends the boundaries of the firm. The

---

[15]In relation to the question of the boundaries and existence of the firm, and the general discussion found in this section, I have been asked whether I thought uncertainty was a necessary and sufficient condition for the existence of the firm. While I cannot attempt a complete answer here, it seems to me that while it may not be sufficient, it is surely necessary. For, as indicated above, in a world of perfect certainty there would be no need for the firm.

institutional (organizational) structure overlays and is intimately related to the production structure in such a way that it is impossible to characterize accurately the production structure without bringing in business organizations. *Organization matters for production.* It is part of the "capital" of any economy. Synergies of joint production (in this general sense) underlie the emergence of excess capacity (economies of experience) that Penrose describes and provide the basis for the "helpful imperfections" identified by Richardson, which constrain the actions of competitors and influence the norms of trade. Synergies of joint production are also at the root of the transactions costs of negotiating and monitoring arm's-length contracts for joint outputs and of avoiding the moral hazards of holdups.

Joint production would not be a problem were it not for the fact that production occurs over time. Time and knowledge belong together. This is Lachmann's axiom, discussed in Chapter 2. "As soon as we permit time to elapse, we must permit knowledge to change" (Lachmann 1976a:127–128, italics removed). It is inconceivable that time should elapse without learning. This is as true of the production process as of anything else. We can see how time and change enter into the production process in at least four different ways.[16]

1. As we have discussed, ongoing processes of joint production contain an element of irreducible indeterminateness in deciding the *relative* contributions of the inputs. It is not possible to know at any point of time what the relative contributions of the various inputs are with any definite "objectivity."
2. Rewarding the factor inputs in terms of the *value* of their marginal products assumes knowledge of the value of the final output per period of time. Yet, since input necessarily precedes output, the value of the latter is a matter of speculation, even assuming that there are no uncertainties attaching to the technical aspects of the process.

---

[16] As Peter Boettke points out, time, jointness, and multiple specificity are all necessary to explain the four indeterminacies (and the implied need for organizational devices to cope with them). If resources were completely homogeneous, no combination problem would exist; similarly, if resources were completely specific, there would be no choices involving variations in the components of combinations. Where resources are heterogeneous and multiply specific, my conclusions follow.

3. Technical and organizational aspects are, however, bound to be uncertain to a greater or lesser degree concerning the quantity or quality of any output. Over time, as learning proceeds, things get done differently, and in ways no one could have expected.
4. Even assuming that 1, 2, and 3 above were not problems, there remains the problem of connecting units of specific input with specific units of output over time, something we discussed in Chapter 4 above.

Echoing some aspects of our discussion of Böhm-Bawerkian capital theory, if the process were fairly divisible and if it were unchanging over time, then with enough time one could (or the market would) vary the input configurations over a sufficiently wide range to be able to solve the imputation problem. Competition would then tend to ensure that each factor was paid the value of its marginal product. When the world is one of constant innovation, and the innovations often come in "lumps" (embodied in indivisible units or nonrival inputs), this is not possible. We shall encounter these issues in our consideration of how firms engage in productive activities below.

Organizations and Change

In a number of contributions, Richard Langlois (for example, 1992; 1995; Langlois and Robertson 1995) has extended the capabilities approach to business organizations to provide a dynamic theory of the boundaries of the firm. He considers the firm to be a device for acquiring and economizing on useful knowledge (see also Demsetz 1991). Firms are able to do this because they are institutions. Institutions, broadly understood, are systems of rule-following behaviors. As we discussed in Chapter 3, rules (or, in the context of the firm, routines) provide a way of acquiring information about the future actions of others, within particular domains (we confidently expect everyone in the United States to drive on the right side of the road). These rules can be understood sometimes as an aspect of human behavior, in the form of tacit knowledge (people follow them unconsciously), or, alternatively, as constraints external to the individual (like private property). In both cases they are conducive to an "orderly pattern of behavior" (Langlois 1992:166).

A firm is an organization embodying a system of (sometimes unarticulated) rules and routines (Vanberg 1992; also relevant is Nelson and Winter 1982). Vanberg considers a firm as a "constitutional system" within which behaviors are conditioned by the written or unwritten rules of the constitution. This constitutional aspect is made necessary by the nature of joint (team) production—the dependencies of teamwork necessitate contractual constraints of certain kinds and duration. Thus the firm's constitution, like Britain's political constitution, is implicit and composed of the understood rules of conduct that facilitate concerted and cooperative action. "The procedural rules that underlie organized or corporate action can justly be viewed as a *constitution* because they *constitute* organizations as corporate actors" (Vanberg 1992:136). Perhaps one way to think of the effect of the constitution of a firm (or any organization) is to suppose that the behavioral response (choice) to certain categories of events is independent of the responding (choosing) individual in that organization. This requires that the individuals of an organization have internalized the rules, routines, procedures, etc., that constitute its constitution, its "culture." Langlois connects this with the capabilities of the firm by "applying the ideas of rule-following to questions of organizational form ... the rules—the routines—that agents follow within an organization embody (often tacit) knowledge that is useful for action. This knowledge constitutes the *capabilities* of the firm" (Langlois 1995:251).

Although the founding of a firm may have been the result of a well-articulated plan (and purpose), there is a sense in which firms are organic rather than pragmatic organizations (Menger 1985). Following Vanberg (1989), Langlois (1992, 1995) has added a dimension to Menger's well-known distinction between organic and pragmatic institutions. The distinguishing feature in Menger was the question of origin. He distinguishes between pragmatic institutions (like firms, clubs, legislation) that were created for specific purposes and organic institutions (like common law, language, money) that are the unintended results of behavior. Hayek, working along this Mengerian theme, distinguishes between orders and organizations according to whether they serve a specific purpose or not. "The rules of an order are abstract and independent of purpose, whereas the rules of an organization are concrete and directed toward a common purpose or purposes" (Langlois 1992:168; Hayek 1973:38).

	Orders	Organizations
Spontaneous	Organic orders (law, language, money)	Organic organizations (firms?, bureaucracies)
Planned	Pragmatic orders (designed constitutions or contracts)	Pragmatic organizations (firms?, clubs)

Table 9.1: Types of institutions

Thus instead of a single-dimensional line we have a two-dimensional matrix of institutional types (see Table 9.1).

Langlois writes

> Both parts of the term *spontaneous order* are of interest. What makes a system of rules spontaneous rather than planned is, in effect, a question of origin.... Unlike an organic system of rules, a pragmatic structure is one set in motion by conscious intention, and thus, in a sense ... is a creature of planning. At the same time, a system of rules in Hayek's theory can be either an *order* or an *organization*. In an order, the rules that guide behavior are abstract and independent of purpose; in an organization, those rules guide behavior toward more or less concrete ends.[17]   (Langlois 1995:249)

It is clear that the firm should be in the right column in Table 9.1. But it is not clear that it fits obviously into either the top or bottom row exclusively and, in an important sense, it is a hybrid. Although it may be a creature of the conscious design of its owner/founder, it almost never develops in a predictable way, especially if it is to be adaptable enough to survive in a dynamic world. As Langlois conjectures, the more dynamic the environment, the more abstract the nature of the organization's constitution needs to be for it to survive, the more it needs to be like an order. Hence the firm is more akin to an organic organization.

To see more specifically how firms evolve, one needs to focus on the capabilities and routines that constitute it. In Langlois's theory the

---

[17]From a "God's eye" perspective or from a public choice perspective the organic/pragmatic dimension might collapse. "[O]ne might easily portray the entire Public Choice theory of politics as undermining a conception of government as a pragmatic institution" (Langlois 1992:169).

determinants of organizational structure are the nature of the capabilities both within and outside the firm on the one hand, and the nature of change and uncertainty that it faces on the other. The story of economic progress and development is the story of the introduction of innovations of various types at various levels: new products, new characteristics of existing products, new methods of production, or some combination of these. In terms of their effects we may distinguish between two types of innovation: *systemic* innovations and *autonomous* (I prefer "stand alone" or decomposable) innovations (Teece 1986; Langlois 1995). Systemic innovations have system-wide implications, they require (if they are to be successful) changes in several related stages of production. This implies that some existing assets would be rendered obsolete and capabilities not previously valued, or perhaps not yet available, would become useful.

This "regrouping" of capital combinations (Lachmann 1978) which constitutes the changing ("mutating") capital structure carries with it implications for the organizational structure. Existing capabilities may be under separate ownership.

> Under this scenario, the business firm arises because it can more cheaply redirect, coordinate, and where necessary create the capabilities necessary to make the innovation work. Because control of the necessary capabilities in the firm would be relatively more concentrated than in a market-based organizational structure, such a firm could overcome not only the recalcitrance of asset holders, whose capital would be the victim of creative destruction, but also the "dynamic" transaction costs of informing and persuading new input holders with necessary capabilities. (Langlois and Robertson 1995:2)

Dynamic transactions costs are the "costs of not having the capabilities you need when you need them" (ibid.:2n.)

According to Langlois this scenario is an accurate description in general terms of the historical development of many of the enterprises that feature in the "second Industrial Revolution" in North America and Germany in the late nineteenth and early twentieth centuries as chronicled in the work of Alfred Chandler (Langlois 1991; Chandler 1977, 1990, 1992). Systemic innovations like the lowering of transportation and communication costs created profit opportunities for those who could create mass markets and take advantage of production economies of scale and scope (steel, farm machinery, meat, soap, and

$$A_1 \to A_2 \to A_3 \to A_4 \to A_5$$
$$B_1 \to B_2 \to B_3 \to B_4 \to B_5$$
$$C_1 \to C_2 \to C_3 \to C_4 \to C_5$$
$$D_1 \to D_2 \to D_3 \to D_4 \to D_5$$
$$E_1 \to E_2 \to E_3 \to E_4 \to E_5$$

——————————————————————————— time

Figure 9.1: Craft production

many others). In an important sense, we see in retrospect that a series of innovations were connected in a complementary way, but these profitable improvements implied the destruction of existing decentralized systems of production and distribution in favor of integration into large-scale production. Integration is seen in many cases to be necessary to overcome the "opposition of vested interests" (Langlois 1995:252), of people doing things the old way.

Organizational structure is here seen to be the result of entrepreneurial innovation. In order to exploit perceived opportunities, entrepreneurs had to change the existing organizational structures in addition to production structures, or, more accurately, in order to effect the latter they had to accomplish the former. An excellent generic example of how altering the organization of production can be a value-creating innovation is provided by Axel Leijonhufvud (1986; see also Langlois and Robertson 1995:ch. 3). Leijonhufvud shows that it is not just (or even necessarily) a matter of using large-scale machinery that accounted for the profitability of factory production. To make the point schematically he contrasts craft production with factory production. In crafts production, craftspeople sequentially complete all the operations necessary to make the product. In factory production, by contrast, each worker specializes in one operation. We recall Adam Smith's pin factory where "the important business of making a pin is … divided into about eighteen distinct operations which, in some manufactories, are all performed by distinct hands" (Smith 1982:4–5, quoted by Leijonhufvud 1986:208).

For example, imagine five distinct operations being performed by five different craftspeople. Each one works at their own pace and differs in skill (both absolutely and relatively) across the different operations. This is depicted in Figure 9.1.

$$A_1 \to B_2 \to C_3 \to D_4 \to E_5$$
$$A_1 \to B_2 \to C_3 \to D_4 \to E_5$$
$$A_1 \to B_2 \to C_3 \to D_4 \to E_5$$
$$A_1 \to B_2 \to C_3 \to D_4 \to E_5$$
$$A_1 \to B_2 \to C_3 \to D_4 \to E_5$$

———————————————————————— time

Figure 9.2: Factory production

Now suppose that we simply rearrange the work as depicted in Figure 9.2. Work previously done in parallel now proceeds in series. Worker A specializes in performing operation 1, worker B in performing operation 2, and so on. We have introduced joint or team production. Each individual now has to work at the pace of the team, making supervision easier. It is important to note, however, that the engineering parameters of the production process have not been changed. The tools are the same in kind (although each worker no longer needs a complete set)[18] and the workers are the same people. Yet we may expect an increase in product. Production is not simply a matter of identifying and combining the inputs (in an unspecified way), unless we broaden what we mean by "input" so as to empty it of all analytical power. As Leijonhufvud pertinently notes, this "sequencing of operations is not captured by the usual production function representation of productive activities; nor is the degree to which individual agents specialize.... Smith's division of labor—the core of his theory of production—slips through modern production theory as a ghostly technological-change coefficient or as an equally ill-understood economies-of-scale property of the function" (Leijonhufvud 1986:209).

The economies achieved by moving from crafts to factory production arise from an increased division of labor, a move from individual to team production. Leijonhufvud enumerates three aspects of this. First, team production results in *product standardization*, workers

---

[18]In this sense the innovation is *capital saving* rather than requiring capital of larger scale. Also, it is possible that the new process may need less "goods in process" inventory. In crafts production, workers may leave goods unfinished as they move from one operation to another, working on a few goods at a time. In team production this does not happen (Leijonhufvud 1986:210).

produce the *same* product. Second, greater coordination is achieved in time sequencing, supervision under a shared set of rules, routines and tacit understandings (that improve over time). Third, the labor of individual workers becomes complementary inputs rather than competitive activities. The absence of any worker will disable the production process.

Recalling the context of Adam Smith's original observations, it has often been noted that *human capital* is intimately involved. Smith explains how specialization improves dexterity, saves time and leads to worker-inspired innovations. To this we should add that specialization may result in the saving of certain kinds of human capital. Workers need no longer possess the skills necessary to make a pin from beginning to end (Leijonhufvud 1986:211). The division of labor is also, in an important sense, a division of (human) capital. In this context it is easy to see how the assumption of a homogeneity of human capital is every bit as misleading as the assumption of homogeneity of physical capital. As the society and the economy progresses, people obviously learn "more" and the knowledge "of the society" is, in a very real sense, greater. But it is also true that, in another sense, individuals do not have to know as much in so far as they are more specialized. This is something we shall examine further in Chapter 11.

An interesting aspect of this example is the fact that the increase in output occurs without any change in the types of inputs (and with fewer capital goods and goods in process) or any change in technology. Although changes in technology may follow upon, or precede, organizational changes, as this example shows, organizational changes themselves can sometimes bring improvements in productivity. This underlines the problems associated with physical notions of the capital stock. In this example, considering capital as being composed of the types and quantities of the inputs fails completely to capture the source of any increase in value that arises. This suggests that *organizational structure is a crucial aspect of the capital structure in general.*

Obviously this example is suggestive of particular types of organizational innovation, one employing a vertical division of labor. It gives one reason that integration of workers may prove profitable. But other forms of profitable organizational change may not be so clear in their implications for organizational type.

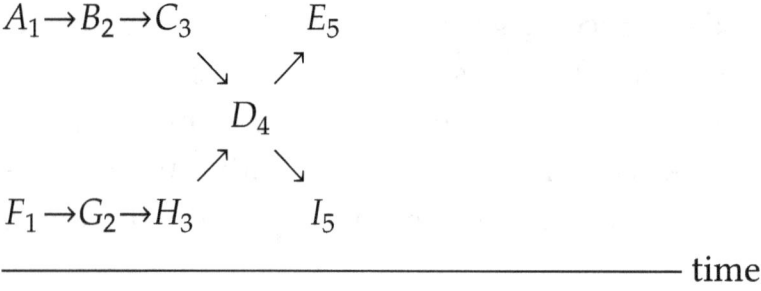

Figure 9.3: Parallel processes and indivisibilities

Leijonhufvud notes that economies are to be gained from judicious horizontal divisions as well. This can result from the indivisibilities that come with prior innovations. So, for example, imagine that one of the stages of production—stage 4—is running at half capacity (a railway car, a telegraph system). Imagine running two parallel production processes as shown in Figure 9.3. There is twice the output of just one process, but the double output comes at the expense of less than twice the inputs, a clear economy of scale of the Lachmann variety. These economies of scale come from organizational change rather than from technology, although the indivisibility that makes it possible may be the result of a technological innovation.

In this example the two "industries" or firms or processes share operation 4. They may not even be the same processes. They may have a common need for operation 4 (like transportation, communication, or electricity) and be quite different in other respects. This is a different type of division of labor. Stage 4 has become a specialized activity on its own. It is clear that these economies of scale depend in a crucial way on the "extent of the market" or on the "throughput" (Lachmann 1996:147–148), that is, on the size of the demand for the services of the various stages that are supplied in indivisible multiples. It is also clear that more complex patterns will most likely emerge—with indivisibilities and crossprocess connections at more than one stage. The degree of returns to scale depends on the amount of excess capacity at each stage. (A similar observation is made by Penrose considering resource combinations within the firm that have to be made up to the "lowest common multiple" (Penrose 1995:72–73)). If the number of stages is held constant, these economies become less and less significant as output is increased and, in this case, approach constant returns to scale in the limit (Leijonhufvud 1986:214). However, an aspect of economic progress is an increasing number of interrelated activities or stages of production (Lachmann 1978:ch. V; see also Chapter 8). Pursuing this line of reasoning, there is then an unending source of scale economies in the market process.

As Leijonhufvud explains (interpreting Smith and Marx), the process of the division of labor is connected to the process of technological change. "As one subdivides the process of production vertically into a greater and greater number of simpler tasks, some of these tasks become so simple that a *machine* could do them.... [We are led to] the *discovery* of ... opportunities for mechanization" (Leijonhufvud 1986:215). If we think of each of the organizational schemes of production such as those discussed above as being one of many possible schemes, then we can easily see the part they could play in an evolutionary process toward greater complexity (a larger and larger number of interdependent productive activities and stages). In effect (paradoxically), greater complexity in production leads to the achievement of greater simplicity and convenience in consumption. (The more complex the central processing unit of the computer, the more user friendly it can be made.)

So, returning to Langlois's dynamic theory of the firm, changes in organizational structure lead (directly and indirectly) in a plausible way to changes in production costs. In the move from craft production to a factory this implies a form of vertical integration, as did the kind of changes required in the Second Industrial Revolution. Integration is favored in situations where changes are systemic and require large-scale entrepreneurial reorganization of existing capabilities and where new required capabilities are not easily available from the market. But more generally, for example in the case of indivisible shared resources, it is not so clear that change leads to integration and may lead in the opposite direction to disintegration or "spinoffs." In many cases the innovations may be local or decomposable. Perhaps the most important examples occur in *modular systems*, like personal computers, stereo sound systems, telephone systems, and the like. "For present purposes, the key feature of a modular system is that the connections of 'interfaces' among components of an otherwise systemic product are fixed and publicly known. Such standardization creates what we might call *external economies of scope*" (Langlois 1992:253). This is a phenomenon of complementarities in consumption (household production) that both

Richardson and Penrose noted. It allows component manufacturers to specialize their capabilities independently but confident of a sufficient market (cf. Richardson 1990).

As economies develop, the capabilities needed for innovation are more likely to be found in the market, and Chandler-type integration may be unnecessary. Even if at first the firm may find it necessary to develop its own marketing and distribution networks and specialized production capabilities, over time, with the growth of knowledge, outside specialists may develop. So integration may be a phase that becomes superseded by disintegration (as happened, for example, in the case of Ford Motor Company). In addition, some of the obsolete existing capabilities may already exist inside the firm and require excision, as in the case of "downsizing" caused by technological restructuring. On the other hand, this situation may account for an element of inertia in some corporations, making it more difficult for them to adapt. As in the computer industry and the illustrative case of IBM, "economic change has in many circumstances come from small innovative firms relying on the capabilities available in the market rather than existing firms with ill-adapted internal capabilities" (Langlois 1995:253).[19]

According to Langlois, the boundaries of the firm are thus not only a matter of transactions costs and moral hazard, but must be seen within a changing environment as a form of strategic adaptation. In the absence of change, knowledge of prices, products, abilities, reputations, and anything else that is important to the (unchanging) production process becomes general, and the need for the firm as an organizing device progressively disappears. (Opportunistic behavior, for example, is less profitable when the same game is repeated many times (Langlois 1992)). But in a dynamic world the capital structure evolves within an evolving institutional and organizational structure.

Implications and Conclusion

As discussed, Langlois's work provides a framework for interpreting the trend toward large-scale integration of industrial structures that

---

[19] The "make or buy" decision may also be influenced by the regulatory structure in the face of competition and change as, for example, in the case of the decision to "outsource" to non-union specialist manufacturers.

occurred at the turn of the century, as well as the opposite sort of trend toward disintegration or divestment as companies move towards concentration on their "core competencies." Some of the specific insights that emerge from this dynamic transaction cost framework are as follows:

1. *Organization matters for production.* The discussion of the article by Leijonhufvud above shows clearly how a simple reorganization of the same inputs can sometimes lead to increases in output.
2. *Indivisibilities that result from systemic innovations imply external economies of scale and scope.* This resonates with Lachmann's (1978) analysis of the evolution of the capital structure. These indivisibilities also explain the emergence of specialized industries, like power, communications, and computing.
3. *When innovations occur which render existing capabilities obsolete or redundant, the response will be either (a) retraining or reorientation, if possible, or (more likely) (b) "downsizing" or (c) inertia and failure, or some combination of the three.*
4. *Product life cycles are often accompanied by organizational-type life cycles.* For example, at the start of the implementation of an innovation a firm may need to develop its own supporting capabilities, sometimes to overcome inertial vested interests, like the production of spare parts or technical support. As the innovation and its implications are diffused and, over time, the knowledge spreads and output grows, these capabilities come to be found in specialists in the market (outside the firm). So the organization first internalizes and then spins off these particular capabilities.
5. *The nature of the organization is influenced by the type of knowledge embodied in the capabilities required and by the nature and type of innovations that it faces.* Examples at two extremes are the hierarchical organization where information flows mainly from the top downwards (requiring that supervisors have as much or more knowledge than their subordinates of what the subordinates need to do) and the participatory organization (where information flows in all directions because team members are highly specialized and use highly specialized knowledge, the usefulness of which depends on the willing contributions of all team members).

In summary: in this chapter we have seen that the neoclassical firm as a "black box production function" bears very little resemblance to that dynamic, enigmatic, ever changing business organization that we know from our everyday experience as the firm. Instead we have learnt from a number of theorists to view it in a different light, as a remarkable organizational device for the achievement of productive activity. The firm, in this view, is "a device for the coordination and use of particular kinds of knowledge, including the coordination of knowledge generation, by the imposition of an interpretive framework" (Loasby 1991:59). It is an important example of the coexistence of equilibrium and change discussed in Chapter 3. As a system of (sometimes tacit) rules, routines, procedures and cues, it evolves over time, but it does so sufficiently slowly, if it is to succeed, to provide a stable, under-standable environment within which decision-makers can act, can conjecture about product types, methods of production, types of inputs, the meanings of market signals, and the like. Each firm, based on its experience (the experience of its members) "acquires a unique character as an interpretive system, construing events and acting on the basis of its interpretations" (Loasby 1991:60). The decision outcomes are thus the results of idiosyncratic interpretation combined with commonly observed information, like market prices, in a generally understood decision-making process that we can characterize as the ongoing calculation of capital value.

The same evolved capabilities that have served some firms in good stead in favoring it to adapt to particular circumstances, may, in other circumstances, prove to be its undoing. Firms used to a particular "way of doing things" may exhibit a degree and type of inertia or narrowness of approach that may render it unsuitable for particular environments. In such situations we get radical organizational change. And this may occur at the market level, where those organizations that happen to have the right configuration and approach will be favored, and at the firm level where those firms that are able to adapt survive. An example might be the emergence of the M-form structure of corporation (Williamson 1985), or the move toward nonhierarchical organizations (Minkler 1993).[20] Often the crucial factor in these shifts is the changing nature of the knowledge utilized by business organizations.

---

[20] Minkler provides an interesting analysis of organizations with "knowledgeable

Knowledge is a key concept in analyzing all productive activity and its organization. This harks back to our discussion of knowledge types in Chapter 2 and suggests a closer look at the meaning and role of productive knowledge in relation to capital,[21] which we consider in Chapter 11 on human capital.

---

workers," that is to say workers who possess not only a degree of "know-how" but moreover the capacity to make decisions in hitherto unencountered situations—"initiative." Such organizations would, under most situations, tend to be participatory rather than hierarchical. So as the nature of productive knowledge changes, so must the nature of the organization. See also Drucker (1993) and (Nonaka and Takeuchi 1995).

[21]This chapter neglects the important relationship between capital and knowledge that emerges when we consider capital goods as embodying the knowledge of how to do certain specific and specialized things. With some justification, capital can be viewed as embodying productive knowledge in the same way as human capital embodies productive knowledge. This leads to a "capital-based" view of the firm. For further explanation and investigation of the important implications of this view, see Lewin and Baetjer (2011).

CHAPTER 10

Organizations, Money, and Calculation

Introduction: Firms and Calculation

The discussion in the previous chapter suggests that firms derive their rationale from the fact that the organization of production matters for its results. By the same token, as the economy changes, and the production structure changes along with it, the advantages of different types of organization will also change. Still, with all the far-reaching economic changes that have occurred, the firm as a category (the modern business corporation) has remained a dominant form of economic organization. It is an institution that is unique to a market ("capitalist") economy. In an important way the market economy owes its success to the business firm.

In his discussion on the feasibility of central planning under state socialism, Mises pointed to the ability of private owners (investors) to calculate profitability as being the indispensable ingredient of a decentralized system, the absence of which accounted for the inevitable failure of a centrally planned one (Mises 1920, 1981, 1966). This was part of the famous socialist calculation debate (Hayek 1935a; Hoff 1981; Lavoie 1985a; Ramsay-Steele 1992) which has recently shown signs of resurfacing (Horwitz 1996; Ramsay-Steele 1996). According to Mises, in a centrally planned economy (in which the means of production were collectively owned) the planners would lack any basis on which to price the means of production. Without private ownership, alternative outputs would not have prices; nor would the inputs required to produce them. Without this, the value of alternative uses would not be discernible. The scope of the debate was considerably broadened by Hayek (in the 1930s) in his consideration of what information would be

---

[This chapter uses material from Lewin (1998).]

necessary for private owners in their calculation of prospective profits, and the observation that much of this information was not simply available to be collected but, in fact, emerged from the market process itself. Abolishing private ownership thus abolished the source of this crucial information, much of it reflected in prices, necessary for basic economic calculation (Hayek 1935a:210–211). Mises wrote in 1927:

> This is the decisive objection that economics raises against the possibility of a socialist society. It must forgo the intellectual division of labor that consists in the cooperation of all entrepreneurs, landowners, and workers as producers and consumers in the formation of market prices. But without it, rationality, i.e. the possibility of economic calculation, is unthinkable.
>
> (Mises 1927:75)

Horwitz (1996) has recently pointed to the connection between these insights and the role of money. In a market economy the existence of money together with the institution of private property facilitate the emergence of money prices which form the basis of the necessary economic calculation that drives the market process. In the light of our discussion about business organizations above, how does the firm, a dominant market institution, fit in with this?

We should recall that the advantages of corporate organization derive from incentive, control, and information issues. By combining resources within the orbit of a single firm, it is sometimes possible to reduce the costs of monitoring and controlling production teams and of avoiding the need to monitor and enforce the fulfillment of specific arm's-length contracts between independent parties. Instead, the firm provides the necessary relative predictability and stability of long-term open-ended contractual obligations with employees.[1] The boundaries of the firm are dynamically and experimentally balanced by these advantages weighed against the advantages of using specialists "from the market." Juxtaposing this line of thinking with the Mises/Hayek rejection of the feasibility of socialist planning and production raises some interesting questions.

---

[1] We have not mentioned the limitation on individual liability provided by the modern joint stock corporation that may also be a factor.

1. On the one hand, if socialism is indeed irrational, in the sense of precluding the ability to perform the necessary calculations, how is it that the firm is not similarly encumbered? After all, is not a state socialist system simply one large firm? And are firms not islands of socialism in a market sea? If so, how does calculation proceed inside the firm?
2. On the other hand, if the market is necessary because it provides the necessary prices for productive calculation, why are firms necessary at all? Why not simply conduct all transactions through market spot and forward contracts?

We have already answered question 2. In a nutshell, there are costs to using the market that are avoided by using the institution of the corporate firm. And these transaction costs are ultimately related to the presence of certain types of irreducible uncertainty. The answer often given to question 1 is more interesting. Of course, it is a *non-sequitur* to conclude that if state socialism is impossible then anything resembling central planning, such as a firm, should also be impossible. In fact, they are not the same things. *Planning within firms proceeds against the necessary backdrop of the market.* Planning within firms can occur precisely because "the market" furnishes it with the necessary prices for the factor inputs that would be absent in a fullblown state ownership situation.[2] And we have already seen what sorts of considerations determine the boundaries between the firm and the market.

The Firm Provides the Necessary Structure for the Calculation of Profit

These answers, however, are not fully satisfactory and raise some further interesting issues. We start by making the important assertion that if the market is necessary for the viability of the firm, the opposite

---

[2]Peter Klein has recently used this type of reasoning in interpreting Rothbard (who in turn was extending Mises on the impossibility of socialist calculation). "[N]o firm can become so large that it is both the unique producer and user of an intermediate product; for then no market based transfer prices will be available, and the firm will be unable to calculate divisional profit and loss and therefore unable to allocate resources correctly between divisions" (Klein 1996:15).

appears to be just as true. That is, *the firm is necessary for the smooth operation of the market process*. This assertion is based on noting the central importance of economic calculation in the market process and the way in which the firm provides for such calculation. We see this by examining the calculation of profits. The calculation of profits is both simple and indispensable for production decisions. It is simple in the sense that the arithmetic is simple, even though the elements that constitute the evaluation are often highly speculative. It is indispensable in that it provides the basis for discrimination between viable and nonviable production projects (cf. Hicks 1973b, as discussed in Chapter 6).

Retrospective Profits

First, consider profit in a retrospective context. That is, how do we decide *which projects have been profitable*? Profit is revenue minus cost.[3] Revenue is the proceeds from the sale of the relevant outputs, and is relatively easy to measure in a monetary economy. Costs, however, present formidable problems that go to the heart of the nature of team production. In a market economy, when inputs are purchased their purchase price serves as the accounting cost. From an economic point of view, it can be seen to represent the market value of opportunities forgone as a result of purchasing the input in question. But what about inputs owned by the firm? How does one determine the costs of using them? What we require is an estimate of the opportunities forgone by using inputs in one combination rather than another (the next best alternative). This requires an estimate of the hypothetical relative contributions of inputs under alternative scenarios. We have already seen that the nature of team production is such that it is impossible to measure objectively the precise contribution of any member of the team (physical or human). If one were required to determine "completely accurate" contributions and to use these contributions as the basis of cost calculations the problem would be insoluble, as with fullblown state ownership devoid of monetary calculation where no clue at all is provided.

---

[3]Recall our discussion of profit as a category of earnings in Chapter 7. Profit depends crucially on the presence of uncertainty. In the present discussion the absence of uncertainty would imply that all earnings (wages, rents, and interest) could and would be contracted for and there would be no residual.

The question is: what is the relevant opportunity forgone? Should it be the value of the net revenue forgone by the firm by doing things one way rather than another, or is it alternatively the net revenue that would be added elsewhere in the economy by redeploying the input in question? This latter measure is an indication of what the input might fetch in the market if it were rented out, and is closer to what we usually understand by cost in the accounting sense. It is also the cost that is relevant for the (actual or prospective) investor in the firm, whose hypothetical alternatives involve moving between firms under the assumption that the firm takes care of the internal allocations. But from the point of view of efficient allocation as seen by the firm, the former measure, using the next best alternative wherever it occurs, is the more relevant.

Thus, in the case of the market firm, the labor inputs are paid according to a(n) (implicit or explicit) monetary contract, and similarly with physical inputs (capital goods) that are rented through the market. We leave aside for the moment the determination of these rental values. From the perspective of the decision-makers in the firm they are "given by the market." For capital goods that are owned, however, the costs associated with their use are more problematic and have to be estimated according to certain accounting conventions. These conventions use procedures to estimate (implicitly) the value of the asset in the current rather than in alternative uses. This implies that a basic ingredient for this conventional calculation is, and apparently must be, the value of the asset itself, which in some way is derived from the estimated value of its estimated alternative possible contributions to output. An alternative way of looking at this is to say, having arrived at a cost for the asset—derived (again mostly implicitly) as the discounted value of its estimated next best output—one must then estimate (in order to arrive at an "accurate user-cost measure") how much of this value is "used up" (per period—its displaced marginal value product) or sacrificed in current production. This is an estimate of how much value is forgone by pursuing this line of production as compared to the relevant alternative (how much revenue net of replacement could have been earned by this asset in the relevant period). There is obviously no "correct" way to do this. So again we are faced with the problem of measuring the relative contributions of the inputs. And we recall again the imputation problem.

In sum, then, where markets exist, the value of the joint output for any project as a whole, once measured (or estimated), is much easier to determine than in the absence of markets. In a sense, one half of the problem is solved: that of valuing an output however measured. As for measuring the (contribution to) output, there is no avoiding certain elements of convention (judgment). *What the institution of the firm does (together with the institutions of money and accounting) is to provide these conventions.* By distinguishing between contractual and owned inputs, one avoids the need to estimate the alternative marginal products of the former. The judgment involved in measuring the latter affects the profit calculation and lends it an unavoidable element of arbitrariness. This means that profit, even measured retrospectively, necessarily contains elements of subjective judgment or convention.

We should distinguish, however, two importantly different aspects of the profit calculation. Profit, understood as the residual after all contractual obligations have been met, but *making no allowance for the costs of use of owned resources*, is, from the perspective of the firm, not arbitrary in the sense just discussed. Market prices provide the necessary "objective" ingredients for a simple calculation. From the "long-term" perspective, therefore, where all capital assets must be used up or completely replaced, profit appears less arbitrary. It is the division between "true profit" and profit unadjusted for user cost that is the problem. However this division is done, it clearly does get done. And the profit calculations that emerge provide a widely accepted (peaceful) way of adjudicating between viable and nonviable projects. This is reinforced in the long term by *the presence or absence of cash flow*. If the short-term division is injudiciously made, the cash flow will eventually become negative as the underestimation of user costs becomes apparent and cash is absorbed in the replacement or repair of capital assets. So, in this way, the firm and the market together provide the indispensable basis for the calculation of profits.

We asserted that market prices provide the cost signal for contractual inputs, while leaving aside how the market price is determined. Of course, in the final analysis, even when a rental price of a durable asset (like a physical capital asset or the price of labor (human capital) services) is determined by contractual arrangement, the terms of the contract, most especially the price, must be determined with reference to exactly the same considerations that are relevant in the case of owned resources, namely the value of opportunities forgone. The market is, after all, just a shorthand reference to the results of decisions taken by everyone else. So what determines these other people's decisions are the same things that determines the firm's. Market prices emerge when assets are generic enough, have enough multiple uses in the market, that people's judgments of their worth become embodied in the stock of information available to decision-makers in general (good examples are the published set of prices for used cars or certain kinds of production equipment or wages for certain kinds of labor services). As such they reflect to some extent the trial-and-error experience of many decision-makers. And as such this kind of information is not available without the market.

Thus, though necessarily subjective and involving elements of entrepreneurial judgment, calculations of profit, involving as they must the imputation problem, are facilitated by the framework provided by at least three interacting institutions, namely the firm, money, and accounting practices, all within the umbrella institution of private property. The indispensable element of judgment involves the attribution of relative shares (contributions) to the inputs, which is necessary to arrive at an estimate of what each input "costs," that is what sacrifice each input entails.

Prospective Profits

This framework provides the basis for the *prospective* calculation of profits as entrepreneurs project, on the basis of past information and conjecture, the emergence of profits in the sense just discussed. And by comparison between prospective projections and retrospective calculations further decisions can be made over time.

Two important notes: First, there is nothing in this account to suggest that the decisions taken with regard to profitability are in a global sense "optimal." Successful projects are viable, not optimal. There is no way to decide, in this open-ended framework, whether Pareto optimality will emerge or not. This is related to the second point (already discussed above in connection with the uncertainties surrounding team production). The prices of contractually purchased factor inputs (labor and capital or land) are sometimes said to be equal to, or to tend to be equal to, their marginal products. In so far as team production does not admit of any simple solution to the imputation problem it is difficult to see how this could happen in any simple way. To be sure, in a market environment of negative feedback, that is to say when certain key aspects of the environment, like the available set of techniques of production, consumer tastes, etc., are unchanging, or changing very slowly, then sufficient variations in adopted techniques are likely to result in the gravitation towards valuations of market traded inputs that, in a meaningful sense, represent the values of their marginal products. This is because, under the postulated conditions, the market provides for "continuous" variations in input and resultant variations, *ceteris paribus*, in output.[4] But this is by no means assured, and in the absence of such "stable" processes, the prices of the factors must be seen to represent simply the market's assessment of their worth. That is, these prices are what people, given their best guesses and estimates, have been willing to pay. As time passes, the prices will change as the projects in which the inputs are employed succeed or fail and to the extent that they are specific to those projects as discussed above. The market prices for inputs are not equilibrium prices, but they do furnish an important and indispensable basis for the calculation of profits. Without market prices, firms could not plan as they do.[5]

---

[4] This is, of course, a nutshell evolutionary argument with a stable equilibrium. It contains the necessary elements of mutation (variation), selection (competition), and replication (continuity in the firm as an institutional entity that replicates certain kinds of behaviors). See Vroman (1995).

[5] In the Hicksian framework developed earlier we might write a general (and necessarily subjective) capital value (vector) function as

$$k_t = k_t(w, \alpha, p, \beta, r, n)$$

indicating, in a general way, the determinants of capital value k_t of any project. The variable r is perhaps especially important because of its macroeconomic significance as the indicator of the relationship between present and future prices of consumption goods. However, the structure of *market prices and wages* in general may affect the project (through p and w) and *technology* (α and β—the types and combinations of inputs and outputs) obviously matters. All of the insights offered by Hicks in terms of intertemporal behavior of k_t follow.

Money and Production: Back to Menger

The ability to calculate profit (both expected and past) is essential to the working of the market process as we know it. It cannot be duplicated by a central planning system. It is a trial-and-error process in which the variables are not only the varied and often spontaneously emerging techniques of production, but also the various incentive information alignments that come with different combinations of firm shapes and sizes and contractual obligations that characterize the market. In addition, the prices for the factor inputs, though not equilibrium prices, bear a crucial connection to the prices of the outputs that they help to produce and, therefore, to the preferences of the consumers who buy them. Producers take their signals from prospective revenues and (implicitly) impute values to inputs when they exercise judgment in the formation of capital combinations. Without the institution of money, this could not happen.

Without money and money prices, producers could not make the calculations necessary for production processes to be initiated and continued. While central planners could use administered prices as the basis for capital projects, the values of these projects would lack any basis in terms of the values of the outputs they produced. The administered prices would not be economically meaningful, not having emerged from a process of individual evaluations. The existence of money, together with private property and the division of labor and capital, is thus indispensable for economic development.

> The phenomenon of money presupposes an economic order in which production is based on the division of labor and in which private property consists not only of goods of the first order (consumption goods) but also in goods of higher orders (production goods). In such a society production is "anarchistic".
>
> (Mises 1981:41)

This statement can be interpreted superficially as suggesting that these various ingredients (money, private property, division of labor, and capital goods) could exist independently and that it is their joint occurrence that ensures decentralized production. An advocate of central planning might wonder why each of these ingredients is so jointly necessary and concoct various substitutes for one or the other (see

Cottrell and Cockshott 1993). This is a misconception. The institutions on which economic development is based do not only exist together, they are inextricably bound up with one another. They are, in an important sense, part of the same institutional nexus; if any one is compromised, they all collapse. So nationalizing the means of production will inevitably lead to a collapse of the monetary system and the unraveling of the fruits of the division of labor and capitalistic production. We can see this by considering how money develops, and of course for this we must go back to Menger.

In Menger's work (1976) we find a full treatment of the question of the origins and development of money. Menger explains how, with the development of trade, certain commodities come to be traded more frequently than others. These products have a high level of marketability. At some point individuals begin to accept these commodities not in order to use or enjoy them but for the purpose of trading them at a later date for what they really want. At that point the product has become money.

Goods derive their value from individuals' appraisal of them. Since different people value different goods differently, trade is mutually advantageous. Wherever people gather together in society, they develop trade. But trade without the benefit of money is severely limited by the need to uncover a double coincidence of wants. In perhaps more revealing terms, trade without money is limited by overwhelming information requirements. By providing a generalized means of purchase, money dramatically reduces the information necessary to conclude any number of transactions. This means that a monetary economy is fundamentally different from a barter economy. It is different precisely because *a barter economy in which the same transactions are accomplished as in an existing monetary economy is literally inconceivable.* It is inconceivable because without money individuals could not acquire the information necessary to conclude the necessary transactions. And without an explanation of how individuals could come by this information we have no methodological basis for postulating such an economy.

What Menger shows, then, is that money facilitates exchange. But he goes further. He shows that money also facilitates production. Without money the degree of specialization would be greatly attenuated because of the increased risks involved. Specialized economic activity (like all economic activity) is conditioned by the individual's perceptions of the risks and benefits available. Specialization implies producing for exchange, i.e., producing more than one intends to consume. In a barter economy specialization is thus limited by what producers believe consumers will be willing to exchange for their (the producers') surplus and to what extent this corresponds to their desires. By committing one's resources to the production of only one or a few commodities a producer risks the accumulation of unwanted stocks because of the inability to find consumers willing to exchange what the producer needs. This risk is considerably reduced in a monetary economy since what the producer (in common with all producers) "needs" is money. Or more accurately, with money producers can be sure of obtaining what they need. Producers may also postpone their consumption decisions. In this way the existence of money supplies the degree of confidence necessary for producers to undertake an increasingly complex set of specialized activities. They need never worry about communicating their desires as consumers to the purchasers of their products. Thus money serves not only to separate the acts of purchase and sale but also to separate the acts of production and consumption.

When Mises writes, "The phenomenon of money presupposes an economic order" with the division of labor, etc., he means, as Menger has shown, that the phenomenon of money develops along with these things and, as Steven Horwitz correctly points out, "[F]rom the start, the existence and use of money is *inherently linked* with private property in the means of production" (1995:8, italics added; see also Horwitz 1996).

It is thus difficult to exaggerate the importance of money in the smooth functioning of a modern economy. The institution of money is intimately related to every other economic, and many noneconomic, institutions. Horwitz (1992) has done some work on the analogies between money and language. But this is not so much an analogy as a vital connection. Money could not exist without language; it is, in a sense, a derivative of language. The use of money, in fact all trade, implies verbal communication. It also implies the use of arithmetic and this brings us back to the question of calculation.

Money and Calculation: The Ability to Budget

Mises claims that the inability to calculate the economic significance of capital projects is what dooms central planning with public ownership of the means of production. Horwitz argues that Mises bases this claim on his understanding of the fundamental properties of money and the emergence of money prices for the heterogeneous means of production. We have discussed above the more precise context of these money prices. For Mises they are "aids to the human mind" in performing the calculations on which actions are based. The crucial point here, it seems to me, is that the institution of money and money accounting allows decision-makers to *budget*. Without the ability to budget, production could not occur, it could not be organized. Budgeting implies an intertemporal framework, the tracking of value over time. It provides the individual planner with meaningful orientation points against which to measure action. The meaningfulness derives from the fact that money prices within the framework of money accounting are *socially* meaningful, they are understood by all market participants, they are part of a shared language or orientation. When money is functioning normally (that is to say when there is no inflation), money prices represent a shared sense of "what things are worth" in the market, what can be got for them. Thus, meaningful money prices in the absence of private property is a contradiction. And it is private property that allows for the orderly development of production activities. By "orderly" we mean widely understood and accepted—peaceful.

We can understand this (once again) in terms of the simple idealized present-value arithmetic that we imagine decision-makers to use when appraising capital projects. The *prospective* capital value of any project (good or process) is thought of as the discounted present value of all of the useful outputs which it is expected to yield over its life. The *retrospective* capital value of the same project is the accumulated value of the investments actually made. Any difference between the two is a capital gain or loss (see Hicks 1973b and Chapter 6). As a result of the occurrence of capital gains and losses, producers alter the capital structure. Successful ventures displace unsuccessful ones. The whole process proceeds peacefully, though not painlessly, as the economy engages in a form of implicit experimentation whose results are calibrated in the form of money.

> In a single firm's accounting statement itemizing the total costs of a project and comparing this total to the revenues received is contained a wealth of scarcity information that neither the accountant not any other agent in the system could ever gather. Each price of purchased, rented, and hired factors reflects a complex tension among diverse plans that have tried to pull the relevant factor into alternative uses. The profit and loss calculus itself then determines whether the particular combination of inputs under consideration yields an output that is expected to pay its way in the market. The fact that all this scarcity information is expressed in quantitative form permits each decisionmaker to test extremely complex combinations of factors for their profitability while simultaneously relying on similar tests being conducted by rival decisionmakers.
> (Lavoie 1985b:71)

The Effect of Macroeconomic Policy on Capital Calculation

One well-known application of Austrian capital theory is the Austrian theory of the business cycle. This theory, developed in different ways by Mises and Hayek, makes use of Böhm-Bawerk's theory of capital as roundabout production. As suggested above (Chapter 8), Hayek uses a simplified version of Böhm-Bawerk's theory to explain how the capital stock becomes distorted as a result of inappropriate monetary policies that reduce the market interest rate below the level that is consistent with the time preferences of the consumers in the economy.

This theory is well known and will not be surveyed or evaluated here. The vision of capital offered in the present work is one that is less abstract, less quantitative, and less aggregative than that of Böhm-Bawerk. In addition, our focus is primarily on the way in which a dynamic society evolves, how its capital structure changes in a peaceful but unpredictable way against the backdrop of a structure of institutions that include a sufficient commitment to the principles of private property. And in this chapter we have considered how it is that individuals are able to make capital project decisions in such an environment. It is of some interest, however, to consider briefly how short-term government policy actions might affect this ability.

We have already noted that inflation, by compromising the ability of money to connote value, will affect the ability of decision-makers to make successful decisions. Inflation, by compromising the institution of money, in effect compromises all of the related institutions, most notably the institution of accounting. In the extreme, in situations of hyperinflation, no capitalist production will take place—the economy will revert to a barter system. But what about less extreme monetary policies that aim only to "stimulate" economic activity by keeping interest rates low?

While it is difficult in a dynamic complex economy to know with any degree of confidence what the typical effects of such a policy might be (as contrasted with the degree of knowledge suggested by the Austrian business cycle theory), we can see immediately how individual business decisions might be affected. We recall that every capital investment decision can be generally characterized by a (necessarily subjective) capital value (vector) function as

$$k_t = k_t(w, \alpha, p, \beta, r, n)$$

indicating, in a general way, the determinants of capital value k_t of any project. We can thus say two things about the reduction of interest rates on the perceived value of any project:

1. As Hicks has explained, a reduction in r will, *ceteris paribus*, increase the value of any project.
2. This effect will (usually, depending on the precise nature of the income flow) be greater for those projects that have a longer time horizon.

Thus, in a situation in which there is a generally perceived decrease in the rate of discount, one may expect a shift toward projects of longer time horizon. In other words, there will be a change in the capital structure and a concomitant change in the pattern of employment. Interest has centered around whether this change is a sustainable one, or whether, because it was precipitated by a change in the supply of money rather than a spontaneous fall in individual time preferences, it is based on an illusion and must necessarily be only temporary.

Clearly, if one makes the assumption that individual time preferences, as expressed on the margin in the market, remain unchanged in the face of the policy, or, at least, remain above the (equivalent) market rate of interest, then it follows trivially, since the shift is based on an illusion, it must be temporary. The increase in production and employment will be reversed and there will be a cycle. The assumed illusion is of the form that the planned time structure of production, the planned arrival times of various products, is out of sync with the planned time structure of consumption. So the discoordination will become apparent when consumer demands in the shorter rather than the longer term go unsatisfied at prevailing prices, and when prices rise the capital values of the longer-term projects will, in general, be adversely affected (as shown in the capital value vector function above, considering w and p). So production plans become undone.

There is no guarantee, however, that the decline in market rates, precipitated by cheap monetary policy, will indeed be taken by investors as a signal of a decrease in time preference. In other words, there is no guarantee that producers in general will decide that r, the appropriate rate of discount for their projects, has fallen. If they regard the policy as inflationary they may well decide that a higher r is appropriate. The policy may be doomed from the start.

Nevertheless, it does seem possible to draw the conclusion that such policies, and particularly *changes* in policies, do introduce an added degree of uncertainty (noise) into individual decision-making. The world is full of changes anyway. Most capital projects will fail in part. To have to factor in an expectation of changes in government policies (interest rates, taxes, regulations, etc.) and their effects places an added burden on the decision-maker. The policies affect not only the viability of capital projects in terms of their straightforward incentive effects (by making them more or less expensive) but they affect their viability also by influencing the degree and type of risk that attaches to the projects. For risk-averse individuals, the attractiveness of any capital value is reduced. And this effect is likely to be greater the longer the time horizon of the project.

In general, short-term macroeconomic policies may be seen to disrupt the longer-term adaptations that we have been analyzing in this book, and are likely to affect adversely the creative dynamism of the economy. Interest rate policy is only one kind of a set of policies whereby the government, to a greater or lesser extent, encroaches on the decision-making territory of private consumers and investors. All of these policies rest on problematic assumptions about the nature of knowledge and incentives. We will return to this in the final chapter.

Conclusion

In this chapter we have investigated the role of money and monetary calculation in the determination of the production structure of the modern economy. We have found that the social institution of money is inextricably bound up with other social institutions like private property and business organizations. The possibility of conceiving theoretically of a system without money, in which all calculation is done in some arbitrary numeraire, should not blind us to the reality that in business organizations it is the ability to calibrate plans and results in the form of money that allows it to function smoothly. Money provides the report card for business. Anything that compromises the reliability of the monetary system thus compromises the functioning of the production system. This is as true for the attempt to impose a collectivist economy without the use of money, reminiscent of the Bolshevik experiment, as it is of the many experiences of inflation. So much has been asserted many times. What we have underlined here is the crucial dependence of ordinary business calculations, for the purpose of undertaking capital investments, on a reliable monetary system.

The ability to make useful calculations to guide decisions thus depends on the stability of certain critical elements of the institutional environment of which money is one and private property is another. The corporate structure also crucially facilitates calculation in providing a cognitive framework, a set of rules and routines (some of them tacit) governing individual behavior of firm members, to guide the decision-makers' expectations. It is important to note that, in addition to these considerations, useful calculation assumes the ability to calculate. Making useful calculations presupposes not only some basic arithmetic and accounting, but also other *forms of knowledge and understanding* relating to the various aspects of the business. Thus in the next chapter we turn to an examination of the nature and importance of human capital.

CHAPTER 11

Human Capital

> Hayek (1945) did not emphasize an even more significant implication of his analysis, although he must have been aware of it. The specialized knowledge at the command of workers is not simply given, for the knowledge acquired depends on incentives. Centrally planned and other economies that do not make effective use of markets and prices raise coordination costs, and thereby reduce incentives for investments in specialized knowledge.
> (Becker and Murphey 1993:306)

Introduction: Human Capital and the Nature of Knowledge

Market economies are characterized by complex capital structures, in which individual complementary capital goods combine, either directly or indirectly through the market process, to produce valued outputs. All production is essentially "team production." We have noted, at various points, the role of knowledge in this process. Knowledge is necessary for action, and, indeed, motivates action. Multiperiod plans involving capital are informed in various ways by the knowledge of the planners. In this chapter we examine in more detail the importance and nature of knowledge in the production of valued outputs. We shall see that the human capital literature, which has developed in the last three or more decades, has much that is relevant to an understanding of capital in general, even more so when a disequilibrium framework is assumed.

We have seen that most production involves the flow of input services for the purpose of producing a flow of valued outputs (or services). (Simple "point input–point output" processes are quite rare.) This input flow is provided by the efforts of physical or human resources, traditionally referred to as labor and capital. Sometimes the identifying difference between labor and capital is the distinction between "original" and "produced" means of production.[1] When considering the role of knowledge in production, one comes quickly to realize, however, that there is little that is "original" in the type of labor effort that is typically provided in modern production processes. It is obvious, first, that human effort in production must be governed by certain types of very specific or general knowledge and that, second, much of this knowledge is intentionally acquired. One is faced, therefore, either with abandoning the distinction between original and produced means (for other reasons this distinction as applied to land is of dubious value), or of treating knowledge *per se* as a separate, produced input. This latter strategy is essentially what the human capital approach does. Knowledge conditions (determines) the type of service that gets "put in," whether from labor or capital. So knowledge is "embodied" in both physical and human resources,[2] although there are some important distinctions in the way in which this happens. And knowledge takes time to acquire. Seen as the *ability* to produce or contribute (directly or indirectly) toward the production of some valued output, knowledge emerges as a special and very important type of capital. (Education considered as a pure consumption good can be accommodated in the above framework if one considers household production, as will become clear below.)

In some ways the term "human capital" is unfortunate. It originates probably from the fact that, in an essential way, knowledge must be embodied in the human mind. There is no human knowledge without a human knower. This aspect of knowledge suggests that it must be thought of as "subjective," although information, from which it derives, is "objective." Knowledge and information, though often used interchangeably, are distinct phenomena.[3] It is knowledge that imbues information with value. Disembodied information, information

---

[1] See the discussion in Chapter 7.   [2] See Baetjer (1998); Lewin and Baetjer (2011).

[3] "We shall use the words information and knowledge respectively to mean the tradable material embodiment of a flow of messages, and a compound of thoughts an individual is able to call upon in preparing and planning action at a given point in time. Our distinction between the two terms thus rests in part ... on that between a socially objective entity and a private and subjective compound of thoughts" (Lachmann 1986:49; see also Lewin 1994:235–236). Also: "Whether applied to comprehensive or noncomprehensive planning, the knowledge problem argument crucially depends on the view that knowledge is not the same as data, that is, given pieces of explicit information" (Lavoie 1985b:57).

without cognition, is valueless. In a sense, knowledge is information transformed into capital and, in fact, *all* capital has a similar knowledge dimension. In this sense, all capital is "human." Capital is *resources* (information and other resources) plus *meaning*, the meaning that humans, by virtue of their purposes, impose on the resources at their disposal. Since knowledge must reside in the human mind, the enhancement in value that it occasions, when applied by humans to physical resources, is naturally referred to as human capital.

Knowledge, of course, in many ways defies characterization. While we may think of it as capital, knowledge as such is never traded, although information is. Knowledge is inevitably dispersed among individuals and can never be collected in a single place. It has aspects that are inexpressible even by the knower, aspects that are *tacit* (Polanyi 1958). This bears on the familiar implications for the impossibility of socialist planning made famous by Hayek (1945). In addition, as Karl Popper has shown, knowledge has an open-ended nature—he referred to knowledge—perhaps unfortunately, given our characterization of knowledge as "subjective"—as being "objective" in nature, meaning that, as we shall show, it has implications beyond the comprehension of any subjective mind (Popper 1972). So when we think of human beings as intentionally acquiring knowledge that is embodied completely within the human mind, we shall have to be a bit careful. Knowledge (or potential knowledge) exists outside of the human mind in the sense that certain machines, for example, embody the potential to produce certain outcomes only if used by someone who "knows how" to use it, but does not necessarily "know why," in a more fundamental sense, certain results are produced. This latter type of knowledge is embodied within the machine. It was put there by someone who presumably knew how to make the machine so that it would work as intended.[4] The question of where *ultimately* the knowledge actually resides would appear to be a metaphysical one, whose answer matters less for our purposes than the fact that knowledge is necessary for production, wherever we may visualize it residing. We need machines of certain physical configurations, embodying certain production potentials, and we need the know-how to operate them. Knowledge of some type, at some level, must *always* be available in any production plan. It

---

[4] See Baetjer (1998).

is inconceivable that a production plan could exist without human knowledge. It is not simply another analogous type of capital in the same way as physical and human resources, which supply the energy and effort for its implementation. So a better term might have been "knowledge capital." While bearing this in mind, for ease of reference and comparison we shall continue to use the term "human capital."

In this chapter I will examine some important aspects of human capital that derive from the existing literature, especially from the work of T. W. Shultz and Gary Becker. We shall see that many of the valuable insights survive when considered outside of the neoclassical equilibrium world of fully consistent plans. More importantly, additional implications emerge as a result of this transplant. I then return, in the next chapter, to the inimitable nature of knowledge touched on above.

Human Capital and the Firm

Business organizations provide for the coordination of resources in production. These resources may be physical or human. In considering either of these types of resources, decision-makers face exactly the same type of decision. In particular, they are concerned about the capital value of any combination of resources, whether they be physical or human, and must take cognizance of the fact that the value of human resources may be enhanced by training and experience. Certainly there are important and significant differences between investments in human as compared to physical resources, but there are important similarities as well.

Knowledge, as we have seen (Chapter 3), comes in many forms. Some knowledge is helpful in all or many different production settings—we will call this *general human capital*. The ability to read and write, to follow instructions, to communicate instructions, etc., are examples. Some knowledge is of value in a limited number of (in the extreme, only one) production settings. We will call this *specific human capital*. Knowledge that relates uniquely to the procedures and routines of a particular firm or to particular production processes are examples. Some forms of general human capital are obtained through specialization in education, in other words, through the devoting of whole units of time (years of schooling) to the acquisition of certain kinds of knowledge. And some forms of general training are provided by firms. On the other hand, specific human capital is obtained mainly on the job, although full-time training courses in specialized subject areas are an exception to this. With both general and specific training, an important difference between human and physical capital is that the owner must be present at the investment stage and the implementation stage. Physical capital can be (and mostly is) produced and used away from its owner. But, at least in an economy without slavery, human capital is tied to its owner. This has some very important implications. It means, first, that firms cannot own human capital, they can only rent its services. As a corollary, it means also that any decision the firm might make with regard to training must be a joint decision taken together with the employee receiving the training. So, it is of some interest to ask when and under what circumstances a firm might pay for specific or general training (Becker 1993:ch. III).

We can examine this by considering the elements of the individual investment-in-training decision. The most important elements relate to earnings. The benefits of training come mainly from enhanced earnings in the post-training period, while the costs come mainly from reduced earnings during the training period. For simplicity we may, for the meantime, ignore the nonpecuniary aspects of training, that is, we ignore any direct satisfaction that the employee may derive from the training process or its results (satisfaction of curiosity, self-esteem, etc.)[5] Also, we assume that the employer's best estimate of the marginal value of the employee's services is reflected in the wage rate paid. In this way, we shall see, both the employee's and the employer's valuation of the costs and benefits of the training are reflected in wage

---

[5]This can be easily accommodated by adding the net nonpecuniary gains to the value of the investment. Adam Smith recognized that differences in nonpecuniary aspects of different jobs would be reflected in market wages. This remains true for jobs that require training. Thus, rates of return from observed wages do not always tell the whole story, not only because outcomes will differ from expectations, but also because wage differences must be adjusted for preferences for and against different kinds of jobs, if the returns are to be taken to imply a net gain to the investor. Still, considering large groups across different occupations does yield important insights.

rates. We recall equation (6.1), the formula for the capital value of any prospective stream of returns from the perspective of point 0:

$$k_0 = q_0 + q_1 R^{-1} + q_0 R^{-2} + \ldots + q_n R^{-n} = \sum_{t=0}^{n} q_t R^{-t} \qquad (11.1)$$

where

$q_t = b_t - a_t$ are the net returns; benefits (b_t) minus costs (a_t)

and

$$R = (1 + r)$$

where r is the rate of discount (time preference). In order to calculate the internal rate of return (IRR) we put $k_0 = 0$.

In the case of investments in training, the costs and benefits have a special pattern. The costs of the investment will be captured by the (estimated) earnings profile that would have been earned in the absence of the training, and this must include any direct out-of-pocket costs. Using our previous notation, $a_t = w_t \alpha_t$ where w_t are the wage rates of the employee's services, α_t, in the absence of training, and $b_t = w'_t \beta_t$, where w'_t are the wage rates of the employee's services (adjusted for any out-of-pocket training costs), β_t, with the benefit of training. Since α_t and β_t refer to the services of the employee (before and after training), these are most conveniently expressed in terms of time units, that is number of hours of input of a particular type of employee service. Thus we may normalize by taking the basic unit to be one (hour, day, year, etc.), then (since $\alpha_t = \beta_t = 1$) equation (11.1) becomes:

$$k_0 = \sum_{t=0}^{n} (w'_t - w_t) R^{-t} \qquad (11.2)$$

The projected gain from training consists of the prospective annual wage differentials each year over the working life (n years) of the employee. The internal rate of return (IRR) or perceived yield is obtained by putting $k_0 = 0$, or

$$k_0 = \sum_{t=0}^{n} \frac{(w'_t - w_t)}{(1 + r)^t} = 0 \qquad (11.2')$$

Call this rate of return r^*. Then the training will be undertaken whenever $r^* > r$, where r is the best perceived alternative, due account being taken of risk, uncertainty, and other relevant factors. It is clear that r^* depends not only on the perceived alternative earnings streams, but also on the perceived length of the payoff period, n. And this payoff period is influenced by the length of life and the degree of labor-force participation of the employee. (We shall consider later how human capital investments may increase the value of time more generally, that is, for time used in- *and* outside of the labor market.)

We may note at this point two other important differences between investment in human and physical capital. Again this is related to the fact that this human capital must be embodied in the human body.

1. Since human life and human working life is finite, it has an important effect on the perceived rate of return in investment in human capital. It is, in general, higher in younger people, and they are likely to predominate in training programs. The finiteness of the payoff period is an important reason for the existence of diminishing returns to investments in human capital. As years of training and schooling are added, the payoff period diminishes by an equal extent (unless the investment lengthens lifespan, as in the case of investments in health, but even then the degree of flexibility is very limited).
2. With each successive investment in human capital, the value of the employee's time in the market is rising. So the value of earnings forgone tends to rise along with the benefits. For example, in the case of formal schooling, a graduate student forgoes more while in school than a high-school graduate.

Thus although, as we shall argue, significant complementarities exist between different types of human capital that are likely to raise the rate of return as investment proceeds, diminishing returns to marginal investments in individuals must eventually obtain, because of the two reasons just given. This is in marked contrast to investments in physical capital in general or in human capital from the economy-wide macro-level point of view, when investments across different individuals can be considered.

It should also be noted, however, that these differences can be overstated, especially in a rapidly changing economy. In a dynamic, rapidly changing world the relevant payoff period for any investment is, more often than not, not the physical life of the human or physical asset, but rather its (shorter) economic life. The scrapping or retooling of machines often comes not so much from the physical depreciation of the asset as from its technological obsolescence. And this is more and more true also of human capital, where individual skills lose their value not so much from physical deterioration or handicap, as from (unexpected, unplanned for) technological change. As the pace of change accelerates, the likelihood that the economic life of a skill is less than its physical life increases, and the need for midlife retraining (with a reduced payoff period) increases. We shall see this phenomenon in our discussion of specific training below. Capital losses (and gains) occur with both physical and human capital in categorically identical ways.[6]

Perfectly General Training

We may now consider the question of who is likely to pay for training. In the case of perfectly general training, it should be clear that the firm is less likely to pay than the employee. The reason is that general human capital is perfectly portable. The training increases (and is known to increase) the value of the employee's services as much in

---

[6]Lachmann asserts:

> The fundamental difference between labor and capital as "factors of production" is of course that in a free society only the services of labor can be hired while as regards capital we usually have a choice of hiring services or buying their source, either outright or embodied in titles to control. The chief justification of a theory of capital of the type presented here lies in the fact that in the buying and selling of capital resources there arise certain economic problems like capital gains and losses. (Lachmann 1978:87n.)

The distinction that Lachmann makes here is surely without substance. The fact that human capital cannot be transferred does not prevent it from being valued in the market by its owners and by its renters. The capital value will vary directly with the rental rate (earnings). Most important, exactly the same considerations that apply to the theory of capital and make it interesting in Lachmann's view apply to human capital. Capital gains and losses most definitely attach to human capital in an uncertain world and are part of the market process of continual re-evaluation of production plans. We shall return to this below.

other (competitive) firms as it does in the one providing the training.[7] Since firms cannot own human capital, they cannot capitalize the value created by buying it, as is the case with physical capital. So the moral hazard problem cannot be solved by "internalizing" the investment process. It is possible for firms to provide the training if they can be insured against the likelihood that the employee will quit and take his skills elsewhere. For these purposes contracts are sometimes fashioned, an example being the armed forces,[8] but enforcement costs can be prohibitive. An easier solution is for the employee to pay. The inalienable property right that the employee has in his skills is the source of his incentive to invest in training by taking a temporary "cut" in earnings.

Thus for firms providing general training with the employee paying, the employee's earnings during the training period would be reduced by the cost of training. Employees pay for general training by receiving wages below what they could receive elsewhere. In this way, current earnings (negatively) include capital investment items. So, unlike formal educational courses (schooling), expenditure for training on the job is "automatically" deducted from earnings. All costs then appear as the value of forgone earnings to workers receiving general on-the-job training and an estimate of their value depends on expectations of future post-training earnings.

Perfectly Specific Training

Specific training illustrates an aspect of the heterogeneity of human capital. As with physical capital, heterogeneity implies complementarity. Specific human capital is valuable in specific combinations of general and specific human capital and physical capital.

---

[7]One does not require a situation of equilibrium here. Irrespective of whether plans exactly match outcomes or not, perfectly general training, like literacy, benefits the individual in a general way, that is, in a variety of situations, to the same extent. Even though the precise benefit may be uncertain, the *differential* benefit, as between one work situation and another, is zero.

[8]Where the military pays for general training, for example for pilots, and does not pay the market wage for graduate trainees, there is a problem of re-enlistment and losses in favor of businesses in the private sector, like the private airlines (Becker 1993:39).

Perfectly specific training increases the expected earnings of the employee only in the firm providing the training. In this case, the employee has a substantially reduced incentive to pay for the training. On the other hand, since the skills obtained are not portable, the firm has a substantially increased incentive to pay for its acquisition. Since the employee's post-training skills are more highly valued in the firm that has provided the training than in the "market," they have a much reduced incentive to quit. Quitting would necessitate taking a pay cut. If the firm could be confident that the employee would not quit in spite of this reduced incentive, it would be prepared to pay the full cost for this training. Since, however, no such absolute assurance could be obtained, the training costs are likely to be shared, even in the case of perfectly specific training.

Where the firm pays all or part of the costs of training, wages during the training period are likely to be more than the "full worth" of the marginal value to the firm of the employee's services and to be less than this "full worth" in the post-training period (where such values can be estimated). This will most likely manifest in the employee earning more than the "market" for his current skills will pay during the training period. And since his skill is specific to the firm, he will earn more than the "market" in the post-training period as well.[9]

Multiple Specificity in Training

In reality, training is seldom likely to be perfectly specific to a particular firm. Rather, the training may have a greater or lesser degree of specificity and this may vary across space and (importantly) across time. A firm that is technologically innovative and pioneers a particular process or product, might, for example, have to provide all

---

[9] As Becker notes, Marshall was clearly aware of the difference between general and specific training.

> Thus the head clerk in a business has an acquaintance with men and things, the use of which he could in some cases sell at a high price to rival firms. But in other cases it is of a kind to be of no value save to the business in which he already is; and then his departure would perhaps injure it by several times the value of his salary, while he could not get half that salary elsewhere.

(Marshall 1949:626, quoted in Becker 1993:44n.)

of a particular type of training itself and would be prepared to do so since the training was of use only to it. As time passed, however, and the benefits of the new process or product became diffused through the economy and imitated by competitors, the training would become more general in nature. This is a risk of which innovative firms are well aware and may be a reason for endeavoring to shift some of the training costs onto the employee. As a general rule the fraction of the training costs paid by firms would be inversely related to the perceived importance of the general component of the training and positively related to the perceived enduring specificity of the training. Firms pay generally trained employees the same wage and specifically trained employees a higher wage than they would get elsewhere.

An important implication of this consideration of specific training is that turnover depends on the wage rate and the degree of specificity. Firms are concerned about the turnover of workers with specific training and would therefore be prepared to offer a premium to prevent it. By the same token, employees are concerned about the possibility of being laid off (or fired). Quits and layoffs in turn affect the expected returns to firms and workers respectively of investments in training. Employees with specific training have less incentive to quit and firms have less incentive to fire them. Accordingly, the quit and layoff rates are inversely related to the amount of specific training possessed, other things constant.

Thus, an unexpected (and isolated) decline in demand could be expected to affect generally trained workers more than those with specific training. Generally trained workers would be laid off before specifically trained ones for two reasons. First, firms have sunk investments costs in specifically trained employees that may be partially recouped in the event that the decline in demand is temporary. Second, if it is indeed temporary, newly hired workers would have to be retrained in the specifics possessed by existing employees, were the latter to be let go. In this sense, labor can be seen as a "quasi-fixed factor of production" (see Oi 1961; Becker 1993:46). Specific training thus implies the existence of a bond between employee and employer which provides a measure of security of service to the firm and job security to the employee. It is, however, a double-edged sword. For the firm, investing in specific training represents a risk in the event that, as noted above, the specificity does not endure. For the employee, investing in specific training is risky to the extent that it ties the employee to a specific employer and its fate. To the extent that a specific product or process loses out in the marketplace and suffers bankruptcy or downsizing, the loss to specifically trained employees is greater than to generally trained ones.

Furthermore, both parties (employees and employers) are subject to the threats of opportunism and holdups noted above in Chapter 9 (Rosen 1991). Shared investment costs require sharing later returns and can lead to problems relating to opportunistic behavior—shirking (thus preventing the collection of the returns) and/or threatening to hold up production. As with specific physical capital, it should be clear that holdup threats can occur on both sides of the market. The firm can hold out the threat of termination of a specifically trained employee in an effort to secure "post-contract" reductions in earnings, and the employee could threaten to quit and take a valuable skill with him in an effort to secure higher earnings. In this regard the situation represents a bilateral monopoly.[10]

Pension plans that incorporate gradual vesting provide a type of insurance to firms against premature quitting of specifically trained workers. Consequently, specifically trained workers would find such plans more valuable than generally trained ones. Similarly, firms are more likely to pay the moving expenses of employees who are or will be specifically trained. Migration is a form of human capital investment, and migration costs are likely to be shared in proportion to the degree of specificity of the employee's skills. Similar considerations attach to the firm's contemplation of investments in the health of its employees. Finally, to the extent that different types of organizational arrangements affect the motivation and performance of employees, this must be seen as a type of (knowledge) capital. Thus, for example, where the conditions are right, firms may be expected to take an interest in and subsidize the consumption of its employees. In less developed countries "an increase in consumption [may have] a

---

[10] This is really just another aspect of the general imputation problem attaching to team production. "Perfectly efficient" imputation would facilitate "perfect learning" of production processes and would thus facilitate perfect coordination and enforcement over time in competitive markets.

greater effect on productivity ... and a productivity advance [may raise] profits more there" than in more developed countries (Becker 1993:57).

Human Capital and the Individual

The investment approach to human capital outlined above thus provides many insights to the type of decisions that firms and employees together face in the production process. This approach can also be used to investigate aspects of individual behavior more generally. Individuals face human capital decisions not only in, or in relation to, the workplace, although traditionally and logically this is the place to start in any investigation. The opportunities available to individuals in the workplace condition and constrain them in the other aspects of their lives. We must begin this more general discussion by visualizing the relationship between individual workers and their earnings over time.

Age–Earnings Profiles

As noted, the "human" aspect of human capital is responsible for important differences between investments in physical and human assets. Both involve considerations of time—intertemporal planning and the evaluation of earnings at different points in time. For investment in individual human capital, however, the elapse of time necessarily suggests aging that cannot be reversed. The tracking of earnings over time is thus often referred to as an age–earnings profile.

Typically, age–earnings profiles (with earnings on the vertical and age on the horizontal axes) are concave to the horizontal axis, suggesting that earnings rise over time at a decreasing rate. This shape suggests that "experience" has value as a form of on-the-job training even in the absence of formal (conscious) training, as earnings increase with tenure and job experience. The fact that the increase tapers off suggests the influence of finite life. The typical shape of the age–earnings profile is a very robust observation, found widely where statistics exist (Becker 1993:12). However, the height and rate of change of the profile varies with circumstances. From a human capital perspective, certain implications emerge.

The age–earnings profiles of less trained workers are likely to be flatter (rise more slowly) than those of trained workers. This is because the age–earnings profile includes the returns to training. The profiles of generally trained workers are likely (other things constant) to be steeper than the profiles of specifically trained workers. With specifically trained workers the firm pays for all or part of the training, thus paying the worker more than their opportunity cost during the training period and less than their opportunity cost after training, thus flattening out the profile. Age–earnings profiles and investments in human capital go a long way towards explaining the personal distribution of earnings (Becker 1993:109ff; Mincer 1974; more below).

Full-time schooling is often a form of investment in general human capital (although there are degrees of specificity that attach to it, the degree of specificity rising usually with the level of education). Thus schooling may be expected to steepen age–earnings profiles. Typically, for example, the age–earnings profiles of college graduates start later and below those of high school graduates, rise much more steeply and rapidly overtake the latter. The same pattern is observed by comparing graduate and college degree earnings profiles. This suggests a phenomenon that we shall examine more closely below, namely that human capital investments are likely to be (sequentially) complementary in nature. College graduates, though sacrificing some earnings growth while in college and thus having to start at a wage below that of their more experienced coworkers who entered the work force right after high school, are able to catch up rapidly as a result of the knowledge that they have accumulated.[11]

Investments and the Allocation of Time over Time

The human capital approach to age–earnings profiles shows that an individual's earnings are not simply given to him as an exogenous constraint. Rather, it is a result of their actions over time with regard to the time he devotes to investing in human capital and other activities.

---

[11] We do not consider here alternative explanations, like the "screening" hypothesis that formal education serves merely to "weed out" already existing abilities. For a convincing (to me) rejection of these types of explanations, see Becker (1993:8).

In this way, the human capital approach integrates many aspects of individual behavior.

The amount of time an individual spends investing in human capital would tend to decline with age for two reasons that we have already discussed.

1. The number of remaining periods, and thus the present value of future returns, would decline with age.
2. The cost of investing would tend to rise with age as human capital accumulation proceeded because the forgone earnings of the individual would rise.

We note now that the rise in the value of the individuals time applies with equal force to the time spent within the household and generally outside of the workplace. Assuming that work was not an end in itself, an increase in the amount of time spent working or investing in human capital would raise the marginal value of "consumption" time to the individual. The age–earnings profile implies an age investment profile. Generally an individual's investment time will rise with age at a decreasing rate, mirroring the path of earnings, but would most likely peak before the peak in earnings. (For a more precise discussion see Becker 1993:70–85.) During time periods when an individual's value of time was rising most, they would tend to economize on other uses of their time. This implies, in addition to forgoing work time and the earnings that come with it, forgoing "leisure" or "consumption" time. Leisure time appears most expensive when one could be buying large increases in "career advancement" with it. As increases in earnings potential taper off, the tradeoff against leisure time becomes less attractive, and eventually the pendulum swings in the other direction with more time being devoted to consumption and leisure at higher ages. The capital theoretic decision is thus seen to apply to this margin of time as well.

The Illiquidity of Human Capital

The above discussion suggests that the investment approach to human capital resources is a powerful and simple tool for explaining a wide range of phenomena. It is predicated on little more than the basic logic of capital value and individual rationality (in the Misesian sense of internal consistency between means and ends). It requires that the individual weigh, in a consistent manner, the costs and benefits of alternative decisions as they see them. Of course, all decisions are taken within a social framework and we have implicitly assumed that these imagined and projected costs and benefits correspond closely to materialized reality. To be sure, investments in human capital, like all investments, may have outcomes that differ to a greater or lesser extent from the planned outcomes on which they were based. As with all actions, they are based, to some extent, on disparate plans and are thus, in part, bound to fail. We shall examine some implications of this below. There are, in addition, some special considerations that attach to human capital, of which we take note at this point.

"Since human capital is a very illiquid asset—it cannot be sold and is rather poor collateral on loans—a positive liquidity premium, perhaps a sizable one, would be associated with such capital" (Becker 1993:91). This is a consequence of the inalienability of human capital and the finiteness of human life. Loans to finance investments can be obtained with greater or lesser ease (on better or worse terms) depending on the degree of confidence that the financiers have in the investment and on the degree to which the alternative value of the investment assets themselves provide some safeguard against the failure of the investment. Assets of a failed business can be separated from the business and sold (redeployed) to help offset the loss. In the case of human capital, however, the asset is inseparable. Furthermore, loans for investment in assets depend on the reputation of the investor. A young investor, anxious to start his own business, must convince the financier that he is creditworthy. If necessary he can postpone the investment a while in order to accumulate a track record and some personal capital. Human capital investments cannot be so easily postponed (Becker 1993:94). Relevant to this is the fact that for investment in human capital the individual must of necessity use his own time (in addition to any other resources and other people's time that may be necessary) in a rather rigid manner in order to accomplish the investment. In other words, there is no substitute for "being there" for a minimum amount of time.[12] In the case of physical capital, a project

---

[12]The necessity of the individual's own time in the investment process prompted Becker to liken the process to the Austrian period of production model. His model is

previously postponed can often be expedited later by increasing the rate of application of inputs.

For these reasons human capital is likely to be much more illiquid and less easily financed. Like other investments there is a greater or lesser degree of uncertainty, depending on the situation. Some of the elements that contribute to uncertainty in the case of human capital have been analyzed.

> There has always been considerable uncertainty about the length of life, one important determinant of the return. People are uncertain about their ability, especially younger persons who do most of the investing. In addition, there is uncertainty about the return to a person of given age and ability because of *numerous events that are not predictable*. The long time required to collect the return on an investment in human capital reduces the knowledge available, for the knowledge required is about the environment when the return is to be received, and the longer the average period between investment and return, the less such knowledge is available.
>
> (Becker 1993:91–92, italics added)[13]

---

said to be "almost identical to those used in the 'Austrian' theory of capital to explain optimal aging of trees or wine. Indeed the main relevance of the Austrian approach in modern economies is to the study of investment in human capital" (Becker 1993:113n.). One may appreciate the point being made here, namely, that in a consideration of investments of human capital one comes to appreciate the importance of time in the investment process and, also, that there is very little scope for substitution when it comes to individual "time." One can learn more or less intensively, but "crash courses" are less effective (productive) than more leisurely ones. Nevertheless, as with the Austrian period of production approach, it can be fundamentally misleading. Time, as such, is never "put in" to anything. Time is not a substance or a resource. Rather it is what happens over time that is important. Sometimes, as with the aging of wine, it happens almost incidentally. Mostly it is a matter of conscious effort or a by-product of such effort, as in the case of the acquisition of tacit skills or "experience."

[13]Becker refers here again to Marshall:

> Not much less than a generation elapses between the choice by parents of a skilled trade for one of their children and his reaping the full results of their choice. And meanwhile the character of the trade may have been almost revolutionized by changes, on which some probably threw long shadows before them, but others were such as could not have been foreseen even by the shrewdest persons and those best aquainted with the circumstances of the trade ... the circumstances by which the earnings are determined are less capable of being foreseen [than are those for machinery]. (Marshall 1949:571; Becker 1993:92)

These remarks suggest that financial markets cannot be relied on as readily with human as with physical capital. The relative illiquidity of human capital also explains aspects of the personal distribution of earnings.

Human Capital and the Personal Distribution of Earnings

Comparison of different age–earnings profiles suggests that different people invest different amounts in human capital. It is clear also that different people invest in different types of human capital. If people were identical in their abilities and opportunities (reflected in an accurate assessment of the returns), we would expect to see everyone investing in the same way and earning the same returns. An explanation of differences in earnings (from work) naturally, therefore, should turn to an examination of differences in abilities and opportunities (including "luck"). This is the approach taken by Becker in a seminal lecture (the Wyotinsky lecture, reprinted in Becker 1993:109ff.).

In this approach differences in the amounts invested by different people in human capital are related to differences in the rates of return available from investing and in the opportunities to finance such investments. Becker calls the former, the differences in rates of return available, differences in ability. It should be clear that "ability" here does not necessarily mean differences in innate capacities, like cognitive ability or IQ, although these may play some part.[14] Rather, it refers to the differential capacities that individuals have for learning and for turning that learning into economically advantageous outcomes, which is obviously a much more complex set of phenomena than ability as measured by any one-dimensional criterion.[15]

---

[14]Recent research into the connection between traditional measures of intelligence and economic success have cast doubt on any simple connection. See, for example, Goleman (1995:ch. 3).

[15]It is possible, of course, that differences in amounts invested in human capital and in type of human capital reflect differences in preferences (however caused). The analysis in the text abstracts from this, in effect assuming that such differences in preferences are less important than differences in abilities and opportunities. Certainly both forces are at work, affecting the demand for human capital. There is very little that one can say systematically about differences in preferences. One suspects that the larger the population under discussion, the less likely that systematic differences

Consider, then, a situation in which all individuals had the same opportunity to invest. Differences in the amounts invested and in earnings from human capital would then be explained solely by differences in perceived rates of return. Indeed, for the same amount invested, more "able" individuals would earn more. But more able individuals would be inclined to invest more (their demand curves for human capital would be higher). Thus, if the marginal cost of investing in human capital were rising (an upward-sloping supply curve) then more able investors would be observed to earn a higher rate of return and would invest more. And the more elastic the supply of human capital (or the supply of financing for human capital), the greater will be the variance in earnings and human capital investment.

If, on the other hand, everyone was equal in ability—investing the same would bring the same rate of return—then differences in earnings and rate of return would be explained by differences in opportunities. This view goes back at least to Adam Smith:

> The difference of natural talents in different men is, in reality, much less than we are aware of; and the very different genius which appears to distinguish men of different professions, when grown up to maturity, is not upon many occasions so much the cause, as the effect of the division of labor. The difference between a philosopher and a common street porter, for example, seems to arise not so much from nature, as from habit, custom, and education. (Smith 1982:28–29)

Smith quotes David Hume as follows: "Consider how nearly equal all men are in their body force, and even in their mental powers and faculties, ere cultivated by education" (ibid.:28, quoting David Hume). Opportunities to invest in human capital will be determined by access to financial markets and by socioeconomic background. Because human capital is rather poor collateral, much human capital investment is financed by parents and other family members. Thus people with the same ability but a superior (more affluent) background would tend

---

in preferences will explain differences in (average) earnings. It is also important to note that differences in rates of return (and therefore earnings) that are observed for individuals who invest the same amounts in the same type of human capital cannot be explained by differences in preferences.

to accumulate more human capital. Conversely, scholarships based on need would work in the other direction.[16]

In reality, both abilities and opportunities differ across individuals. Abler persons tend to invest more than others and the distribution of earnings would be very skewed to the right even if ability were symmetrically distributed and people had "equal" access to finance. In fact, abilities and opportunities may even be positively correlated, in that more able people are more likely to have access to loans and other types of financial assistance. This would tend to reinforce the explanation of why earnings distributions are positively skewed.

Human capital investments serve partially as inheritances.

> Inheritances appear to be received by only a small and select part of the population because small inheritances are invested in human capital and therefore are not reported in inheritance statistics. As the amount inherited by any person increased, a larger and larger fraction would be invested in physical capital. This can explain the sizable inequality in reported inheritances and can contribute to the large inequality in physical capital and property income. (Becker 1993:148)

Age–earnings profiles together with the above considerations explain also why earnings inequality appears to increase with age. Abler and more fortunate people who invest more (and for a longer time) in human capital take longer to reach their peak earnings. The absolute gap (though not necessarily the proportional gap) between people with different amounts invested in human capital rises with age.

---

[16]The presence of state subsidies for education and other human capital investment would normally set up compensating variations in private investments. For example, parents might be inclined to spend less of their after-tax dollars on human capital investment in the presence of subsidies to their children. As we have discussed, human capital is poor collateral. Therefore investments are unlikely to be financed to the full extent desired by poorer parents (were they better collateral) in the absence of state assistance. Thus, state assistance is likely to result in more (of certain types) of human capital (at the expense of other types of expenditure) than would be accumulated otherwise.

Conclusion

This common framework helps explain many aspects of individual human behavior and their outcomes.[17] We have yet to consider the full implications of rapid change for human capital investment decisions. Before we do, however, we should take note of the role of human capital in the economy as a whole.

Human Capital and the Economy

When we shift our view from the individual to the economy, we must take account of the way in which the knowledge possessed by different individuals is combined in joint and related projects. One is drawn naturally to the concept of the division of labor.

Recognition of the phenomenon of human capital and its role in the economy is clear in Adam Smith's treatment of the division of labor in the *Wealth of Nations*. He gives the following as (two out of the three) reasons that the division of labor leads to an increase in output (increasing returns): that the specialized individual worker both improves in dexterity over time and may be expected often to discover improved methods of production (Smith 1982:17–18). We have already seen an example of this in our discussion of the firm and of the connection between the division of labor and the acquisition of knowledge (human capital) by the worker and also in our discussion of Lachmann's capital theory and his reinterpretation of Böhm-Bawerk's notion of increasing roundaboutness. The division of labor appears to be involved, implicitly or explicitly, in many aspects of capital theory. In addition, as Carl Menger has pointed out, "Adam Smith has made the progressive division of labor the central factor in the economic progress of mankind" (Menger 1976:72).

Menger goes on, however, to criticize Smith. He points out that even in primitive societies labor is efficiently specialized, yet the improvement in production is not such as is typical of technologically

---

[17] The work of Gary Becker and his collaborators has extended this approach to the search for explanations of observed outcomes relating to intergenerational individual and family mobility and aspects of family economics in general. We shall have an opportunity to visit some of this below.

progressive societies.[18] Production may be efficient within the given state of the arts; progress consists in breaking out of the existing framework, in visualizing and implementing new methods of production. To be fair, it seems to me that Smith does indeed imply this in his third reason for the importance of the division of labor ("the inventions of common workmen," etc. (Smith 1982:19–22)). Be that as it may, the point is that the division of labor occurs within a given, known way of doing things and it is primarily through changes in the latter that progress occurs.

> The quantities of consumption goods at human disposal are limited only by the extent of human knowledge of the causal connections between things, and by the extent of human control over these things. Increasing understanding of the causal connections between things and human welfare, and increasing control of the less proximate conditions responsible for human welfare, have led mankind, therefore, from a state of barbarism and the deepest misery to its present stage of civilization and wellbeing, and have changed vast regions inhabited by a few miserable, excessively poor, men into densely populated civilized countries. *Nothing is more certain than that, the degree of economic progress of mankind will still, in future epochs, be commensurate with the degree of progress of human knowledge.*
> (Menger 1976:74, italics added)

What, presumably, Smith would argue is that advances in knowledge (human capital accumulation) and the division of labor are intricately connected.

This is the theme of some recent work (Becker and Murphey, reprinted in Becker 1993) integrating human capital, coordination of team production, and economic progress. Becker and Murphey argue that the degree of the division of labor is governed not only by the

---

[18]"We may assume that the tasks in the collecting economy of an Australian tribe are, for the most part, divided in the most efficient way among the various members of the tribe. Some are hunters; others are fishermen; and still others are occupied exclusively with collecting wild vegetable foods.... We may imagine the division of labor of the tribe to be carried still further, so that each distinct task comes to be performed by a particular specialized member of the tribe. [The improvement in allocation and the increase in production that results from this] is very different from that which we can observe in actual cases of economically progressive peoples" (Menger 1976:72–73). Essentially the same point was made at length by T. W. Schultz (1964).

extent of the market, as Smith would have it, but also by "the costs of combining specialized workers." We have already discussed problems of team production that manifest in principal-agent difficulties, free riding, communication difficulties, and the like. Becker and Murphey suggest that these considerations "imply that the costs of coordinating a group of complementary specialized workers grows as the number of specialists increases" (ibid.:300). More specifically:

> The productivity of specialists at particular tasks depends on how much knowledge they have. The dependence of specialization on knowledge available ties the division of labor to economic progress since economic progress depends on growth in human capital and technologies. (ibid.:300)

As societies progress, they become more complex in the sense that tasks become more specialized. This echoes the views of Lachmann and Böhm-Bawerk. It is in this sense that progress implies a greater degree of roundaboutness. We see this in the specialization of the professions (for example, in physicians with their specializations and subspecializations) and in the way in which new industries develop. Much of this increased specialization "has been due to an extraordinary growth in knowledge" (ibid.:307). This knowledge embodied in the human capital of specialized workers not only raises the average product of each worker, but also raises the marginal product of the larger team. Teams may be within or between firms. Specialized members of a team who are employed by the same firm get coordinated by the rules and routines of the firm. Specialists who are employed by different firms have their activities coordinated by contracts and other agreements across firms.

The modern market economy, as Hayek (1945) has pointed out, facilitates the coordination of larger, more complex teams than would be possible in other types of economy. And larger and more complex teams facilitate economic progress.[19] So teams get larger and workers become more specialized and expert over a smaller range of skills as

---

[19] "It is the extensive cooperation among highly specialized workers that enables advanced economies to utilize a vast amount of knowledge. This is why Hayek's emphasis on the role of prices and markets in combining efficiently the specialized knowledge of different workers is so important in appreciating the performance of rich and complex economies" (Becker and Murphey 1993:308).

human capital and technology grow. While, in Smith, causation goes from the division of labor to greater knowledge, in Becker and Murphey it also goes from greater general knowledge to a more extensive division of labor and greater task-specific knowledge.

There are important complementarities between different types of human capital.[20] In particular, general knowledge is usually complementary with investments in task-specific knowledge (adding another dimension to the distinction between specific and general human capital discussed earlier). Thus, increasing general knowledge increases the demand for specific knowledge. By the same token, increases in general scientific and other knowledge, together with the decline in coordination costs that a mature market system brings, raise the benefits from greater specialization. Declining transportation costs, raising the effective size of the market, are seen by Becker and Murphey as an alternative and additional explanation, but this may be equally seen

---

[20] Although he often does not seem to see the significance of this and, indeed, sometimes claims to assume exactly the opposite, Becker (and his collaborators in this work) clearly see human capital as a *heterogeneous* structure, much in the same way as Lachmann thinks of physical capital structures, that is in which the elements are crucially complementary. Another example: "An important function of entrepreneurship is to coordinate *different types* of labor and capital" (ibid.:305, italics added). Perhaps surprisingly, this is clearly recognized by the founder of the concept of human capital, T. W. Schultz, who states:

> I have argued ... that while a strong case can be made for using a rigorous definition of human capital, it will be subject to the same ambiguities that continue to plague capital theory in general, and the concept of economic growth models in particular. [Particularly problematic] is the assumption, underlying capital theory and the aggregation of capital in growth models, that capital is homogeneous. Each form of capital has specific properties: a building, a tractor, a specific type of fertilizer, a tube well, and many other forms not only in agriculture but also in all other production activities. As Hicks has taught us, this capital homogeneity assumption is the disaster of capital theory. It is demonstrably inappropriate in analyzing the dynamics of economic growth ... whether capital aggregation is in terms of factor costs or in terms of the discounted value of the lifetime services of its many parts.... One of the essential parts of economic growth is thus concealed by such capital aggregation. (Schultz 1981:10–11)

It does not seem as though this insight has permeated the human capital literature in general.

as a particular aspect of the growth of knowledge and a decrease in coordination (communication) costs.

It is important to emphasize that the incentive to invest in knowledge depends partly on the degree of specialization. In this way the essential and vital complementarities between different types of knowledge is brought out. At the economy level, investments in knowledge are not subject to diminishing returns in the usual way that investments in physical capital are thought to be (but remember our discussion on growth theory above in Chapter 5). Greater knowledge raises the productivity of further investment in knowledge (ibid.:312). Greater specialization enables workers to absorb knowledge more easily, which tends to offset the tendency toward diminishing returns. Thus, complementarities obviously exist within as well as between individual workers. One has to learn how to learn and, having done so, can learn more easily and productively (we will return to this below).

According to Becker and Murphey, the increasing returns associated with the division of labor and the accompanying accumulation of knowledge are garnered by increasingly more "roundabout" production of human capital. All people who help produce human capital are called "teachers." The human capital of the economy is "produced" over many succeeding generations. "The human capital of workers in later periods is produced with more 'roundabout' methods, and hence longer lineages, than the human capital of workers in earlier periods" (ibid.:316). So the effects of human capital accumulation on the degree of specialization implies that members of more roundabout sectors tend to specialize in a narrower range of tasks. This provides some insight into the "evolution" of human capital. All surviving human capital is of relatively old vintage-lineage.

Becker and Murphey's vision complements the endogenous growth literature (see Chapter 5) in explaining the absence of any tendency toward diminishing returns in expanding economies and in explaining why human capital tends to migrate toward them rather that toward less developed and more slowly expanding economies. Rates of return on investment in knowledge depend on the costs of coordinating specialized workers.

> Countries with lower coordination costs due to stabler and more efficient laws, or other reasons, not only have larger

outputs, but they also tend to grow faster because lower costs stimulate investments in knowledge by raising the advantages of a more extensive division of labor. (ibid.:314)

In sum, "An analysis of the forces determining the division of labor provides crucial insights not only into the growth of nations, but also into the organization of product and labor markets, industries and firms" (ibid.:318).

Human Capital and the Family

Introduction

Among the changes that have occurred in the twentieth century, perhaps none is more profound than the changes that have occurred in the nature and role of the family in the economy and in society as a whole.

> The family in the Western world has been radically altered —some claim almost destroyed—by events of the last three decades. The rapid growth in divorce rates has greatly increased the number of households headed by women and the number of children growing up in households with only one parent. The large increase in labor force participation of married women has reduced the contact between children and their mothers and contributed to the conflict between the sexes in employment as well as in marriage. The rapid decline in birth rates has reduced family size and helped cause the increased rates of divorce and labor force participation of married women. Conversely, expanded divorce and labor force participation have reduced the desire to have large families. (Becker 1991:1)

Among those women who were married for the first time in the 1950s, less than 15 percent have been divorced, whereas the comparable number for those first married in the 1980s is around 60 percent. The average household size has declined by one-third since the end of the nineteenth century. Female-headed households increased from 15 to 31 percent of all households (in the United States) between 1950 and 1987. Labor force participation rates of women, especially married women, rose precipitously in all of the advanced economies of the world in the postwar period (see Becker 1991 and the references therein).

Economists have generally not shown much interest in the family, and where they have it has been primarily from the point of view of population growth. Changes in fertility are a major determinant of changes in population growth and these affect not only the size of the population at any given point in time but also the age composition of the population through time. In this regard the most famous contribution is that of Malthus. Even here, however, subsequent to the discrediting of the dire predictions of Malthusian theory, economists paid very little attention to the determinants of population growth and simply took it to be "exogenously given," as, for example, in growth economics. The human capital "revolution" introduced a new and richer perspective on population questions. The human capital approach in fact began with this new look at population. In a very influential article Jacob Mincer (1962) argued persuasively that the labor force participation of married women was determined not only by their earnings but also by the earnings of their husbands, the number of children they have, and other aspects of the family. In this way it was seen that population influences the economy not only by its size and composition but in a more detailed way by the degree and type of participation of the elements of the population in work and other activities. And these, in turn, are the results of "endogenous" forces: basic economic decisions involving intertemporal planning.

While economists are used to analyzing the decisions of economic agents with regard to their consumption patterns, hours of work, investment prospects, and the like, they have tended to ignore those decisions relating to marriage, children, health, and other "personal" matters. But this dichotomy between "personal" and "economic" matters is surely an artificial one that can be maintained only at the risk of ignoring important aspects of both. People, after all, do not make such decisions in isolation one from the other. Rather, they make and change lifetime plans involving jointly work, marriage, leisure, children, and retirement. Each of these decisions influences and is influenced by the others in ways on which economic reasoning can throw considerable light. This is the project of the "family economics" that Gary Becker deals with in much of his work and most particularly in his *A Treatise on the Family* (1991, second enlarged edition).

Children

The unprecedented rise in labor market opportunities available for women in this century (as caused, for example, the rapid expansion of the service sector), manifesting in an increase in the relative wage rate earned, has changed the value of time spent in the home by both husband and wife. This is the major cause of the increased participation of married women in the labor force. The traditional division of labor between husband and wife has become less advantageous or "more expensive." More families have decided that they cannot afford for the wife not to work and forgo the second source of income. This increase in the opportunity cost of the wife's time has meant that all those things that are produced in the household that intensively use her time have become "more expensive." This includes children.

Childcare is a very time-intensive activity, especially involving the time of the mother when the child is still young. Thus the decline in fertility, according to this perspective, is simply a reflection of a decline in the demand for children. It is a reflection also of a shift, with urbanization, of the changing role of children in the family. Whereas in traditional societies children are an important source of wealth, both in the form of labor and as a form of social security, in modern urbanized societies this is no longer true. Children are desired more exclusively as ends in themselves and can no longer be relied on as sources of wealth. This reinforces the effect of an increasing cost of time in making them more expensive.[21]

The decline in the average size of the family has been accompanied by an increase (both absolutely and relatively) in the amount spent on (invested in) the smaller number of children. There has been a shift away from "quantity" to "quality" (Becker 1991:ch. 5). In important respects this development stands the Malthusian model on its head. It is true that, other things constant, an increase in incomes leads generally to an increase in the demand for children and therefore to an increase in family size, which reduces income per capita. What Malthus neglects are the implications of an increase in the value of

---

[21] An explanation in terms of the advances in the technology of birth control has been investigated and found wanting. There is historical evidence to suggest that effective forms of birth control have always been readily (cheaply) available (Becker 1991).

time. Other things are not constant when incomes rise as a result of an increase in earnings from work (as contrasted, for example, with an increase in property or inherited income). A rise in the earnings rate of a family member increases the cost of using that member's time in household activities, and when this applies to women, the implication is a substitution effect away from children toward other types of expenditure that (if it is strong enough) will outweigh the Malthusian income effect. In addition, with rising incomes and the changing role of children, there is a tendency to "want more for one's children," that is, an increase in the demand for "child quality."

We saw earlier that differences in earnings among people could be explained by the interaction of "abilities" and "opportunities." We can see now that these "abilities" are most likely largely determined by the kinds of family decisions that we are discussing. The quality and quantity of human capital invested in children is profoundly influenced by parents' lifetime decisions concerning family size, labor force participation and the division of labor in the home, investments in physical and financial assets, and the success or failure of marriages.

The Family and the Division of Labor

Considering the family as a productive unit, one gains insights into the type and extent of the division of labor within it. As expected, at any point of time, the division of household tasks for the accomplishment of mutually beneficial outputs is determined by the perceived comparative advantages of the various family members. We abstract here from the question of how, and by whom, decisions within the family are made, although clearly this is a relevant determinant of the allocation of tasks. Given a particular decision-making regime, the perception of comparative advantages will be important. The same principles that govern the identification of the gains from trade in an international trade context (or in any market context) operate as well within organizations in general and within the family in particular. And just as has been recently emphasized in the international trade literature (Krugman 1991), so with the family, the degree and type of specialization is, at least in part, endogenously determined over time by the investment decisions of the traders. Resources are not simply given.

The rising wage rates of married women has meant an increase in the cost of their home time and an economizing of it within the family. This has implied a *reduced* division of labor within the household, a greater sharing of traditionally specialized tasks. This has, as we have seen, also implied a decline in the size of families; a reduction in the number of children per family. These developments have, in effect, reduced the gain from marriage and increased the likelihood of divorce. And an increase in the likelihood of divorce has, in turn, reduced the advantages of specialization within the family.

The incentive to invest in human capital specific to a particular activity is positively related to the time that one anticipates will be spent on that activity. The traditional division of labor between men and women, with men specializing in the accomplishment of market-oriented tasks and women specializing in the accomplishment of household-oriented tasks, is predicated on the assumption that men would spend a sizeable proportion of their time in the labor market and, more importantly, that women would spend the bulk of their time in the home. As a result, men tended to invest primarily in market-specific human capital and women in household-specific human capital. Thus the traditional division of labor may not be the result of (large) intrinsic differences between people in general, or between the sexes in particular, but, rather, are the path-dependent result of decisions to specialize. Because of complementarities in learning and between different types of specific human capital, investments in specialized human capital produce increasing returns and thereby provide a strong incentive for the division of labor even among basically identical people. Initially small differences between people become, over time, transformed into large observed ones (Becker 1991:57ff.).

Divorce

As the amount of time that women anticipate spending in the home has gone down, their incentive to invest in household-specific human capital has diminished and this has reinforced the move away from the traditional division of labor. In addition, as the probability of divorce has risen, the incentive of women to invest in "marriage-specific" human capital has likewise diminished. To some extent the acquisition of market skills by women is a type of "divorce insurance," as it is they who are most likely to obtain custody of any children and to have to provide for them (the degree of contributions by divorced fathers being notoriously low). Expectations of divorce are, in this way, partly self-fulfilling—the perception of reduced gains from marriage has led to a reduced commitment to marriage.

There is an element of paradox in this. It is almost as if, to some extent, people marry in the expectation of getting divorced. Yet, fundamentally, divorce is a result of plan failure; it is an indication that the marriage has failed. It is, in this sense, an indicator of disequilibrium in the "marriage market." Another way of looking at it is to see the gains from marriage as having become more uncertain, inviting the provision of more contingency planning. Just as rapidly changing technologies have implied the expectation of a reduced tenure within firms, the disappearance of the career track, so these same changes have implied a "reduced tenure" of marriage. Women are more economically mobile, more committed to market production, and less able to rely on the contributions of their potential spouses. They therefore invest less in marriage and get divorced much more often. And, while it is true that men are investing more in household- and marriage-specific human capital than they used to, this is much too weak to offset the much larger change in the status and role of women. (See Horwitz and Lewin (2008) for a more extensive discussion.)

Conclusion: The Evolution of the Family

The momentous changes in the family—in fertility, divorce, and the division of labor—can thus be seen as a response (to some extent an unconscious one) to the rapid changes of our technologically advanced society and the uncertainty that it implies.

Traditional societies have enormous problems coping with uncertainty and changes in knowledge (Becker 1991:ch. 11). Societies exemplified by traditional farming and hunting (fishing) economies do not experience rapid and cumulative changes in techniques. In such societies, the family, or more accurately the kinship group or extended family, is very important in protecting members against uncertainty. The family serves as both a social and a productive unit. The characteristics of the members of the group are well known and their behavior is easily (inexpensively) monitored since they live together or close by. Elders are venerated because of their knowledge, the value of their specific human capital. This knowledge is particularly valuable in stationary societies where it can be passed down to younger generations through the family, mainly via the cultural inheritance of children, nephews, and other young relatives. In such societies occupational tracks across generations coincide with families. Families can be considered as small, specialized schools that train graduates for particular occupations and accept responsibilities for attesting to qualifications and suitability for certain tasks, especially where such is not easily ascertained (ibid.:344).

In dynamic economic environments, where technologies, incomes, and opportunities change rapidly, the knowledge accumulated by older members of society is much less useful, especially to younger members. The young face a different and continually changing environment. General human capital (acquired in large schools) becomes much more valuable. The ability to adapt becomes crucial. The importance of kinship thus declines. Market insurance replaces reliance on the family. Market contracts replace informal family contracts. Members of the kin scatter. Individualism replaces group identity.

There is some indication that the above trends in fertility, divorce, and the division of labor may be slowing down and even partially reversing, perhaps with a renewed appreciation or reappraisal of the costs they have entailed. In particular, as Becker has argued, families tend to be held together by altruism, by sharing of concerns across family members, and those families that behave more altruistically tend to be more socially and economically successful. Altruism is in this way "selected."

> [A]ltruistic parents tend both to have larger families and to spend more on each child than selfish parents with equal resources.... If children "inherit" culturally or biologically a tendency to be like their parents, families with greater altruism would become relatively more numerous over time.
> (Becker 1991:8–9)

It remains to be seen what this implies for the nature of the family in the future.

CHAPTER 12

Human Capital, the Nature of Knowledge, and the Value of Knowledge

Introduction: The Implicit Tension

> To create knowledge is not to fathom or command it or own it. All knowledge is born, and forever dwells, behind a veil that is never shed. After their birth, bodies of knowledge remain forever unfathomed and unfathomable. They remain forever pregnant with consequences that are unintended and cannot be anticipated. (Bartley 1990:32)

Having reviewed some of the implications of the human capital approach, we may now return to an unfinished theme started in the introduction to the previous chapter. Human capital refers to the perceived value of accumulated knowledge in various contexts. Yet, as has been noted at various points in this work, knowledge is a very difficult phenomenon to analyze. The term "knowledge" encompasses an enormous amount. It underlies every action, every thought. It is riddled with paradoxes and self-references. On the one hand, it is certainly clear, as suggested above, that an essential aspect of economic development and progress lies in the existence and growth of vast bodies of knowledge. On the other hand, although knowledge is often consciously and purposefully acquired ("produced"), in recognition of its necessary role as a facilitator of growth and development, there are aspects of knowledge that cannot be purposefully acquired because they cannot be perceived ahead of time. There is a real sense in which "knowledge of knowledge" is an impossibility. In this section we attempt a resolution of this implicit tension. How can knowledge at once be consciously produced and an unfathomable phenomenon?

Part of the resolution lies in recognizing that the phenomenon we refer to as "knowledge" is jam-packed with many diverse subphenomena. There are many different dimensions that emerge when knowledge is "unpacked." Along some of these dimensions knowledge can be shown to be fallible, unfathomable, inexpressible, and tacit.

Knowledge is Fallible

One dimension along which one can think about knowledge is its truthfulness, its fallibility. Following the work of Karl Popper, it is widely (though perhaps not universally) held that knowledge is and must always be fallible. Today's valid theories may be refuted tomorrow. Although he was talking primarily about scientific knowledge, Popper's work can be (and has been) applied to knowledge in general with science seen as a metaphor for all knowledge.

> My interest is not merely in the theory of scientific knowledge, but rather in the theory of knowledge in general. Yet the study of the growth of scientific knowledge is, I believe, the most fruitful way of studying the growth of knowledge in general. For the growth of scientific knowledge may be said to be the growth of ordinary human knowledge *writ large.*
>
> (Popper 1989:216)

All knowledge, according to Popper, is accumulated by trial-and-error elimination of error. In scientific endeavors the elimination of error is more conscious than in everyday life, but the process is essentially the same. An implication is that all bits of knowledge, all theories, are at base "conjectures" held with a greater or lesser degree of confidence. And conjectures can never be positively justified or verified, although they can (ideally) be refuted. All knowledge is thus tentative to some degree. There can be no ultimate and absolute knowledge. Knowledge is always fallible.[1]

A model in which human capital is purposefully accumulated in response to the accurate perception of its benefits is thus, if we follow Popper, an inadequate depiction of the truth. More importantly, it

---

[1] For an interesting application of Popper's ideas to the understanding of entrepreneurship see Harper (1996).

would seem to be inappropriate as an aid to understanding how and why knowledge is accumulated. For such a model presupposes that a particular and certain (infallible) stock of knowledge exists (or could be produced) and is available to be replicated and distributed. Yet if, on the contrary, all knowledge is tentative, how is it that people are able to make decisions regarding the acquisition of something whose properties are inherently and radically (as opposed to probabilistically) uncertain?

Knowledge is Unfathomable

A related but distinct and more subtle dimension that can be used to think about knowledge is its understandability, its fathomability. The unfathomability of knowledge transcends its fallibility. "Understanding" is related to but is different from knowledge. It is not easy to explain what understanding is (one suspects, to anticipate, that there is an element of tacitness to it). Various aspects of cognition defy verbal expression. Bartley hazards:

> To understand what a theory asserts will require, among other things, understanding its logical implications, its content and its context, what historical problem situations it addresses, what problems it can solve, and how it interconnects logically with other theories. Among these preconditions for understanding, the hardest to understand (sic), and to characterize and convey adequately, is the idea of *content*, even though, or perhaps because, we all have an intuitive idea of what must be involved.
> (Bartley 1990:34)

In exploring ways to characterize content, Bartley defines two related concepts, *logical content* and *informative content*. Together they make up the *objective content* of a theory or body of knowledge.

1. The *logical content* of a theory (or a body of knowledge) is all the non-tautological consequences that can be logically derived from it. All statements that follow logically from it as well as further implications that result from combining this theory with other theories proposed or assumed are part of its logical content. "It is well known that the logical content of any theory must be infinite" (ibid.:35).

2. The *informative content* of a theory is the set of statements that are *incompatible with it*. It is also infinite. The more a theory forbids the more it says. To say that it will either rain today or it will not is not very informative and does not exclude very much of interest.

The logical and informative contents are distinct but related. The elements of the informative content of a theory stand in a one-to-one correspondence to the elements of the logical content of a theory. This can be seen by realizing that for every element in either set there is, in the other set, its negation. "Hence the logical and informative content of a theory increase and decrease together" (ibid.:36). To explain the infinite size of the informative content of any theoretical system, and therefore of its logical content, Bartley uses the well-known example of the relationship between Newton's and Einstein's theories of gravitation.

> Call Newton's theory N and Einstein's E. Any statement or theory that is incompatible with N will belong to the informative content of N, and similarly, any statement or theory that is incompatible with E will belong to the informative content of E. Since Newton's and Einstein's theories are mutually incompatible, each belongs to the informative content of the other. [But] Einstein's theory is not simply incompatible with Newton's, it is historically connected with it in the important sense of having superseded it. It has superseded it in the sense that Newton's theory is inadequate to the facts, and that Einstein's theory appears to come closer to the truth. This illustrates that *any* new theory that supersedes a reigning theory ... has to belong to the informative content of the superseded theory. [Thus we may say] any existing theory includes in its informative content any theory that will eventually supersede it, and in its logical content the denial of any theory that will eventually supersede it.
> (ibid.:36–37)

This should be sufficient to illustrate the sense in which it can be claimed that knowledge is a product not fully known (or knowable) to its creator. Theoretical systems have objective content beyond the accessibility of any individual mind. The full extent of a theory can never be fathomed. The content of Newton's theory is not identical with Newton's thoughts or opinions about it.

Bartley points out that the meaning and relevance of any theoretical system, in the sense of the common understanding of it at any particular time, is in an important way a historical matter, as well as partly a matter of logic. The significance of a theory "depends on what has been discovered, *at a certain time*, in the light of the prevailing situation, about the theory's content; it is, as it were, a projection of this historical problem situation upon the logical content of the theory" (Popper 1976:28). Bartley calls this projection the "accessed slice" of the objective content of a theory.

The historical relevance of a theory suggests that its meaning has little to do with the particular words and terms used in it. Almost any statement may be rendered in different terms without change in meaning. In fact, meaning and objective content are not identical. The meaning, relevance, and common understanding, and thus also the *economic value*, of a theory (or a body of knowledge) "shifts as we uncover more of, or gain access to a larger slice of, its objective logical and informative content" (Bartley 1990:38).

Knowledge existing at any point in time is reflected in the "knowledge objects" to which it gives rise. Books, tapes, and computer programs are obvious examples. But in an important sense, a pharmaceutical drug, a machine, or a bunch of keys are also "knowledge objects."

> What is crucial [in our present context] about an item of objective knowledge—a book, or a pill, for instance—is its *potential* for being understood, or being utilized in some way that has not yet been imagined, a potential that may exist without ever being realized. (ibid.:44)

Bartley is here (unconsciously) pointing toward the essential and sequential complementarity of knowledge elements and an important and unnoted implication of this. The value of any item of knowledge depends crucially on what is already known. Expectations of the prospective value of any knowledge object depend on what has already been learnt about it in existing applications. So, for example, the valuable use of many medical drugs arises out of imaginative conjectures and serendipitous extensions to applications other than those for which they were created (like the use of blood pressure medicine to aid in the growth of hair). So the creation of the objects or, indeed, the teaching of any theory, could not have been completely connected to and could not have taken full account of their prospective uses (because of the impossibility of acquiring the knowledge on which those uses will depend); although retrospectively one can (in principle) trace out the changing influences on their values. Since knowledge as a product is sequentially complementary, and since future knowledge is unavailable, the productivity of knowledge can never really be known ahead of time. One may again question the sense in which individual motivations can be captured in observed (calculated) rates of return to the accumulation of human capital.

The fact that knowledge is unfathomable, that its objective content is beyond the reach of any human mind, is another aspect of the difference between information and knowledge. As we have noted, information may be traded although knowledge may not. We see now that information is pregnant with meaning but that meaning may not always be, and frequently will not be, available to any individual, because its objective content is infinite. It is the content of knowledge that, in a sense, extends beyond the individual knower, not the knowledge itself, which is subjective and contextual. What is valued in the marketplace is the accessed slice of any particular body of knowledge.

> Demand for an item of knowledge, to the extent that it is available in the marketplace, will be based on dispersed subjective understandings or estimates of, or preferences for, its accessed slice, and on speculations about its potentialities. It will not, and cannot be based on its objective—unfathomable and autonomous—logical and informative content. This is not available or readily accessible for anyone to value.
>
> (Bartley 1990:48)

Knowledge is Tacit

Knowledge can also be thought about in terms of its explicitness. It has been recently acknowledged in a number of different contexts—in the philosophy of science (Polanyi 1958),[2] economics and political econ-

---

[2] Polanyi (1958) (and related work) is the best known, but the work of many diverse and often seemingly inconsistent philosophers of science like Popper, Kuhn, and Lakatos all arguably imply a similar conclusion with regard to the question of tacit knowledge. For a remarkable—though necessarily incomplete—survey that motivates this position, see Lavoie (1985b:appendix).

omy (Hayek 1979), and even recently in the theory of business management and organization (Nonaka and Takeuchi 1995)—that knowledge is, at least in large part, tacit in nature. This distinction between tacit and explicit knowledge is related to the dimensions of fallibility and fathomability. Our acceptance of and our understanding of bodies of knowledge rest necessarily on tacit (unarticulated and frequently inarticulable) rules, conventions, and inclinations. The question raised here is, if tacit knowledge is, as it must be, part of human capital, how is it valued and how is it produced? If we do not even "know" what it really is, how is it that we are able to "teach" it? If it cannot be taught, how is it transmitted and acquired?

A particularly relevant and well-known application of the importance of tacit knowledge emerged from the "second round" of the socialist calculation debate, particularly in the work of Hayek (and the seminal article that followed it, surely one of the most widely quoted articles in economics (Hayek 1945)). It has since permeated (as we saw above) into the theory of the business organization, particularly in the prolific work of Herbert Simon and of Oliver Williamson.

Hayek argues that *the* economic problem does not consist in achieving the best allocation of resources among the various means available, as though the means and ends were somehow given and known.

> The economic problem of society is ... not merely a problem of how to allocate "given" resources—if "given" is taken to mean given to a single mind which deliberately solves the problem set by these "data." It is rather a problem of how to secure the best use of resources known to any of the members of society, for ends whose relative importance only these individuals know. Or to put it briefly, it is a problem of *the utilization of knowledge* which is not given to anyone in its totality.
> (Hayek 1945:77, italics added)

Knowledge is dispersed and it is specialized. Individuals have special knowledge of "time and place" and they are often not even aware of the knowledge that they have. The implications of this for the impossibility of central planning have been well covered (see, for example, Lavoie 1985a,b; Kirzner 1992:ch. 6). The fact that much of our knowledge is tacit and inarticulate and unconscious, places insurmountable barriers in the way of would-be central planners trying to duplicate the achievements of decentralized market systems. It is not simply a problem of the technical difficulty of collecting and processing all of the relevant information. It is, furthermore, the impossibility of being able to:

1. extract from this information the necessary knowledge;
2. know what needs to be known when the individuals in possession of the necessary knowledge might not even be aware that they have it;
3. gather the necessary information when much of it has yet to be generated by the market process.

The market, indeed, is a process that coordinates inarticulate knowledge by continual, and implicit, trial and error. The "knowledge" possessed by different individuals is often inconsistent. How, then, could it possibily be centralized?

The tacitness of knowledge is thus of singular importance in understanding the market process. Its importance is further enhanced by a realization that *all articulated knowledge rests on unarticulated foundations.* The component parts of any statement accepted as true (one plus one equals two) include undefined words which cannot be completely defined. Requiring a complete articulation of all terms pushes us into either an infinite regress or into circular reasoning.[3] And, moreover, the very act of formulating any general statement necessarily requires using rules of proper statement formulation which are themselves inarticulate. For example, in describing real situations we must always select certain abstract qualities to which we wish to draw attention. This implies that nothing can be completely articulated, since the very process of articulation involves abstracting from real features of the phenomenon being described (Lavoie 1985b:60; also Hayek 1967 and 1973). Perhaps the most graphic illustration of the necessity of tacit knowledge is the way that children learn language. A child, who usually does not learn the rules of grammar early in life, if ever, can nevertheless construct grammatically correct sentences. This is evidence of the kind of tacit knowledge that underlies all articulated

---

[3]"It was ... Alfred North Whitehead (1968:95) who so concisely pointed out ... 'there is not a sentence which adequately states its own meaning. There is always a background of presupposition which defies analysis by reason of its infinitude'" (Lavoie 1985b:60).

knowledge. "It is only because our minds are capable of operating according to effective rules of which we are unaware that we are able to learn to speak a language" (Lavoie 1985b:61). Another example is the act of riding a bicycle and other acquired skills. "Articulation, then, is just one kind of skill that we learn without knowing precisely how we accomplish it" (ibid.:62).

The fact that all knowledge is in part tacit and that all explicit knowledge rests on tacit foundations, implying that knowledge can never be made fully explicit, raises interesting questions for the economics of information in general and human capital in particular.

Equilibrium and the Nature of Knowledge

Many aspects of the human capital model suggest the assumption that agents operate in a context of equilibrium. In particular, there is the suggestion that the data historically observed in the labor market on earnings in relation to education and training are to be thought of as valid and accurate guides to the decisions that brought the data about (and, for that matter, to decisions relating to the current future). This implies that the projections that motivated the decisions are borne out by the outcomes that resulted and that there are no inconsistencies in the perceptions and plans of the various decision-makers. It implies, in short, a Hayekian equilibrium (see Chapter 3).

If this were true, we would have to conclude that the human capital approach not only abstracts from important aspects of time and change, it also begs certain important questions raised by the nature of knowledge discussed above. If knowledge is fallible, unfathomable, and tacit, it must be a product whose value cannot be fully known ahead of time and whose value is continually changing. The analogizing of knowledge to a consciously produced product is fraught with pitfalls and paradoxes arising out of the fact that it is a product of unknown quality and form. So we must ask, how do the seemingly valuable insights of the human capital approach apply in a disequilibrium world?

The world as we know it is, and must be, in disequilibrium, in the sense that individuals at any given moment are operating under different and often inconsistent expectations and theories. The outcomes that we observe, in the labor market and elsewhere, are the results of individual decisions that have been, and are bound to be, to a greater or lesser extent, mistaken. Just as observed financial portfolios do not represent, except in a trivial sense, optimal portfolios (i.e., those that would have been chosen if all the knowledge now available were available at the time of decision), so portfolios of human capital cannot be optimal. Capital gains and losses are, and must be, experienced as part of the market process. The market value of accumulated knowledge is an outcome that is (with rare exceptions) different from its anticipated value, to the extent that it can be anticipated.

I would suggest, however, that in order to make sense of our (tacit?) understanding of the market process, of our very real conviction that people do accumulate education and training in the reasonable expectation of economic (and other) gain, we re-examine our understanding of equilibrium and the nature of knowledge. As was suggested in Chapter 3, rather than seeing equilibrium as an all-or-nothing proposition, we should realize that we are, in relation to the various aspects of our lives and the decisions we take, *simultaneously* in both equilibrium and disequilibrium. It will be recalled that I suggested a simple tripartite taxonomy of knowledge. Knowledge type 1 (K1) is knowledge of the laws of nature; knowledge type 2 (K2) is knowledge of "social laws," of conventions, routines, customs, etc.; and knowledge type 3 (K3) is knowledge of specific and unique events that have occurred (history) or will occur. Knowledge types 1 and 2 are knowledge of an abstract kind, knowledge of general principles (related to the natural world—apples fall from trees to the ground; or related to the social world—people stop at red lights, dollar notes are a generally accepted means of payment), whereas knowledge type 3—historical knowledge and expectations or anticipations—is knowledge of specific unique events.

It should be clear that K1 and K2 are necessarily fallible, unfathomable, and involve tacit elements, many of which are the evolved result of spontaneous social interaction. Even knowledge of the natural world is fallible, as we have seen following Popper. At any point of time there will, however, be a (more or less widely) shared understanding of "how the world works," in Bartley's terms the "accessed slices" of the various bodies of knowledge, and this will inform and help coordinate individual actions in important ways. Similarly, with "social laws" of behavior, many of which will be tacit, to the extent that they are widely "understood" they will serve to harmonize important aspects of individual plans. With regard to K3 we expect there to be inconstancy and disequilibrium. Since individuals' plans are multilayered they could be, and, we contend, are, in equilibrium with respect to some aspects (like what they will do or not do if profits are not earned—they will not go to war, or resort to theft) while they are in disequilibrium with regard to other aspects (like being unable to anticipate accurately the level of profits, or, indeed, the returns to investment in education). As we have seen, however, the disequilibrium aspects do not incapacitate the decision-making abilities of economic agents precisely because such decisions are taken within an institutional environment that provides K1 and K2 with meaningful content.

Calculated rates of return on investments in human capital represent historical outcomes, but these historical outcomes will inform individual decisions to the extent that such outcomes are regarded as reliable guides to the future. A priori, there is very little that one can say in general about how likely this is. It is clear that individuals do look at educational opportunities as opportunities for economic advancement. Some of these opportunities will be regarded as more speculative than others. For example, investments in general human capital—generalized training that is not specific to any firm or industry, or generalized education (such as high school)—will generally be regarded as being more secure than an investment in more specialized, specific training. Investments in general training may be regarded as investments in K1 and K2 (their accessed slices), as may some investments in certain types of specific training. The uncertainty that attaches to the value of acquiring different types of knowledge is a function not only of the changing fortunes of different products, services, and the technologies associated with them, but also to the shifting sands of the validity of different principles and theories as new slices are accessed. The above discussion relating to general and specific training certainly continues to apply. One should emphasize, however, that cost and benefit calculations should be interpreted from a prospective perspective in so far as they are motivators of decisions. Every such decision is an entrepreneurial decision, with a greater or lesser degree of speculation involved. In this regard, human capital is no different from physical capital.

There remains the question of how tacit knowledge may be purposefully acquired. Clearly not all such knowledge can be. To the extent that we have knowledge of which we are not aware, we cannot have been aware of acquiring it. But there are types of tacit knowledge of which we are aware. Although we may not know exactly (from the point of view of physics) how it is that we learn to ride a bicycle, we do know what we have to do in order to learn. The connection between practice (experience) and performance provides a pragmatic or practical guide for very accurate decision-making, even though we may not know why. Through trial and error we discover better or worse ways of teaching language. Apprenticeships and internships of a very informal nature are often effective even if they mean simply providing the right environment for the spontaneous emergence of certain skills.

Conclusion

Summary

A world in which all individual plans, in every relevant detail, are mutually consistent, is a world in which economic analysis is greatly simplified. It is a world devoid of essential change. All economic values have universal and unambiguous meaning. The capital stock, that set of productive instruments in combinations that give effect to universally perceived productive techniques, has an unambiguous value. Each productive instrument can be unambiguously valued in terms of its clearly identified contribution to the valued production of which it is a part. And any contemplated difference (one hesitates to call it a change) in any of the parameters of the system, like the height of any interest rate, will have predictable and definite effects on the value of the capital stock and the other values in the system.

Such a world, although it strains the imagination and renders nonsensical the meaning to be attached to the passage of time, is, nevertheless, illuminating as a contrast. And although it is seldom postulated so graphically, it does form the basis of much theorizing in capital theory and in economic theory generally. It is the implicit basis for a conception of capital as a substance, analogous to a physical substance, whether valued in terms of time, labor hours, or any other metric. And it is the basis for the world of "perfect competition" so popular in contemporary theorizing, in which no competition actually occurs and in which no innovation is possible, no mistakes made.

An equilibrium world, in the above sense, makes the connection between capital and time manifest in such a way that capital can actually (and somewhat misleadingly) be expressed in terms of time. In such a world one can characterize every productive process as a process that culminates in the production of a particular output at a particular time. It is thus possible to connect every input to a specific part of every output, and since each output has an unambiguous value, it is possible to impute exhaustively and accurately that value to the specific inputs, and it is thus possible to calculate for how long on average each input remains in the productive pipeline.

In this book I have tried to suggest that such a treatment of capital is inadequate and that to the extent that it has encouraged us to think in terms of capital stocks as "longer" or "shorter" it has been unfortunately misleading. Outside of equilibrium such notions have no ready application. Furthermore, to think of capital in these terms, that is in terms of equilibrium, encourages thinking of capital accumulation as an automatic process of value accretion. It encourages a kind of "capital illusion," an implicit conviction that by providing the necessary financial capital, or even the specific tangible instruments for various capital combinations, one automatically can achieve the kind of value creation that characterizes the "capitalistic" economies of our real world.

I have suggested a view of capital that is firmly rooted in individual planning in a disequilibrium world. Such a view sees value creation as the result of individual decisions and suggests that to understand how such value is created, one cannot avoid looking at the decision-making environment. The decision-making environment necessarily includes the institutions of the economy and the knowledge of the decision-makers. Both of these are part of the "capital" of the economy. I have suggested a view of capital as a structure rather than a stock. In the first instance, the capital of an economy is embodied in the largely undesigned network of capital combinations of individual capital goods and human resources. This structure operates within a superstructure of (many undesigned) institutions like the institution of money, of private property, commercial law, and, crucially, the private firm. Within the private productive organization that we refer to generically as the firm, capital combinations get made and changed against a backdrop of shared "ways of doing things" that serve to coordinate individual actions by harmonizing their expectations. Certainly such institutions as firms and the law are not rigid, unchanging restraining devices. They do change. But they change slowly enough to provide a reliable backdrop for effective decision-making. So the capital structure operates within an institutional structure. This institutional structure encompasses and gives meaning to the financial structure, the set of financial instruments and practices that facilitate the formation and mutation of the capital structure. The financial structure is volatile and cannot be designed; but in its absence the capital structure has no meaning and no value.

Finally, the productive structure as a whole, encompassing the capital structure (narrowly understood) and the institutional structure (including the financial structure), must also be seen to include the value of human capital. In fact the human capital structure is arguably the most essential (and the most difficult to replicate) ingredient of the entire productive structure. Human knowledge has value. It is an asset. The human capital structure is, however, indescribably complex and unfathomable. While it is possible to understand how individual decision-makers invest profitably in certain types of knowledge acquisition, human capital as a whole remains an unpredictable amalgam of diverse incommensurate elements, many of which are unknown, unarticulated, and unpredictable. It is one of the strengths of a market system that it is able (and has been seen empirically to be able) to evolve the kind of human capital structures necessary to form the capital structures that have brought the kind of creation of value that many have characterized as nothing short of miraculous.[4]

Implications for Policy

If the above vision is correct, then the accumulation of capital is more than a quantitative phenomenon. Adding to the capital of an economy is a complex multidimensional process. It involves not only, or primarily, the addition of existing capital equipment but rather the introduction of progressively more technically advanced equipment, the production of which is made possible by an institutional environment in which the discovery of such technical advances is encouraged. One

---

[4]In this book I have also suggested that the above conception of equilibrium is, in a sense, too broad. That is, it encompasses too much by requiring that *all* expectations of *everyone* be consistent. I have suggested that more restricted view in which some expectations must be, and others must not be, mutually consistent. In short, I have suggested that the real world of capital accumulation is one that is simultaneously both in and out of equilibrium.

must be clear that what is involved is indeed "discovery" rather than the implementation of already known techniques. I am suggesting that the process involves a real Popperian "growth of knowledge."

Capital accumulation thus necessarily involves "knowledge accumulation." It is true that capital accumulation involves the introduction of more "roundabout" or more "complex" methods of production, as Böhm-Bawerk and Lachmann have suggested. The real question, however, is how do we come to know about these new and improved methods? If the characterization of knowledge as fallible, tacit, and unfathomable is correct, then knowledge in general is not something that can be planned for in a concrete way. It is a product whose value and character cannot be fully known to its owner. This has profound implications.

The superior performance of capitalistic economies thus cannot be logically "proved." The resort to the efficiency properties of perfectly competitive economies is not only irrelevant and misleading, it is actually counterproductive. For the perfectly competitive model suggests that knowledge is a standardized product equally available to everyone, including would-be central planners (as was quickly recognized by the socialist protagonists in the socialist calculation debate). The superior performance of capitalist economies rests, rather, on the fact that they do not rely on central planners (policy-makers) knowing very much at all. It is, as Hayek realized (1945), rather that capitalist economies are able to effect a division of knowledge that facilitates the accumulation and division of capital. Knowledge is, in effect, economized on. But it is also true that capitalist economies "know more." The most significant aspect of accumulation is in fact the (largely undesigned and unplanned) accumulation of knowledge.

This has relevance to the efficacy of piecemeal economic planning, whether it be interest rate engineering, antitrust regulation, antipoverty planning, or environmental husbandry. To be effective, policy-makers must have or must be able to acquire knowledge of the relevant economic future; of techniques, of preferences, of values. In addition, since government action requires resources that would otherwise be available to private individuals who would be, implicitly through the competitive process, experimenting with various techniques and theories, the extent of "discovery" displaced by such government action is inestimable. There is literally no way to estimate the "cost" of government, since a crucial part of that cost is the loss of valuable knowledge. Knowledge lost cannot be known about.

This is relevant also to the problem of economic development. The "transition to capitalism" cannot be simply bought. Capital equipment can be bought. Buildings can be built. Experts can be hired. But respect for private property cannot be produced. A system of laws that interprets and innovates property rights cannot be easily acquired. A functional monetary system cannot be centrally designed and implemented—the money has first to be accepted. And the necessary human capital structure in all its subtleties and depths cannot simply be replicated. Some transfers can be simply taught, others can be painfully acquired—"learning by doing" or by immersion in "other cultures"—other aspects are more elusive. Prosperity is a miraculous and improbable evolutionary outcome. If it can be transferred at all, it will be by allowing and encouraging the local population to evolve its own particular brand privately.

Bibliography

Ahiakpor, J. W. C. 1997. "Austrian capital theory: Help or hindrance?" *Journal of the History of Economic Thought* 19 no. 2: 261–285.

Alchian, A. and H. Demsetz. 1972. "Production, information costs, and economic organization". *American Economic Review* 62 no. 5: 772–795.

Alchian, A. and S. Woodward. 1988. "The firm is dead; long live the firm: A review of Oliver Williamson's *The Economic Institutions of Capitalism*". *Journal of Economic Literature* 26 no. 1: 65–79.

Arthur, W. B. 1989. "Competing technologies, increasing returns and lock in by historical events". *Economic Journal* 99: 116–131.

———. 1994. *Increasing Returns and Path Dependency in the Economy*. Ann Arbor: University of Michigan Press.

Baetjer, H. 1998. *Software As Capital: An Economic Perspectives on Software Engineering*. Los Alamos: IEEE Computer Society.

———. 2000. "Capital as embodied knowledge: Some implications for the theory of economic growth". *Review of Austrian Economics* 13 no. 1: 147–174.

Bartley, William Warren, III. 1990. *Unfathomed Knowledge, Unmeasured Wealth: On Universities and the Wealth of Nations*. La Salle, IL: Open Court.

Barzel, Y. 1982. "Measurement costs and the organization of markets". *Journal of Management* 17: 99–120.

Becker, G. S. 1971. *Economic Theory*. New York: Alfred A. Knopf.

———. 1991. *A Treatise on the Family*, second edition. Cambridge: Harvard University Press.

———. 1993. *Human Capital*, third edition. Chicago: University of Chicago Press.

Becker, G. S. and K. Murphey. 1993. "The division of labour, coordination costs, and knowledge". manuscript, 1993. Reprinted in Becker (1993). [1989].

Bergson, H. 1965. "The Possible and the Real", in *An Introduction to Metaphysics: The Creative Mind*. Totowa, NJ: Littlefield, Adams, 1965. Trans. M. L. Andison. [1946].

Blaug, M. 1974. *The Cambridge Revolution: Success or Failure?* London: Institute for Economic Affairs.

Boettke, P. J. and D. L. Prychitko, eds. 1994. *The Market Process: Essays in Contemporary Economics*. Brookfield, VT: Edward Elgar.

Boettke, P. J., D. L. Prychitko, and S. Horwitz. 1994. "Beyond Equilibrium Economics: Reflections on the Uniqueness of the Austrian Tradition" in Boettke and Prychitko (1994).

Böhm-Bawerk, E. von. 1959. *Capital and Interest*. South Holland: Libertarian Press. 3 vols in 1.

Buchanan, J. M. and Y. J. Yoon, eds. 1994. *The Return to Increasing Returns*. Ann Arbor: University of Michigan Press.

Chandler, A. D. 1977. *The Visible Hand: The Managerial Revolution in American Business*. Cambridge, MA: The Belknap Press of Harvard University Press.

———. 1990. *Scale and Scope: The Dynamics of Industrial Capitalism*. Cambridge, MA: The Belknap Press of Harvard University Press.

———. 1992. "Organizational capabilities and the theory of the firm". *Journal of Economic Perspectives* 6 no. 3: 79–100.

Chiles, T. H., A. H. Bluedorn, and V. K. Gupta. 2007. "Beyond creative destruction and entrepreneurial discovery: A radical austrian approach to entrepreneurship". *Organization Studies* 28 no. 4: 469–493.

Chiles, T. H., C. S. Tuggle, J. S. McMullen, L. Bierman, and D. W. Greening. 2010. "Dynamic creation: Extending the radical austrian approach to entrepreneurship". *Organization Studies* 31 no. 1: 7–46.

Clark, J. B. 1893. "The genesis of capital". *Yale Review* : 302–315.

———. 1988. *Capital and Its Earnings*. New York: Garland. [1888].

Coase, R. 1937. "The theory of the firm". *Economica* (new series) 4: 386–405.

Collis, D. S. and C. A. Montgomery. 1998. *Corporate Strategy: A Resource Based Approach*. New York: McGraw-Hill.

Cottrell, A. and W. P. Cockshott. 1993. "Calculation, complexity and planning: The socialist debate once again". *Review of Political Economy* 5 no. 1: 73–112.

Currie, M. and I. Steedman. 1990. *Wrestling with Time: Problems in Economic Theory.* Ann Arbor: University of Michigan Press.

Dahlman, C. 1979. "The problem of externality". *Journal of Law and Economics* 22: 141–162.

Day, R. H. and P. Chen. 1992. *Nonlinear Dynamics and Evolutionary Economics.* Oxford: Oxford University Press.

Demsetz, H. 1991. "The Theory of the Firm Revisited" in Williamson and Winter (1991).

Dolan, E. G., ed. 1976. *The Foundations of Modern Austrian Economics.* Kansas City: Sheed and Ward.

Dorfman, R. 1959. "Waiting and the period of production". *Quarterly Journal of Economics* 73: 351–367.

Drucker, P. F. 1993. *Post Capitalist Society.* New York: Harper Business.

Ebeling, R. M. 1986. "Towards a Hermeneutical Economics: Expectations, Prices, and the Role of Interpretation in a Theory of the Market Process" in I. M. Kirzner, ed. *Subjectivism, Intelligibility and Economic Understanding: Essays in Honor of Ludwig M. Lachmann on his Eightieth Birthday.* New York: New York University Press, 1986.

———. 1997. "Money, Economic Fluctuations, Expectations and Period Analysis: The Austrian and Swedish Economists in the Interwar Period" in W. Keizer, B. Tieber, and R. van Zip, eds. *Austrian Economics in Debate.* New York: Routledge, 1997.

Evans-Prichard, E. E. 1951. *Social Anthropology.* London.

Faber, M. 1979. *Introduction to Modern Austrian Capital Theory.* New York: Springer-Verlag.

———, ed. 1986. *Studies in Austrian Capital Theory, Investment and Time.* Berlin, Heidelberg and New York: Springer-Verlag.

Fetter, F. A. 1977. *Capital, Interest and Rent: Essays in the Theory of Distribution.* Kansas City: Sheed, Andrews and McMeel. Ed. with intro. by Murray N. Rothbard.

Foss, N. J. 1994. "The theory of the firm: The Austrians as precursors and critics of contemporary theory". *The Review of Austrian Economics* 7 no. 1: 31–65.

———. 1995. "The economic thought of an Austrian Marshallian: George Barclay Richardson". *Journal of Economic Studies* 22 no. 1: 23–44.

———. 1996a. "Post-Marshallian and Austrian economics: Toward a fruitful liaison?" *Advances in Austrian Economics* 3: 213–221.

———. 1996b. "Austrian and Post-Marshallian Economics: The Bridging Work of George Richardson" in N. J. Foss and B. J. Loasby, eds. *Capabilities and Coordination: Essays in Honor of G. B. Richardson.* London and New York: Routledge, 1998.

Garrison, R. W. 1979a. "Comment: Waiting in Vienna" in Rizzo (1979).

———. 1979b. "In defense of the Misesian theory of interest". *Journal of Libertarian Studies* III no. 2: 141–150.

———. 1985. "A Subjective Theory of A Capital Using Economy" in O'Driscoll and Rizzo (1996).

———. 1988. "Professor Rothbard and the Theory of Interest" in W. Block and L. H. Rockwell. *Man, Economy and Liberty: Essays in Honor of Murray N. Rothbard.* Auburn: Ludwig von Mises Institute, 1988.

Goleman, D. 1995. *Emotional Intelligence.* New York: Bantam.

Grossman, G. M. and E. Helpman. 1990. "Trade, innovation and growth". *American Economic Review* 80 no. 2: 86–91.

———. 1994. "Endogenous innovation in the theory of growth". *Journal of Economic Perspectives* 8 no. 1: 23–44.

Hahn, F. H. 1984. *Equilibrium and Macroeconomics.* Cambridge, MA: MIT Press.

Harcourt, G. C. 1991. *Some Cambridge Controversies in the Theory of Capital.* London: Ashgate.

Harcourt, G. C. and N. F. Laing. 1971. *Capital and Growth.* Middlesex: Penguin.

Harper, D. A. 1996. *Entrepreneurship and the Market Process: An Enquiry into the Growth of Knowledge.* London: Routledge.

Hausman, D. 1981. *Capital, Profits and Prices: An Essay in the Philosophy of Economics.* New York: Columbia University Press.

Hayek, F. A. 1933. *Monetary Theory and the Trade Cycle.* London: Jonathan Cape.

———. 1935a. *Collectivist Economic Planning: Critical Studies on the Possibilities of Socialism.* London: Routledge. 1935.

———. 1935b. *Prices and Production.* London: Routledge and Kegan Paul. 1935.

———. 1937a. "Investment that raises the demand for capital". *Review of Economic Statistics* 19: 174–177.

———. 1937b. "Economics and knowledge". *Economica* (new series) 4. Reprinted in Hayek (1948).

———. 1939. *Profits, Interest and Investment.* London: Routledge.

———. 1941. *The Pure Theory of Capital.* Chicago: University of Chicago Press.

———. 1945. "The use of knowledge in society". *American Economic Review* 35 no. 4. Reprinted in Hayek (1948).

———. 1948. *Individualism and Economic Order.* Chicago: University of Chicago Press.

———. 1967. *Studies in Philosophy, Politics and Economics.* London: Routledge and Kegan Paul.

———. 1973. *Law Legislation and Liberty.* Vol. 1. Chicago: University of Chicago Press.

———. 1979. *Law Legislation and Liberty.* Vol. 3. Chicago: University of Chicago Press.

Hennings, K. H. 1987a. "Eugen von Böhm-Bawerk". Entry in *Capital Theory (The New Palgrave).* New York: Macmillan, 97–107. 1987.

———. 1987b. "Capital as a factor of production". Entry in *Capital Theory (The New Palgrave).* New York: Macmillan, 108–122. 1987.

———. 1987c. "Maintaining capital intact". Entry in *Capital Theory (The New Palgrave).* New York: Macmillan, 200–205. 1987.

———. 1987d. "Roundabout methods of production". Entry in *Capital Theory (The New Palgrave)*. New York: Macmillan, 232–236. 1987.

———. 1997. *The Austrian Theory of Value and Capital: Studies in the Life and Work of Eugen von Böhm-Bawerk*. Brookfield, VT: Edward Elgar.

Hicks, J. R. 1946. *Value and Capital*. Oxford: Oxford University Press. (1st edn 1939).

———. 1965. *Capital and Growth*. Oxford: Oxford University Press.

———. 1973a. "The Austrian Theory of Capital and its Rebirth in Modern Economics", in *Carl Menger and the Austrian School of Economics*. Oxford: Clarendon Press, 1973. Reprinted in J. R. Hicks (1983) *Classics and Moderns: Collected Essays on Economic Theory*, vol. III. Cambridge, MA: Harvard University Press, 96–102.

———. 1973b. *Capital and Time: A Neo-Austrian Analysis*. Oxford: Oxford University Press. 1973.

———. 1976. "Some Questions of Time in Economics", in Tang, A. M., F. M. Westerfield, and J. S. Worley, eds. *Evolution, Welfare, and Time in Economics*. Lexington: Brooks, D. C. Heath, 1976.

Hodgson, G. M. 1988. *Economics and Institutions: A Manifesto for Modern Institutional Economics*. Philadelphia: University of Pennsylvania Press.

———. 1993. *Economics and Evolution: Bringing Life Back Into Economics*. Ann Arbor: University of Michigan Press.

Hoff, T. J. 1981. *Economic Calculation in the Socialist Society*. Indianapolis, IN: Liberty Press. [1949].

Horwitz, S. 1992. *Monetary Evolution, Free Banking, and Economic Order*. Boulder, CO: Westview Press.

———. 1994. "Hierarchical metaphors in Austrian institutionalism: A friendly subjectivist caveat". Unpublished manuscript.

———. 1995. "Economic calculation in the theory of money and credit: Money and Mises's critique of planning". Unpublished manuscript.

———. 1996. "Money, money prices, and the socialist calculation debate". *Advances in Austrian Economics* 3: 59–77.

Horwitz, S. and P. Lewin. 2008. "Heterogeneous human capital, uncertainty, and the structure of plans: A market process approach to marriage and divorce". *The Review of Austrian Economics* 21 no. 1: 1–21.

Ingrao, B. and G. Israel. 1990. *The Invisible Hand: Economic Equilibrium in the History of Science.* Cambridge, MA: MIT Press.

Kaldor, N. 1985. *Economics Without Equilibrium.* New York: M. E. Sharpe.

Kirzner, I. M. 1966. *An Essay on Capital.* New York: Augustus M. Kelly.

———. 1976. "Equilibrium Versus Market Process" in Dolan (1976).

———. 1990. "Knowledge problems and their solutions: Some relevant distinctions". *Cultural Dynamics* Reprinted in Kirzner (1992).

———. 1992. *The Meaning of Market Process: Essays in the Development of Modern Austrian Economics.* London and New York: Routledge.

———. 1993. "The Pure Time-Preference Theory of Interest" in J. M. Herbener, ed. *The Meaning of Ludwig von Mises: Contributions in Economics, Sociology, Epistemology and Political Philosophy.* Auburn: Ludwig von Mises Institute, 1993.

———. 1994a. "On the Economics of Time and Ignorance" in Boettke and Prychitko (1994).

———. 1994b. *Classics in Austrian Economics.* London: William Pickering. 1994. 3 vols.

———. 1996. *Essays on Capital and Interest: An Austrian Perspective.* Aldershot: Edward Elgar.

———. 1997. "Entrepreneurial discovery and the competitive market process: An Austrian approach". *Journal of Economic Literature* XXXV no. 1.

———. 2009. "The alert and creative entrepreneur". *Small Business Economics* 32 no. 2: 145–152.

Klein, P. 1996. "Economic calculation and the limits of organization". *Review of Austrian Economics* 9 no. 2: 3–28.

Knight, F. H. 1936. "The quantity of capital and the rate of interest". *Journal of Political Economy* 44: 433–463.

Kregel, J. A. 1976. *Theory of Capital.* London: Macmillan.

Kresge, S. and L. Wenar, eds. 1994. *Hayek on Hayek: An Autobiographical Dialogue.* Chicago: University of Chicago Press.

Krugman, P. 1991. *Geography and Trade.* Cambridge, MA: MIT Press.

Lachmann, L. M. 1938. "Investment and costs of production". *American Economic Review* 28: 469–481. Reprinted in Lavoie (1994).

———. 1939. "On crisis and adjustment". *Review of Economics and Statistics* 21: 62–68. Reprinted in Lavoie (1994).

———. 1941. "On the measurement of capital". *Economica* 8: 367–377. Reprinted in Lavoie (1994).

———. 1944. "Finance capitalism". *Economica* 11: 64–73. Reprinted in Lavoie (1994).

———. 1947. "Complementarity and substitution in the theory of capital". *Economica* 14: 108–119.

———. 1948. "Investment repercussions". *Quarterly Journal of Economics* 63: 697–713. Reprinted in Lavoie (1994).

———. 1971. *The Legacy of Max Weber.* Berkeley, CA: Glendessary Press.

———. 1973. "Sir John Hicks as a neo-Austrian". *South African Journal of Economics* 41 no. 1: 54–62.

———. 1976a. "On the Central Concept of Austrian Economics: Market Process" in Dolan (1976).

———. 1976b. "From Mises to Shackle: An essay on Austrian economics and the kaleidic society". *Journal of Economic Literature* XIV.

———. 1978. *Capital and its Structure.* Kansas City: Sheed, Andrews and McMeel. [1956].

———. 1979. "The flow of legislation and the permanence of the legal order". *ORDO* 30 no. 1: 69–70.

———. 1986. *The Market as Economic Process.* Oxford: Basil Blackwell.

———. 1992. "Socialism and the market: A theme of economic sociology viewed from a Weberian perspective". *South African Journal of Economics* 60: 24–43. (Posthumously published paper).

———. 1994. "On the Economics of Time and Ignorance" in Boettke and Prychitko (1994).

———. 1996. "Time complexity and change: Ludwig M. Lachmann's contributions to the theory of capital". *Advances in Austrian Economics* 3: 107–165. [1968].

Lachmann, L. M. and L. H. White. 1979. "On the recent controversy concerning equilibration". *Austrian Economics Newsletter* 2 no. 1.

Langlois, R., ed. 1986a. *Economics as a Process: Essays in the New Institutional Economics.* New York: Cambridge University Press. 1986.

———. 1986b. "The New Institutional Economics: An Introductory Essay" in Langlois (1986a).

———. 1991. "The capabilities of industrial capitalism". *Critical Review* 5 no. 4: 513–530.

———. 1992. "Orders and Organizations: Toward an Austrian Theory of Social Institutions" in B. Caldwell and S. Böhm, eds. *Austrian Economics: Tensions and Directions.* Dordrecht: Kluwer, 1992.

———. 1995. "Do firms plan?" *Constitutional Political Economy* 6 no. 3: 247–261.

Langlois, R. and L. Robertson. 1995. *Firms, Markets and Economic Change: A Dynamic Theory of Business Institutions.* London: Routledge.

Lavoie, D. 1985a. *Rivalry and Central Planning: The Socialist Calculation Debate in Perspective.* Cambridge: Cambridge University Press. 1985.

———. 1985b. *National Economic Planning: What is Left?* Washington DC: Cato. 1985.

———, ed. 1994. *Expectations and the Meaning of Institutions: Essays in Economics by Ludwig Lachmann.* New York: New York University Press.

Leijonhufvud, A. 1986. "Capitalism and the Factory System" in Langlois (1986a).

Lewin, P. 1994. "Knowledge, expectations and capital: The economics of Ludwig M. Lachmann". *Advances in Austrian Economics* 1: 233–256.

———. 1995. "Methods and metaphors in capital theory". *Advances in Austrian Economics* 2B: 277–296.

———. 1997a. "Capital in disequilibrium: A reexamination of the capital theory of Ludwig M. Lachmann". *History of Political Economy* 29 no. 3: 523–548.

———. 1997b. "Rothbard and Mises on interest: An exercise in theoretical purity". *Journal of the History of Economic Thought* 19: 1–19.

———. 1997c. "Hayekian equilibrium and change". *Journal of Economic Methodology* 4 no. 2: 245–266.

———. 1997d. "Capital and time: Variations on a Hicksian theme". *Advances in Austrian Economics* 4: 63–74.

———. 1998. "The firm, money and economic calculation". *American Journal of Economics and Sociology* 57 no. 4: 499–512.

Lewin, P. and H. Baetjer. 2011. "The capital-based view of the firm". *Review of Austrian Economics* (forthcoming). Published online April, 2011.

Liebowitz, S. J. and S. E. Margolis. 1994. "Network externality: An uncommon tragedy". *The Journal of Economic Perspectives* 8 no. 2: 133–150.

Lindahl, E. 1929. "The Place of Capital in the Theory of Price" in Lindahl (1939a).

———. 1939a. *Studies in the Theory of Money and Capital.* London: George Allen and Unwin. 1939.

———. 1939b. "The Dynamic Approach to Economic Theory" in Lindahl (1939a).

Loasby, B. 1991. *Equilibrium and Evolution: An Exploration of Connecting Principles in Economics.* Manchester: Manchester University Press.

———. 1994. "Evolution within equilibrium". *Advances in Austrian Economics* 1: 69–11.

Lucas, R. E. 1990. "Why doesn't capital flow from rich to poor countries?" *American Economic Review* 80 no. 2: 92–96.

Lutz, F. A. 1967. *The Theory of Interest.* Dordrecht: D. Reidel.

Machlup, F. 1958. "Equilibrium and disequilibrium: Misplaced concreteness and disguised politics". *Economic Journal* 68. Reprinted in F. Machlup. *Essays in Economic Semantics.* New York: W. W. Norton, 1967.

Maclachlan, F. C. 1993. *Keynes' General Theory of Interest: A Reconsideration.* London and New York: Routledge.

Marshall, A. 1949. *Principles of Economics.* London: Macmillan.

Masten, S. E. 1991. "A Legal Basis for the Firm" in Williamson and Winter (1991).

McCloskey, D. N. 1985. *The Rhetoric of Economics.* Madison: University of Wisconsin Press.

Menger, C. 1976. *Principles of Economics.* New York: New York University Press. [1871].

———. 1985. *Investigations into the Method of the Social Sciences with Special Reference to Economics.* New York: New York University Press. [1883; trans. 1963].

Mincer, J. 1962. "On-the-job training: Costs, returns and some implications". *Journal of Political Economy* 70 no. 5: 50–79.

———. 1974. *Schooling, Experience and Earnings.* New York: Columbia University Press.

Minkler, A. P. 1993. "Knowledge and internal organization". *Journal of Economic Behavior and Organization* 21 no. 1: 17–30.

Mises, L. von. 1920. "Economic Calculation in the Socialist Commonwealth" in Hayek (1935a).

———. 1927. *Liberalism in the Classical Tradition.* Irvington on the Hudson, New York: Foundation for Economic Education. (Reprinted 1985).

———. 1957. *Theory and History.* New Haven: Yale University Press.

———. 1966. *Human Action.* Chicago: Henry Regnery. [1949].

———. 1971. *The Theory of Money and Credit*, ninth edition. New York: Foundation for Economic Education. [1912].

———. 1981. *Socialism.* Indianapolis, IN: Liberty Classics. [1922].

Nelson, R. R. and S. G. Winter. 1982. *An Evolutionary Theory of Economic Change.* Cambridge, MA: Harvard University Press.

Nonaka, I. and H. Takeuchi. 1995. *The Knowledge Creating Company.* Oxford: Oxford University Press.

O'Driscoll, G. P. and M. J. Rizzo. 1996. *The Economics of Time and Ignorance.* London: Routledge. [1985].

Oi, W. 1961. "Labor as a quasi fixed factor of production". Unpublished dissertation, University of Chicago.

Orosel, G. O. 1987. "Period of production". Entry in *Capital Theory (The New Palgrave).* New York: Macmillan, 212–219, 1987.

Pellengahr, I. 1986a. "Austrians Versus Austrians I: A Subjectivist View of Interest" in Faber (1986).

———. 1986b. "Austrians Versus Austrians II: Functionalist Versus Essentialist Theories of Interest" in Faber (1986).

———. 1996. *The Austrian Subjective Theory of Interest: An Investigation into the History of Thought.* Frankfurt: Peter Lang.

Penrose, E. T. 1995. *The Theory of the Growth of the Firm.* Oxford: Basil Blackwell. [1959].

Polanyi, M. 1958. *Personal Knowledge: Towards a Post Critical Philosophy.* Chicago: University of Chicago Press.

Popper, K. R. 1972. *Objective Knowledge: An Evolutionary Approach.* Oxford: Oxford University Press.

———. 1976. *Unended Quest: An Intellectual Autobiography.* La Salle, IL: Open Court.

———. 1989. *Conjectures and Refutations.* London: Routledge. [1963].

Progogine, I. and I. Stengers. 1984. *Order Out of Chaos: Man's New Dialogue With Nature.* New York: Bantam.

Ramsay-Steele, D. 1992. *From Marx to Mises: Post Capitalist Society and the Challenge of Economic Calculation.* La Salle, IL: Open Court.

———. 1996. "Between immorality and unfeasibility: The market socialist predicament". *Critical Review* 10 no. 3: 307–331.

Ricardo, D. 1973. *The Principles of Political Economy and Taxation.* London: The Guernsey Press. [1817].

Richardson, G. B. 1972. "The organization of industry". *Economic Journal* 82: 883–896.

———. 1990. *Information and Investment: A Study in the Working of the Competitive Economy.* Oxford: Clarendon Press. [1960].

Rizzo, M. J. 1979. *Time Uncertainty and Equilibrium: Exploration of Austrian Themes.* Lexington: D. C. Heath.

———. 1990. "Hayek's four tendencies toward equilibrium". *Cultural Dynamics* 3: 12–31.

———. 1992. "Equilibrium visions". *South African Journal of Economics* 60 no. 1: 117–130.

———. 1994. "Time in Economics" in P. J. Boettke, ed. *The Edward Elgar Companion to Austrian Economics.* Brookfield, VT: Edward Elgar, 1994.

———. 1996. "Introduction" in O'Driscoll and Rizzo (1996). [1985].

Robinson, J. 1956. *The Accumulation of Capital.* London: Macmillan.

Romer, P. M. 1990. "Are nonconvexities important for understanding growth?" *American Economic Review* 80 no. 2: 97–103.

———. 1994. "The origins of endogenous growth". *Journal of Economic Perspectives* 8 no. 1: 3–22.

Rosen, S. 1991. "Transactions Costs and Internal Labor Markets" in Williamson and Winter (1991).

Rothbard, M. N. 1970. *Man, Economy and State: A Treatise on Economic Principles.* Los Angeles: Nash.

———. 1975. *America's Great Depression*, third edition. Kansas City: Sheed and Ward. [1963].

———. 1977. "Introduction" in Fetter (1977).

———. 1987. "Time Preference", in *The New Palgrave: A Dictionary of Economics.* New York: Macmillan, 1987. Reprinted in Richard Ebeling, ed. (1991) Austrian Economics: A Reader. Hillsdale: Hillsdale College Press.

Samuelson, P. A. 1962. "Parable and realism in capital theory: The surrogate production function". *Review of Economic Studies* 39: 193–206.

Schultz, T. W. 1964. *Transforming Traditional Agriculture.* New Haven: Connecticut University Press.

———. 1981. *Investing in People: The Economics of Population Quality.* Berkeley, CA: University of California Press.

Schumpeter, J. A. 1947. *Capitalism, Socialism and Democracy*, second edition. New York: Harper.

———. 1954. *History of Economic Analysis.* New York: Oxford University Press.

———. 1961. *The Theory of Economic Development.* Cambridge, MA: Harvard University Press. Trans. Redvers Opie. [1934].

Scully, G. W. 1992. *Constitutional Environments and Economic Growth.* Princeton: Princeton University Press.

Selgin, G. A. 1988. *The Theory of Free Banking: Money Supply Under Competitive Note Issue.* Totowa, NJ: Rowman and Littlefield.

Shmanske, S. 1994. "On the relevance of policy to Kirznerian entrepreneurship". *Advances in Austrian Economics* 1: 199–222.

Smith, A. 1982. *An Inquiry into the Nature and Causes of the Wealth of Nations.* Indianapolis, IN: Liberty Classics. [1776].

Solow, R. 1956. "A contribution to the theory of economic growth". *Quarterly Journal of Economics* 70 no. 1: 65–94.

———. 1994. "Perspectives on growth theory". *Journal of Economic Perspectives* 8 no. 1: 45–54.

Sorokin, P. A. 1964. *Sociocultural Causality, Space, Time: A Study of Referential Principles of Sociology and Social Science.* New York: Russel and Russel. [1943].

Sraffa, P. 1960. *Production of Commodities by Means of Commodities: Prelude to a Critique of Economic Theory.* Cambridge: Cambridge University Press.

Steele, G. R. 1996. *The Economics of Friedrich Hayek.* London: Macmillan.

Stiglitz, J. E. 1987. "The causes and consequences of the dependence of quality of price". *Journal of Economic Literature* 25.

Teece, D. 1982. "Towards an economic theory of the multi-product firm". *Journal of Economic Behavior and Organization* 3: 39–63.

———. 1986. "Profiting from technological innovation: Implications for integration, collaboration, licensing, and public policy". *Research Policy* 15: 285–305.

Vanberg, V. 1989. "Carl Menger's evolutionary and John R. Commons's collective action approach to institutions". *Review of Political Economy* 1. Reprinted in Vanberg (1994).

———. 1992. "Organizations as constitutional systems". *Constitutional Political Economy* 3 no. 2: 223–254. Reprinted in Vanberg (1994).

———. 1994. *Rules and Choice in Economics.* London: Routledge.

Vaughn, K. I. 1992. "The problem of order in Austrian economics: Kirzner vs. Lachmann". *Review of Political Economy* 4: 251–274.

———. 1994. *Austrian Economics in America: The Migration of a Tradition.* Cambridge: Cambridge University Press.

Vroman, J. J. 1995. *Economic Evolution: An Enquiry into the Foundations of New Institutional Economics.* London: Routledge.

Whitehead, A. N. 1968. *Essays in Science and Philosophy.* New York: Greenwood Press. [1947].

Williamson, O. E. 1985. *The Economic Institutions of Capitalism.* New York: Free Press.

Williamson, O. E. and S. G. Winter, eds. 1991. *The Nature of the Firm: Origins, Evolution, and Development.* Oxford: Oxford University Press.

Yeager, L. B. 1976. "Toward understanding some paradoxes in capital theory". *Economic Inquiry* 14: 313–346.

———. 1979. "Capital Paradoxes and the Concept of Waiting" in Rizzo (1979).

Index

A

action, 31–32
    competitive vs. complementary, 32
    dependence on rules, 42–43
    predictability, 38–39, 42, 45
Ahiakpor, James W. C., 56, 243
Alchian, Armen, 158, 159, 243
Arthur, W. Brian, 40, 144, 243
asset specificity, 158–159
Austrian School, 23, 49, 64, 98
Austrian theory of the business cycle, 126
average period of production, 63–78

B

Baetjer, Howard, xii, 175, 194, 195, 243, 252
Bartley, William Warren, III, 225, 227–230, 234, 243
Barzel, Yoram, 159, 243
Becker, Gary, vii, 12, 17, 193, 196, 197, 201–203, 205–207, 209, 210, 212–218, 220, 222–224, 243
Bergson, Henri, 36, 244
Bierman, Leonard, 145, 244
Blaug, Mark, 88, 244
Bluedorn, Allan C., 145, 244
Boettke, Peter, viii, 162, 244
Böhm-Bawerk, Eugen von, 5, 9, 11, 49, 57, 61, 63–71, 73–78, 79, 80, 88, 89, 92, 93, 95, 96, 97, 110, 112–114, 126, 127, 141–143, 147, 189, 213, 215, 240, 244, 247, 248
Buchanan, James M., 144, 244
budget, 46–47, 188–192

C

capital
    capital accumulation, 14, 54, 55, 56, 59, 67, 74, 77, 86, 117, 123, 138–139, 142–145, 149, 207, 214, 217, 230, 239, 240, 255
    capital goods, 3, 48, 52, 53, 60–67, 72, 76, 102, 104, 105, 113, 117–119, 121, 129, 131–134, 136, 138, 143, 169, 175, 181, 185, 193, 238
    capitalist economy, xi, 5, 7, 51, 58, 59, 64, 72, 122, 148, 177, 186, 238
    capital stock, 5, 6, 54–58, 64, 65, 72–74, 76, 91, 95, 103, 104, 126, 128, 129, 131, 132, 142, 157, 169, 189, 237, 238
    capital structure, xi, 3, 11, 60, 62, 71, 72, 73, 126–128, 130, 131, 134–142, 144–146, 147, 151, 156, 166, 169, 172–173, 188, 189, 190, 193, 216, 238, 239, 241, 250
    capital theory, vii, xi, xii, 4–7, 10, 11, 19, 49, 51, 53, 54, 63–64, 69, 78, 79, 88, 91, 93, 95, 96, 110, 113, 120, 121, 123, 125, 126, 127, 128, 130, 139, 144, 148, 163, 189, 200, 209, 213, 216, 237, 243, 250, 251, 252, 255, 257
    human capital, vii, 3, 11, 12, 33, 85, 86, 155, 169, 175, 182, 192, 193–200, 201–224, 225–226, 230, 231, 233–235, 239, 241, 243, 248
Chandler, Alfred, 151, 166, 172, 244
Chen, Ping, 144, 245
children, 220–221
Chiles, Todd H., 145, 244
Clark, John Bates, 5, 70, 71–73, 244

Coase, Ronald, 148, 158, 244
Cockshott, W. Paul, 186, 245
Collis, David S., 148, 244
constant returns to scale (CRS), 10, 81–84, 152, 170
constrained maximum, 15, 17
convergence to equilibrium, 22, 24, 26–30, 40, 42, 86
Cottrell, Allin, 186
Currie, Martin, 31, 35, 37–38, 245

D

Dahlman, Carl, 158, 245
Day, Richard H., 144, 245
Demsetz, Harold, 148, 159, 163, 243, 245
discounted marginal value product (DMVP), 118
disequilibrium, xii, 8, 11, 13, 24, 25, 28, 29, 31, 34, 45, 46, 48, 50, 51, 104, 120, 129, 131, 132, 133, 135, 138, 139, 194, 223, 233, 234, 235, 238, 252
division of labor, 9, 11, 55, 56, 67, 141, 142, 145, 168–171, 178, 182, 185–187, 211, 213–218, 220–224
divorce, 222–223
Dolan, Edwin G., 23, 245, 249, 250
Dorfman, Robert, 73, 245
Douglas, Cobb, 80
Drucker, Peter F., 175, 245

E

Ebeling, Richard M., viii, 39, 79, 245, 255
endogenous change, 10, 27–29, 154, 217, 219, 221, 246
Endogenous Growth Theory, 81–84
equilibrating tendencies, 7, 13, 27
  and Austrian economics, 7
  "long-run" stationary state, 9, 59
equilibrium, 8
  absence of, 14
  as a "balance of forces", 16, 17
  as a result of plans, 32
  definition, 13, 15–18
  effect of time, 21, 26
  empirical nature, 23
  general equilibrium, 15

equilibrium *(cont.)*
  implications of, 19–21
  individual vs. system, 20
  intertemporal equilibrium, 16, 21
  micro and macro, 20
  momentary equilibrium, 17
  partial equilibrium, 15
  static equilibrium, 15
  supply and demand, 16
  temporary equilibrium, 16
  tendency toward, 14, 25, 36
  volitional aspect, 18
equilibrium price, 28–30
  market-clearing price, 24
  price discrepancies, 28, 47
  supply and demand, 29
Evans-Pritchard, Edward E., 44, 245
evenly rotating economy (ERE), 117–119
exogenous change, 28–30, 80, 87, 89, 206, 219

F

Faber, Malte, 70, 94, 110, 113, 245, 254
Fetter, Frank A., 78, 112–114, 115
firm, vii, 2, 11, 86, 99, 100, 120, 123, 126, 135, 137, 141, 145, 148, 149, 151–175, 177–185, 189, 192, 196, 197, 200–206, 213, 215, 218, 223, 235, 238, 243, 244, 245, 246, 251, 252, 253, 254, 256, 257
Foss, Nicholai J., 126, 246

G

Garrison, Roger W., viii, 62, 73, 110, 112, 246
Goleman, Daniel, 210, 246
Greening, Daniel W., 145, 244
growth theory, 11, 53, 74, 78, 80, 81, 88, 89, 93, 217, 246, 256
Gupta, Vishal K., 145, 244

H

Hahn, Frank H., 19, 246
Harcourt, Geoffrey C., 88, 246
Harper, David A., viii, 226, 246
Hausman, Daniel, 76, 247

Hayek, Friedrich A., xii, 8, 11, 13, 14, 18–24, 26, 27, 31, 34, 42, 44, 45, 48, 70, 71, 73, 74, 78, 88, 95, 96, 98, 105, 119, 123, 126–131, 139, 145, 147, 149, 160, 164, 165, 177, 178, 189, 193, 195, 215, 231–233, 240, 247, 250, 252, 253, 255, 256
   definition of equilibrium, 8, 13, 14, 18, 27
   effect of time on equilibrium, 21
   Monetary Theory and the Trade Cycle, 126
   Prices and Production, 126
   The Pure Theory of Capital, 126
   equilibrium tendencies, 22
   existence of equilibrium, 22
   individual and system equilibrium, 20
Hennings, Klaus H., 63–65, 74, 247
Hicks, John R., 10, 21, 49, 53, 54, 57, 90, 92, 93–107, 156, 180, 184, 188, 190, 216, 248, 250, 252
   Capital and Growth, 93
   Capital and Time, 93, 95, 96
   Pure Theory of Capital, 11
   Value and Capital, 93
   Fundamental Theorem, 100–101, 106
   intertemporal equilibrium, 21
   neo-Austrian approach, 10
Hodgson, Geoffrey M., 144, 248
Hoff, Tigre J., 177, 248
Horwitz, Steven, viii, 27, 40, 41, 177, 178, 187, 188, 223, 244, 248
human capital, *see* capital
Hume, David, 211

I
interest, 109–120
internal rate of return (IRR), 99, 101, 102, 106–107, 197

J
Jevons, William Stanley, 57, 127
joint production, 156

K
Keynes, John Maynard, 4, 7, 94, 126, 129, 137, 253
Kirzner, Israel, M., viii, xii, 8, 13, 17, 23–28, 40, 78, 88, 91, 105, 110, 112, 113, 115, 116, 126, 129, 139, 145, 231, 245, 249, 256, 257
   definition of disequilibrium, 24
Klein, Peter, 179, 249
Knight, Frank H., 5, 70–73, 249
Knowledge capital, 3, 225–236
   informative content, 227, 228
   logical content, 227, 228
   objective content, 227
Kregel, Jan A., 53, 59, 64, 249
Kresge, Stephen, 131, 250
Krugman, Paul, 40, 221, 250
Kuhn, Thomas S., 230

L
Lachmann, Ludwig M., vii, xi, xii, 11, 13, 16, 23–28, 35, 37, 40, 41, 43, 53, 54, 59, 73, 78, 94, 95, 99, 105, 116, 123, 126, 127, 128, 130–146, 147, 149, 150, 151, 156, 159, 162, 166, 170, 171, 173, 194, 200, 213, 215, 216, 240, 250, 251, 252, 257
   Capital and its Structure, 131–146
   Lachmann's axiom, 26, 27, 35, 43, 162
Laing, N. F., 88, 246
Lakatos, Imre, 230
Langlois, Richard, 123, 147, 153, 158, 160, 161, 163, 164, 165, 166, 167, 171, 172, 251
Lavoie, Donald C., viii, 177, 189, 194, 230–233, 250, 251
Leijonhufvud, Axel, 167–171, 173, 251
Lewin, Peter, xii, 3, 13, 23, 26, 32, 35, 79, 93, 110, 114, 127, 130, 131, 175, 177, 194, 223, 248, 251, 252
Liebowitz, Stan J., 40, 252
Lindahl, Erik, 35, 252
Loasby, Brian, 42, 123, 155, 156, 174, 246, 252
Lucas, Robert E., 80, 85, 252
Lutz, Friedrich A., 74, 76, 79, 252

M

Machlup, Fritz, 15, 19, 20, 252
Maclachlan, Fiona C., 113, 253
Malthus, Thomas, 59, 219, 220, 221
Margolis, Stephen E., 40, 252
market-clearing price, 24
marriage, 222–223
Marshall, Alfred, 24, 123, 126, 135, 148, 202, 209, 246, 253
Marx, Karl, 171, 254
Masten, Scott E., 158, 253
McMullen, Jeffrey, 145, 244
measurement cost approach, 159
Menger, Carl, 9–11, 40, 49, 60–65, 71, 73, 92, 95–97, 123, 125–127, 129, 147, 164, 185–187, 213, 214, 248, 253, 257
    Time Structure of Production, 60–63
Mincer, Jacob, 12, 206, 219, 253
Minkler, Alanson P., 174, 253
Mises, Ludwig von, 11, 32, 34, 46, 47, 78, 110, 112–114, 115, 126, 129, 157, 177, 178, 179, 185–189, 207, 246, 248, 249, 250, 252, 253, 254
modern growth theory, 74, 80
Montgomery, Cynthia A., 148, 244
multiple specificity, 134, 145, 159, 162, 202
Murphey, Kevin, 193, 214–217, 243

N

Nelson, Robert R., 164, 253
neo-Austrian, 10, 93, 248, 250
neo-Ricardian, 9, 10, 19, 49, 59, 76, 78, 79, 88–91, 92, 101, 102, 147
net present value (NPV), 98–99
Nonaka, Ikujiro, 175, 231, 253

O

O'Driscoll, Gerald P., 20, 27, 28, 34, 246, 254, 255
Oi, Walter, 203, 254
On the Principles of Political Economy and Taxation, 9
Orosel, Gerhard O., 70, 254

P

Pellengahr, Ingo, 110, 114
Penrose, Edith T., 11, 123, 147, 149, 154–156, 162, 170, 172, 254
Polanyi, Michael, 160, 195, 230, 254
Popper, Karl, 195, 226, 229, 230, 234, 240, 254
price
    as a measure of worth, 46
    as a mode of calculation, 46
    as a social institution, 46
    changes in, 47
    discrepancies, 28, 47
    effects within disequilibrium, 46
processes of convergence, 40–43
"production function" approach to capital, 9, 79–92
    capital intensity, 89, 101
    capital reversing, 89
    challenge to, 88–91
    complete production function, 82
    constant returns, 10
    diminishing returns, 10, 56, 89
    endogenous change, 10, 27, 28
    Endogenous Growth Theory, 81–84
    limitations, 86–88
    partial production function, 83
    technological change, 10
profit, 10, 50, 117–120
    prospective profits, 183–184
    retrospective profits, 180–183
Pure Theory of Capital, 11, 126
Pure Time Preference Theory (PTPT), 10, 109–117

R

Ramsay-Steele, David, 177, 254
Ricardo, David, 5, 9, 49, 54, 57–60, 62–64, 73, 75, 92, 93, 96, 123, 147, 254
Richardson, George B., 11, 123, 149–154, 155, 156, 162, 172, 246, 254
Rizzo, Mario J., viii, 20, 23, 26–28, 34, 36, 246, 254, 255, 257
Robertson, Paul L., 153, 158, 160, 161, 163, 166, 167, 251
Robinson, Joan, 79, 255

INDEX

Romer, Paul M., 80, 81, 83, 85, 255
Rosen, Sherwin, 204, 255
Rothbard, Murray, 78, 110, 112–114, 117, 118–119, 126, 179, 245, 246, 252, 255
roundabout methods of production, 9, 11, 52, 61, 62, 65–68, 70, 74, 78, 97, 113, 126, 142–144, 147, 189, 213, 215, 217, 240, 248

S
Salerno, Joseph, viii, 157
Samuelson, Paul A., 90, 255
Schultz, Theodore W., 12, 196, 214, 216
Schumpeter, Joseph Alois, xii, 128, 134, 147, 256
Scully, Gerald W., 88, 256
Selgin, George A., 40, 256
Shackle, George L. S., 25, 250
Shmanske, Steven, 17, 18, 256
Simon, Herbert, 231
Smith, Adam, 8, 9, 11, 49, 51, 53–58, 74, 75, 91, 93, 123, 140, 142, 145, 167–169, 171, 197, 211, 213, 214–216, 256
    corn economy, 53–57, 74, 140, 145
Solow, Robert, 80, 83, 84, 87, 256
Sorokin, Pitirim A., 37, 38, 256
specific human capital, 195
Sraffa, Pierro, 57, 79, 256
steady-state economics, 9, 103–104, 117
Steedman, Ian, 31, 35, 37–38, 245
Steele, Gerhard R., 143, 177, 254, 256
Stiglitz, Joseph E., 19, 256

T
Takeuchi, Hirotaka, 175, 231, 253
technical information, 150
Teece, David, 123, 148, 166, 256
theory of the firm, *see* firm
time, 60–63, 66, 70, 71, 73, 75, 91, 94–96
Treatise on the Family, A, 219
Tuggle, Christopher, 145, 244

U
Uniform Rate of Profit, 57–60

V
Vanberg, Victor, 164, 257
Vaughn, Karen, viii, 26, 257
Vroman, Jack J., 184, 257

W
Wealth of Nations, 8, 213
Wenar, Leif, 131, 250
Whitehead, Alfred North, 232, 257
Wicksell, Knut, 79, 96, 127
Wieser, Friedrich von, 129
Williamson, Oliver E., 123, 148, 160, 174, 231, 243, 245, 253, 255, 257
Winter, Sidney G., 148, 160, 164, 245, 253, 255, 257
women in the workforce, 218–222
Woodward, Susan, 158, 243
Wyotinsky Lectures, 210

Y
Yeager, Leland B., 88, 90, 110, 257
Yoon, Yong J., 144, 244